Constance Fenimore Woolson

♣

Constance Fenimore Woolson

❧

HOMEWARD BOUND

Sharon L. Dean

The University of Tennessee Press ❧ Knoxville

Frontispiece: Constance Fenimore Woolson, from Clare Benedict, *Five Generations (1785–1923),* vol. 2 (3 vols., London: Ellis, 1929–30).

Letters from the Samuel Mather Family Papers are reprinted by permission of the Western Reserve Historical Society. Letters from the Katharine Loring Papers are reprinted courtesy of the Beverly Historical Society and Museum. Quotations from *The Claremont Woolsons* by Elinor Colby are made by permission of the Claremont, N.H., Historical Society. Quotations from a letter owned by the Fiske Free Library, Charemont, N.H., are made by permission. Correspondence with Kathleen Reich of Rollins College is quoted by permission of Kathleen Reich.

Part of chapter 3 originally appeared as "Constance Woolson's Southern Sketches" in *Southern Studies* 25, no. 3 (Fall 1986). It is reprinted here by permission.

Part of chapter 5 originally appeared as "Gender Implications in Henry James's 'The Pupil' and Constance Woolson's 'A Transplanted Boy'" in *InSight* 1, no. 1 (1992), published by Rivier College.

Part of chapter 6 originally appeared as "Homeward Bound: The Novels of Constance Fenimore Woolson" in *Legacy* 6, no. 2 (Fall 1989): 17–28. Reproduced by permission of The Pennsylvania State University Press.

Part of chapter 7 originally appeared as "Women as Daughters; Women as Mothers in the Fiction of Constance Woolson" in *Critical Essays on Constance Fenimore,* edited by Cheryl B. Torsney, © 1992 by Cheryl B. Torsney. Used with permission of Twayne Publishers, an imprint of Macmillan Publishing Company.

Part of chapter 9 originally appeared as "Constance Fenimore Woolson and Henry James: The Literary Relationship" in *Massachusetts Studies in English* 7, no. 3 (1980).

The paper in this book meets the minimum requirements of the American National Standard for Permanence of Paper for Printed Library Materials. ∞   The binding materials have been chosen for strength and durability.

Library of Congress Cataloging-in-Publication Data

Dean, Sharon L., 1943–
    Constance Fenimore Woolson: homeward bound / Sharon L. Dean.—1st ed.
       p.   cm.
    Includes bibliographical references and index.
    ISBN 0–87049–898–3 (cloth: alk. paper)
    1. Woolson, Constance Fenimore, 1840–1894—Criticism and interpretation.
2. Women and literature—United States—History—19th century. 3. Women in literature. I. Title.
PS3363.D43   1995
813'.4—dc20
                                          95–4332
                                            CIP

For my parents

Contents

✤

Acknowledgments

♣

The origins of this book date back more than twenty years to when I began to write my dissertation on the portraits of women in the fiction of canonized male writers. At the time I had no language to define my study as feminist, but I have since come to realize that I was re-reading "the masters" from a woman's point of view. To my dissertation advisor at the University of New Hampshire, Philip Nicoloff, I owe my first note of thanks. Not only did he support my early groping toward a feminist perspective, he also taught me to love American literature.

My dissertation led me into the work of Henry James and a one-sentence reference to Constance Fenimore Woolson. I returned to that sentence after commencement and began my slow research into this woman whose life and writing I have also grown to love. For support in this research I have many to thank, from colleagues within academia to interested friends and a supportive family. I wish to acknowledge the staff at the Western Reserve Historical Society for granting me access to the Samuel Mather Family Papers; Katherine Pinkham, curator of the Beverly Historical Society and Museum, for help with the Woolson–Katharine Loring connection; Colin Sanborn of the Claremont Historical Society, and Marilyn Nagy of the Fiske Free Library, Claremont, New Hampshire, for information on Woolson and Clare Benedict; and Kathleen Reich, archivist at Rollins College, not only for access to Rollins's collection, but also for her shared interest in Woolson. I owe special thanks to a number of people at the University of Tennessee Press: Meredith Morris-Babb, acquisitions editor, for her early support of the project; Stan Ivester, managing editor, and freelancer Karin Kaufman for copyediting; and Marilyn Kallet for valuable suggestions in the last stages of the manuscript. For their reading of earlier drafts of the manuscript, I am indebted to Melissa Pennell of the University of Massachusetts–Lowell and Dennis Berthold of Texas A&M University. Their comments were honest, useful, and encouraging; without them, this book would have lacked much of its shape and context.

I wish also to thank Rayburn Moore for his encouragement and for his early work on Woolson. Victoria Brehm, Alice Petry, Cheryl Torsney, and Joan Weimer have shared their interest in and their knowledge about Woolson: they have become attached friends. Many at Rivier College also deserve thanks: the administration for supporting me in a sabbatical leave; France Kelleher and Margaret Payne of the Regina Library for gracious help with interlibrary loan; colleagues both in and out of the English Department for their interest; and students for confirming that Woolson merits inclusion in the curriculum. Judith Stanford deserves a special note of thanks for working toward including Woolson in literature anthologies, as does Patsy Roberts for reminding me of ways to turn my scholarship to my teaching.

On a more personal level, I would like to thank Deb Christenson and Joan Plummer for our literary tours and conversations as well as Allain Schnable and son Zachary and Lauretta Daley and son Malcolm for listening on our walks. Lauretta also read early drafts of the manuscript and offered many probing questions and insights. I thank my daughter Emily, whose love for exercise helped me to see how much a difference exercise made in Woolson's life, and my son Michael, whose study of geology caused me to notice Woolson's geological knowledge. Finally, I thank my husband Ron, who has been with me since those twenty-plus years ago when I began my interest in Woolson and who has shared with me the kind of home that Woolson would have valued.

Introduction

♣

A hundred years ago, instead of writing this book that aims to recover the name of Constance Fenimore Woolson, I might be waiting for the latest *Harper's* to arrive with a new story by this woman who regularly earned reviews in such major outlets as the *New York Times, Atlantic, Nation,* and *Scribner's.* I might have talked with a few of the 750 people in my town, Brookline, New Hampshire, about the story or have asked if someone had checked out one of Woolson's novels from the public library. I might be just a touch proud of that library, founded in 1877, in the first state to mandate public libraries for all townships and of Woolson's family roots in New Hampshire. But it is now the latter part of the twentieth century, and though Brookline has still not grown beyond three thousand people, I suspect that fewer of these than a hundred years ago would recognize Woolson's name—and these few would strain to recover it from a conversation they had with me about my book project. I hope that my library, looking very nineteenth century in its recent move to the old Methodist Church, will purchase my book to replace the ones by Woolson it must long ago have sold in a fundraiser. I hope that the Fiske Free Library in Claremont, New Hampshire, will do the same, and I am grateful that the Historical Society in Claremont rescued the copies of Woolson's books that the library had stamped "discard" in the 1960s, along with books about Woolson by her niece Clare Benedict. And I hope that with my book Woolson's name will inch forward toward the recognition it deserves.

Unfortunately, Woolson's name has been lost to more than the general population of small-town New Hampshire. Even at conferences focusing on American literature, I find few scholars who recognize it. "Constance Who?" they ask, then, "Is she any good?" At exchanges like this, I bite my tongue. Why, I ask myself, is Woolson still so marginalized and how did she become lost in the first place? The few of us who have in the last ten years dedicated much time and energy to recovering Woolson have some theories. Cheryl Torsney summarizes them: her lack of a close relationship with another woman that has come to be known as a "Boston marriage"; her failure to be associated with the local color of one region; her position as a woman born midcentury between the domestic novelists and the "New Woman" novelists; the lack of an autobiography and of a psychobiography to generate interest.[1] While these may explain the continued obscurity of Woolson, they do not explain why after her death she so quickly faded from literary annals.

I like to speculate that one of the reasons for Woolson's disappearance rests with her niece Clare Benedict. Benedict's adoration of her aunt became a lifetime agenda of marketing: she wrote a three-volume history of the Benedict-Woolson ancestry, with one of the volumes devoted entirely to Constance.[2] She also gathered letters and notices in appreciation of her aunt and of her own work on her aunt's behalf, which she collected in a book called *Appreciations,* one of the strangest books I have ever seen and one that she had printed by a vanity press.[3] Benedict donated her books about her family and her aunt to numerous libraries, and many of the recognitions in *Appreciations* are thank-you letters for her donations. She frequently visited the library in Claremont, New Hampshire, her aunt's birthplace, and the Claremont Historical Society now possesses many books from Woolson's personal library.[4] Benedict also spent much time and money arranging for a monument in her aunt's memory on Mackinac Island[5] and a house in her name at Rollins College in Winter Park, Florida, which holds the largest collection of Woolson memorabilia.

The impression one gets reading through the Rollins correspondence is that Benedict began to be more of a burden than an asset. She persistently directed the college on the use of the Woolson collection and recalled much of it from Rollins when she felt it was not being cared for properly. Rollins healed those wounds and eventually received the twenty-five thousand dollars plus interest it expected from Benedict's will, money set aside for the upkeep of Woolson House. After Cheryl Torsney visited Rollins and exposed the sorry state of the Woolson House in a notice in *Legacy* in 1985,[6] Rollins refurbished it, even rescuing Woolson's desk from a campus fraternity. It is now used as an English Department lounge, but Kathleen Reich, an archivist at the college, informs me that no members of that department wish to pursue Woolson studies. Despite her lobbying, faculty who put together a collection of Florida writers omitted Woolson, even though she has been identified as the first novelist of Florida.[7]

Those who have tried to rekindle an interest in Woolson often have done so because of her connection to Henry James or because of a local interest. In the 1920s, Fred Lewis Pattee, a New Hampshire native, included her in his book *The Development of the American Short Story*. After teaching at Pennsylvania State University, whose library is named for him, he taught at Rollins College, and he wrote the Dedicatory Address for the Constance Fenimore Woolson English House at Rollins.[8] In 1940, Lyon N. Richardson tried to rekindle interest in Woolson studies at a "propitious" time, the anniversary of her birth. His connection was to Western Reserve University in Cleveland, Ohio, where Woolson lived for nearly thirty years; the university, now called Case Western Reserve University, is adjacent to the Western Reserve Historical Society, which houses most of the Woolson papers.[9] Richardson wanted to correct some of the work done in 1934 in a full-length study of Woolson, John Dwight Kern's *Constance Fenimore Woolson: Literary Pioneer*. Kern's advisor at the University of Pennsylvania, Arthur Hobson Quinn, had valued Woolson,[10] and Kern developed his own interest in Woolson with much the same agenda as Richardson: both aimed to "[awaken] some measure of enthusiasm with which her fiction was greeted by contemporaries, and [to rescue] her memory from the almost complete oblivion which has overtaken it" (Kern 179). These men, however, were working in a climate that was still seeking midcentury to establish American literature as a legitimate area of academic study, a canon-formation battle that had begun as early as the 1920s.[11] As American literature became legitimized it is not surprising that it became largely comparable to the white, male canon of British literature.

Thirty years after Kern tried to gain more notice for Woolson, Rayburn Moore, primarily a James scholar, published his Twayne study and, then, an edition of her novella *For the Major,* bound with selected short stories.[12] The late sixties and early seventies saw reprints of much of her work, but these came from neither popular nor mainstream university presses. These are not books we would expect to find stocked at our local Barnes and Noble.[13] What may have added to poor sales is the fact that Moore's collection and critical study coincided with the publication of Leon Edel's brutally negative assessment of Woolson and her fiction in his biography of Henry James, so that those who began to hear her name understandably marginalized her.[14]

By the mid-1960s, Woolson had been lost, as most writers become lost once their books have been pushed aside by the mass of readers who turn to more current ones. She had missed her entry in the academy, that guardian and creator of the literary canon, because of a pesky niece, because of a battle that had white, male American literature as its offering for canonization alongside white, male British literature, and because of the harsh words of a soon-to-be canonized literary biography. In the 1970s and 1980s feminists missed her because of her birth date and her solitary life and, I surmise, because they were loath to discuss someone who had been labeled as a protégée of a male who had been labeled Master. The late 1980s and early 1990s promise to rectify feminist neglect. Besides Torsney's 1988 book, Joan Weimer has gathered a selection of Woolson's short fiction for the American Women Writers Series of the Rutgers University Press,[15] and Torsney has edited *Critical Essays on Constance Fenimore Woolson,*[16] which contains original reviews of her work, some of Woolson's own reviews of novels, and samples of criticism from most decades in the twentieth century.

Woolson will never receive the respect she deserves until others join Torsney and Weimer and begin to see her as a culmination of an earlier era rather than as a failure of modernity. Male scholars, too, need to give her serious attention, and, whether male or female, scholars need to widen their scope of discussion beyond women's issues. To do this, Woolson's work needs to be more easily available. What might help most in triggering a greater interest in this work is a widely anthologized piece—"Felipa," "Miss Grief," or "A Transplanted Boy" are good candidates—in college literature anthologies. The anthologizing of stories like Charlotte Perkins Gilman's "The Yellow Wallpaper," Sarah Orne Jewett's "The White Heron," Mary Wilkins Freeman's "A New England Nun," and Kate Chopin's "The Story of an Hour" have cemented these names in numerous future scholars. The students I teach have responded well to Woolson, whether they are English majors or not, so an anthologized piece would seem appropriate.[17]

One of the aims of this book is to generate enough interest in Woolson to trigger reissues of her work. Another is to generate more scholarly interest like that begun by Torsney and Weimer. I also hope that this book will broaden interest to include nonspecialists. Woolson was a popular writer in her day and, as several of my nonspecialist friends have testified, remains someone who still can be read for enjoyment. She provides a window into the society of the late nineteenth century, one that was remarkably like our own at the end of the twentieth century as it struggles to redefine women's roles, to respect ethnic and racial differences, and to cope with new technologies, shifting demographics, and the increasing factionalism of different regional and social groups.

When I aim to connect nineteenth-century issues to a broad audience of twentieth-century readers, I reflect my attitudes toward the nature of literature and the historical study of literature. In "'But is it any *good?*': Evaluating Nineteenth-Century American Women's Fiction," Susan Harris draws on Hans Robert Jauss and articulates a view I share: "literary works," she writes, "continuously interact with their readers to create, over time, new moral and aesthetic perceptions."[18] Literature, in other words, not only reflects certain perceptions and values but also creates them. To study literature is to understand how books reflect their historical context and to see how they can reflect and re-shape our own times. During the course of her discussion, Harris references the critical view that early-nineteenth-century novels by women structured themselves around plots involving happy-ending marriages that were acceptable to the publishing establishment at the same time that the plots subverted these expectations by spending most of their time examining themes that supported more autonomy for women. "Challenges to the public definition of women's place," says Harris, "are embedded in texts' structures and accessible only to readers who are predisposed to grasp them" (48).

By the end of the century, women novelists no longer had to bury their themes so that only the predisposed could grasp them. The early work served as models for them to re-envision the status of women and to write about it in more open ways. Here again, we can see Woolson as lying midway between the domestic novelists of the early part of the nineteenth century and the new novelists at the end. Even more than that of the domestic novelists, her work may have pushed women to protest openly the status quo in their writing. Elizabeth Ammons has studied how seventeen of these turn-of-the-century women form an identifiable group that moved women's writing out of the field of the professional into the more consciously artistic. The writers she discusses include one born before Woolson (1840)—Frances E. W. Harper, 1825—and two born just a decade later than Woolson—Sarah Orne Jewett, 1849, and Kate Chopin, 1851. Although Ammons names Woolson as a precursor for these writers, she excludes her from her discussion, perhaps because, unlike Harper, she brings no ethnic diversity, because, unlike Jewett and Chopin, she came of age before the Civil War, and because, unlike all seventeen of the writers, she ended her career by the early 1890s. But Ammons's discussion of the lives and the thematic concerns of turn-of-the-century women should lead us to see just how forward-looking Woolson was. Like them, she was "educated, worldly, career-oriented," and chose to de-emphasize marriage and children as necessary elements for a woman to lead a meaningful life. And like them, she consciously addressed issues that Ammons identifies as relating to questions about women's power: for example, she centers *Jupiter Lights* around the links between sexual exploitation, violence, and women's silence; she frequently writes about women's roles as mothers and daughters; she depicts how ethnicity, race, and class impact on women's lives; and she writes often and probingly about what it means to be a female artist.[19]

Woolson's birth in the middle of the nineteenth century may actually have given her an advantage for achieving the quality, if not the current fame, of her fiction. One of Harris's criteria for evaluating fiction by nineteenth-century women is to see how well it strikes a balance between the antithetical aims of the socially approved marriage plot and the textual undercurrents that subvert that plot. Woolson neither hides her thematic agenda nor turns it into the polemical agenda it often became at the end of the nineteenth century in, for example, a writer such as Charlotte Perkins Gilman. With the exception of "The Yellow Wallpaper," Gilman wrote pieces that are more sociological treatises on the need for women to assert themselves than they are thickly textured fiction. Whether specifically writing about women's themes or not, Woolson is as good as she is because she places people in situations that raise questions and she provides various avenues of response that cannot be pigeonholed as freeing or imprisoning. Throughout her work and her life, she illustrates what Harris says of the best of nineteenth-century women's texts and their anticipation of twentieth-century women's issues: she shows women in conflict with fixed and emerging definitions of the self, and she struggles to learn "how to nurture and protect a self that has only just become aware of its own possibility and that is trying to work out the parameters of its obligations to others" (55). The struggles of Woolson's characters—the major ones primarily, though not exclusively, female—are our struggles, and experiencing vicariously how they struggled we may learn how better to face the challenges of our own times.

To say that literature—or at least some literature—helps us to make sense of our world assumes that we read, and teach, literature as if it can approach a vision of reality that is temporarily true, even if part of us knows that our own perceptions are relative to how we are situated in our particular time and place. In his introduction to his major study of New England literary culture, Lawrence Buell discusses how such a vision underlies the branch of literary criticism evolving as new historicism. Where new criticism, semiology, and deconstruction foreground the text, the latter two emphasizing the relativism of the sign system of the text, old versions of historicism foreground a culture its practitioners believed could be presented objectively. Buell, like many contemporary literary scholars, looks to the anthropologist Clifford Geertz and his notion of "thick description" to reach a truce between "absolute relativism" and "naive objectivism," quoting Geertz's splendid metaphor: to abandon the search for objectivity because complete objectivity is impossible is "like saying that as a perfectly aseptic environment is impossible, one might as well conduct surgery in a sewer."[20]

Like these new historicists, I, too, seek a truce between "absolute relativism" and "naive objectivism." At the same time, I recognize that objective readings of enlarged cultural texts are no more possible than the objective readings of literary texts that new criticism strove to achieve. In fact, new historicism may simply be new criticism writ large not only onto creative literature but onto local newspapers, legal and medical documents, instructional manuals, private letters and journals, town records, et cetera. Having exhausted reasonable interpretations of canonized literary texts, critics centered for almost two decades on the arbitrariness of language systems and embarked on a process of deconstructing interpretive certainty in favor of constructing uncertain, but clever, readings. But this began to generate a scholarly community ready to collapse under the weighty language of theory and increasingly out of touch with the vast majority of readers. New historicism is beginning to allow critics avenues into literary study applicable to a larger community of readers. It is not without its own set of dangers: we can never recover the full texture that generated a work of art, and some of what we think we recover may be simply coincidental. Still, the field of inquiry is so large as to seem inexhaustible and carries with it avenues for connecting the literature of the past to our present lives. For example, if we uncover nineteenth-century legal documents pertaining to the right to privacy and read nineteenth-century literature in light of the public perception of these legal documents, we may increase our understanding of our own debates about the right to privacy.[21]

Although I am drawn to new historicism, my approach to Woolson can claim only minimal use of its methods. My "thick description" of nineteenth-century culture is on the thin side because, at this juncture in Woolson studies, we need to know more about the general shape of her work before we can understand how her culture can enrich our readings of the details of that work. Along with reader-response theorists, I know that my reading of Woolson, of primary nineteenth-century documents, and of secondary texts about the nineteenth century are fluid, shaped and reshaped by my experiences and beliefs and by my awareness of new data. In fact, at each stage of writing this book I have learned new things that are relevant and that have made their way into the book by the happy coincidence of my hearing about them. At the same time, I have had to leave many avenues unexplored. For example, when I learned that Hawthorne had written a book titled *A Book of Autographs* based on discussions of handwriting analysis in *Godey's Lady's Book,* I wondered whether Woolson had this in mind when she wrote a satirical description of a character's handwriting and, if so, whether this has any implication beyond the satirical.[22] I left this unexplored, knowing that it will be relevant only when a significant number of people have read the story in question.

Besides new historicism, I am also drawn to reader response theory, which has begun to generate a new form of subjective literary criticism that Diane Freedman calls an "alchemy of genres."[23] A variety of academic and cultural trends have contributed to the development of subjective criticism. The blurring of the boundaries of academic disciplines that pushed literary scholars into fields such as anthropology and cultural history, which underlie new historicism, has also led them into narrative modes of telling the stories they have found. Increasing disillusion with the exclusionary voice of deconstructive and poststructural theoretical approaches has led some critics to risk the humanizing "I." The impact of feminism and the establishment of women as visible members of the academy have moved some toward the personal voice as they attempt to articulate how they connect to specific literary texts. Many who are now entering the academy have been trained not only in literary theory but also in the teaching of writing, a discipline that has been emphasizing personal narrative and expressive forms of writing for over twenty years. I use subjective methods of criticism sparingly in this book, but I am grateful that they have allowed me to break through the myth of objectivity and situate myself in a small New Hampshire community that persists in making me see Yankee roots in a largely rootless author who left New Hampshire at birth. But I also fear them as self-indulgent in a book whose aim is to recover Constance Woolson, not to examine the life of Sharon Dean. Joan Weimer has taken the opposite approach in *Back Talk: Teaching Lost Selves to Speak.*[24] The book is a personal memoir of recovery from a debilitating back operation, but because Weimer is a Woolson scholar, she uses her firm grounding in Woolson's biography and fiction to develop an imagined dialogue with a writer who helped her move toward both psychological and physical wholeness. Weimer's book and her approach should influence others to do what its subtitle suggests: teach lost selves to speak. But it will not, nor does it intend to, advance the literary study of Woolson.

Drawing on the method of subjective literary criticism, I begin my study of Constance Fenimore Woolson aware that it is shaped by my position as a privileged, white New England female. Because I have managed to combine home and rootedness with an evolving career, I read Woolson in light of her struggle with these values. By organizing around issues relating to this struggle, I place more demands on writer and reader than I would with a chronological pattern, but I believe this thematic approach reveals more about the milieu that generated Woolson's fiction and thus more about the nuances of the fiction. I devote chapter 1 to biographical matters, then move into four chapters that loosely follow Woolson's physical movements from the Great Lakes region of the United States, to the southern United States, to Europe. Chapter 2 focuses on Woolson's vision of the myth of Eden, on how this myth connects to the nineteenth-century romance writing of Cooper and Hawthorne, and on how she abandoned the romance genre for a more realistic vision of a non-Edenic United States. Chapter 3 moves from the Edenic myth into a discussion of the actuality of place, focusing on how Woolson relates to the domestic realists of the early nineteenth century and the local-color realists who gained prominence after the Civil War, and on how realism became a more compatible literary home for her than romance. Centering on how region shapes the way Woolson views home in the context of her characters' personal relation to place, this chapter moves from Woolson's lake country stories, which she wrote while living in the South, to her southern stories and her decreasing sense of belonging to a community. Where the northern stories foreground community within regional tensions, the southern ones foreground the tensions and the breakdown of community after the Civil War. Chapter 4 follows the same pattern of north to south, but shifts the emphasis from physical place to ethnic tensions within diverse communities, mirroring Woolson's increasing perceptions about issues of diversity that were emerging with the continued displacement of American Indians, the abolition of slavery, and the influx of new immigrant groups into the United States. The chapter ends with Woolson's continued treatment of diversity in her European fiction and thus bridges into chapter 5, which analyzes the center of Woolson's European experience: her relationship with Henry James, with the American expatriate community, both literary and otherwise, and with her increasing vision of herself as a homeless wanderer.

Always keenly aware of gender issues, in Europe Woolson foregrounds her position as a lone female in a foreign country where the American feminist agenda did not play itself out and where the social milieu forced her to be discreet in her relations with James. Thus I move in chapters 6 through 9 to discussions of Woolson's treatment of women in particular roles: as wives, as daughters and mothers, as widows and spinsters, and as artists. These chapters move my treatment of Woolson from a more physical and public locale into the increasingly private world she inhabited as she became more isolated from family and friends because of her transient life-style and her increasing deafness. As her public world became silenced, her private world found an increasingly powerful voice in her writing. In her life and in her fiction, Woolson journeyed from a vision of homogeneous, regional communities, limited and stifling but also comfortable for many, through an increased vision of the diversity and tension embedded in the national and international communities, to a vision of herself as an outsider to all communities.

Throughout her career, Woolson pursued themes involving communal and individual homes, which have prompted me to borrow my title, *Homeward Bound,* from her great-uncle, James Fenimore Cooper. It is a title that Woolson also used for one of her travel sketches from Mentone, Cairo, and Corfu.[25] The title aptly describes a woman who, Odysseus-like, moved forward, away from a home she felt bonded to and bounded by, toward a metaphorical literary space she could name as home. The ensuing chapters attempt to trace that journey through an analysis of a fictional oeuvre that provides insights into the nineteenth century and that may help us to shape the century that is looming before us.

I

A Woman in Search of a Home
❧

I should like to turn into a peak when I die;
to be a beautiful purple mountain,
which would please the tired, sad eyes
of thousands of human beings for ages.
— Constance Fenimore Woolson,
"Reflection," 24 December 1893

Constance Fenimore Woolson's life is marked by gravestones. It began on March 5, 1840, in Claremont, New Hampshire, where she was born the sixth child of Charles Jarvis and Hannah Cooper Pomeroy Woolson. In an old cemetery behind what was once the Universalist Church in Claremont, stand two small headstones that touch each other and bear the names of sisters who died in the month of her birth: "Julia Campbell Woolson, Died, March 21, 1840, .E. 2 years" and "Gertrude Elizabeth Woolson, Died, March 22, 1840, .E. 4 years." A third stone has been broken off from the other two and lies face down in the grass. Lifted up, it reveals, dimly, the name of a third sister: "Ann Cooper Woolson, Died, April 3, 1840, .E. 5 years." Four thousand miles away, in a Protestant cemetery in Rome a marble coping, filled in with violets and ivy that surround a Celtic cross, bears at its foot the inscription "Constance Fenimore Woolson, 1894." In fifty-three years, Woolson traveled far—from New Hampshire to Cleveland, Ohio, and much of the newly settled land along the Great Lakes; from Ohio to Florida and much of the post–Civil War South; from Florida to Italy, England, much of the European Continent, and even a part of North Africa. In fifty-three years, she watched most of her family die—her parents, seven of her eight sisters, her one brother, and two brothers-in-law. Henry James called her a woman who had "a constitutional, an essentially, tragic and insane *difficulty in living*—; an element rendered unspeakably touching by her extraordinary consideration of others."[1] John Hay, the writer, politician, and biographer of Abraham Lincoln, wrote that she was a "thoroughly good, and most unhappy woman, with a great talent, bedeviled by disordered nerves"; she "did much good and no harm in her life, and had not as much happiness as a convict."[2] Yet for all her melancholy and her habit of solitude, Constance Woolson remained involved in life. She was an amateur botanist who closely observed the varied landscapes she traveled through, and was as much a social psychologist as an artist in her observations of the people who occupied these landscapes. As she wrote once to Alice James's companion Katharine Loring, "Do not local habits & local ways amuse you? To me they are full of entertainment" (BHSM, 19 Sept. 1890).

Woolson's nomadic life, which gave her so many opportunities for observing local habits and local ways, was nurtured from infancy by parents who had settled in Claremont, where Jarvis Woolson had been raised, only after their enlarging family began to demand a permanent home. Before Constance was a year old, they left that town, perhaps to escape the New England winters, perhaps to outride their sorrow over their three dead children.[3] They rode until they reached Cleveland, a growing town that Hannah liked well enough to try to build a new life in, especially since an old friend from Claremont had settled there. Clara Benedict, Woolson's Cleveland-born sister and the only sibling to survive her, wrote that "'something' went out of" their mother after the deaths of her babies so that the surviving children never knew what she "had really been" (Benedict 1:42). Still, Hannah recovered enough to bear not only Clara but also another daughter, Aleta, who died in infancy, and a son, Charlie. She created a home for the family, complete with family dogs who received burials to which neighborhood dogs were invited;[4] she joined the family on vacations on Mackinac Island, Michigan; and she kept up her own habit of writing, a legacy perhaps of her relationship to her great-uncle, James Fenimore Cooper. Like Hannah, Jarvis Woolson also developed in Constance a sense of home. When O. F. R. Waite of Claremont asked for information about him for the Claremont town history, Woolson wrote that she would like to write the sketch herself, adding that, although she had visited Claremont only for a few days as a girl, "I know both New Hampshire & Vermont well, from my father's loving descriptions; he never liked the West; he was always homesick for the hills of New England."[5] The sketch Woolson wrote appears in the Claremont town history and in Benedict's *Five Generations* (1: 94–101). It reveals her deep attachment to this man who was probably descended from one of the piratical settlers of Wollaston, Massachusetts, memorialized as Merry Mount in Hawthorne's "Maypole of Merrymount." In Cleveland, Jarvis Woolson fought his feeling of exile from his New England roots through his love for reading and writing, through physical activity, and through the habit of travel, all coping strategies that he taught his daughter.

We know little about Jarvis and Hannah Woolson's parenting style, but it reflects the beliefs advocated in the mid-nineteenth-century version of Dr. Spock, Lydia Maria Child's *Mother's Book*.[6] By midcentury, the shift from seeing children as miniature adults, of little interest until they reached the age of reason, to individuals with needs unique to childhood had taken place. Jean-Jacques Rousseau's *Emile* (1762), one of the books that precipitated the change, was nearly a hundred years old, and children and childhood play had become standard subjects for art, literature, and study evidenced in the paintings of Woolson's contemporary Mary Cassatt, in the poems of Wordsworth, and in the educational theories of Bronson Alcott. Echoing the kind of childhood we perhaps idealize for the Alcott girls from our own childhood reading of *Little Women,* Child's book advocated the freedom of outdoor recreation for both boys and girls. The Woolson parents taught their children to enjoy a rich outdoor life, one that Constance maintained throughout her adulthood primarily through the activities of walking and rowing. They also valued education for their daughters. Constance attended the Cleveland Female Seminary, where her interest in the outdoors gained scientific legitimacy from the school's founder Samuel St. John, a specialist in biology, chemistry, geology, and natural history, and where her writing was encouraged by teacher Linda Guilford, the author of books about the school and about education. Although at age eighteen Woolson left Cleveland for Madame Chegaray's School, a fashionable New York academy attended mostly by southern women, she maintained the physical and intellectual habits her life in Ohio had inculcated in her.

Another of Woolson's habits was the independence to make choices about her personal life, something her parents at least tacitly encouraged in all the children. For example, although the Woolsons disapproved of their daughter Emma's marriage to Rev. Jarvis Carter because of an obscure illness he had, they supported her in it. The marriage of the three daughters, however, only added to the sorrow of the Woolson family: both Carter and Emma died shortly after their marriage; Georgiana Woolson, married to Samuel Mather, an indirect descendent of Increase and Cotton Mather, died of tuberculosis at age twenty-two shortly after giving birth to her second child; and the youngest daughter, Clara, was widowed when her husband, George Benedict, died in a train accident, leaving her with a young child to care for. It was to the widowed Clara and the unmarried Constance that Hannah Woolson looked for financial and emotional support after her husband died. At this time, daughters and parent changed roles, with Constance taking the majority of the responsibility for her mother.

Woolson's pattern for facing a life marked with pain begins to take shape after her father's death, when she developed the habits of writing, of traveling, and of guarding her solitude. By this time, she had had a brief romance with a childhood friend, Zeph Spaulding, who had become a colonel in the Union army.[7] We do not know who broke off the relationship, though the plots of two of her stories, "Hepzibah's Story" and "Wilhelmina," and of her novel *Anne* suggest that Spaulding made the break. There is no evidence, however, that Woolson felt any long-term heartbreak over the ended affair, and, in fact, in later years she considered it a fortunate escape from an unsuitable marriage. Nor do we know what prompted Woolson to consider herself a spinster after this affair, but she willingly accepted this role and the caretaking of her mother after her father's death. With his death, she began to write and publish, at first travel sketches that she sent to the *Daily Cleveland Herald* from New York in 1870 and 1871, and then a children's novel, *The Old Stone House* (1872), drawn from reminiscences of her childhood. When Woolson committed herself in 1873 to traveling in a warmer—and less costly—southern climate with her mother, she also committed herself to becoming the kind of writer she wished to be. She abandoned children's literature altogether, considering herself unsuited for it, but continued to write travel sketches throughout her life, perhaps because she traveled so extensively and it was a natural way to supplement an income she always found insufficient. Many of her feelings about the landscapes she observed as she traveled also found their way into her poetry. But she directed most of her energy from 1873 on into the five novels and fifty-eight stories published during her lifetime or posthumously.

Woolson gained several advantages from her years in the South with her mother. Here, she observed even more differences in character and culture than she had in the lake country and these differences inform the strongest thematic strands of her work. Her training in geology and the natural sciences informed her observations of new landscapes, so that her fiction uses color and light in a filmlike technique that creates lush scenic backgrounds. As an unmarried northern woman in the South, Woolson gained an outsider's view of the problems of Reconstruction as well as the sense of what it meant to be an outsider—by region, by gender, and by marital status. In the South, she also met the poet and critic Edmund Clarence Stedman, whose lifelong friendship aided her career, and the southern poet Paul Hamilton Hayne. She corresponded with both men, and they began to serve as the literary sounding board her father had been for her before his death.

The opportunity to cultivate what was to become her greatest literary friendship came after the death of Hannah Woolson when Constance, devastated at first but also freed from obligation to an ailing and aging mother, embarked for Europe, armed with a letter of introduction to Henry James. Clara Benedict claims that she accompanied her sister abroad after their mother's death because Constance was so emotionally disturbed by that death (Benedict 3:567). This is likely because Woolson's letters about her mother and her feelings when she died indicate a strong attachment and profound grief. However, Woolson also found familial attachments limiting to her own freedom. She, Clara, and Clare became traveling companions in Europe, but their tastes, especially in terms of climate, were incompatible. The extent of their incompatibility is reflected in a letter to Henry James in which Woolson, only half-jokingly, writes that "my sister has not enjoyed my being shut up in my own rooms, invisible until evening. . . . She greatly detests all my MSS, and has already presented me with a new dress and round-hat, so that I shall not look too 'literary.'"[8] The letter goes on to note that, if she lived in the United States, she would choose as home Florida, Mackinac Island, or Cooperstown, all three of which her sister hated.

Woolson's letters about Clara and Clare often echo with the strain of accommodating to them. We can speculate from this that she had also felt this way toward her mother—bound by as well as bound to her—and that, after her mother's death, she felt some degree of freedom, at the age of thirty-nine, to at long last pursue her own life-style. That life-style included long work hours, solitary walks, carefully regulated social connections, and deeply cultivated friendships, largely through correspondence, with a few people. Partly because of the attachment to travel that she had learned from childhood and partly because of economics, Woolson never maintained a permanent home in Europe. But she did seek semipermanent homes, preferring to rent apartments that she could furnish to her liking and in which she could employ her own cook rather than finding herself at the mercy of hotel dining. Despite her solitary habits, Woolson did not avoid society completely. Her fiction about Americans in Europe reflects her interest in diversity, and her close observation categorizes the various types of Americans in Europe: cultured, intellectual Americans who settled for long periods in one European city; the *nouveau riche* on grand tours whose obligatory visits to galleries and ruins were frenzied and superficial; and Americans who were stretching their limited means and hoping to marry their children to wealthy Europeans.

One of the reasons Woolson had limited patience with society was her sense of awkwardness over her increasing deafness. She maintained her closest friendships through letters: to her family, especially her nephew Sam Mather who handled her finances; through the Mather connection, to John Hay; to Stedman and Hayne from her days in the South; to Francis Boott and his daughter Lizzie, who in her thirties married a painter from Kentucky named Frank Duveneck and who lived near Woolson in Florence; and to Henry James, and to a lesser degree, both Alice James and her companion Katharine Loring. Letter writing was crucial for her, not just because she was removed from the people she cared about, but also because writing is a comfortable way for a person hard of hearing to communicate.

Woolson's nomadic and solitary life was also marked by anxiety over her brother Charlie, whose name she also spells *Charly* and *Charley*. Charlie is mysterious enough within the family that Clare Benedict left him, alone of the children who reached adulthood, out of the family tree that prefaces *Five Generations,* her three-volume sketch of the family, though she did not excise the few references to him from the volume itself. What letters survive mentioning Charlie talk about him in terms of anxiety. Jarvis Woolson, in an undated letter to Georgiana's child, Sam Mather, takes pains to ask Sam to maintain contact with Charlie, who believes himself important at a foundry and warehouse, because "[e]very one, in this world, finds a *firm friend* their best earthly possession. In *grief, sickness,* or *trouble,* there is nothing like a true friend." Hannah Woolson wrote, also to Sam, in 1875, that Charlie, according to a letter he sent her, "has become quite aged in his looks" and, in 1878, that she feels "great anxiety" about his health and about the fact that Charlie cannot come to her because he will not throw away "all the chances he has worked so hard for, the past year." And during her first years in Europe, Woolson wrote to Sam that she is "anxious . . . that [Charlie] should do well with his farm this next season. The winter seems to depress him."[9]

The anxiety about Charlie was well founded. Joan Weimer has found evidence that Woolson believed he had taken morphine (*MG* xvi), and Cheryl Torsney says that the circumstances of his death in California in 1883 suggest suicide.[10] A letter from Woolson to Sam Mather reveals just how distraught she was over Charlie's death. It made her "suffer more than [she had] ever suffered"; she was "so extremely unhappy for a number of weeks that [she] did not know where to turn"; she read and then destroyed a "sort of diary" that he sent her just before his death that "showed suffering so piteous that it broke [her] heart" (WRHS, 16 Jan. 1884).

Whatever the exact circumstances of Charlie's life and death, he probably suffered from a tendency toward depression that both he and Constance inherited from their father. Cheryl Torsney has traced Woolson's depressions and suggested she had Seasonal Affective Disorder, an interesting conjecture given Woolson's belief that Charlie suffered more in the winter months.[11] Over and over in her personal correspondence and her fiction, Woolson mentions depression and its hereditary nature. The clearest letter is one to Sam Mather:

> What you write shows one that underneath all lies the one thing that I have known and preached for years . . . that thing is that *we* as a family *cannot* do what many other people can, without breaking down. We cannot go without sleep, we cannot overtax ourselves; we cannot "overdo" in any way. If we persist either from ignorance or obstinacy, we only break down. But on the other hand, if we will only take good care of ourselves, we are able to do as much as most people each day, and have, too, better health than most people; that is, fewer illnesses in the course of the years. But we cannot, must not, transgress. (Benedict 2:36–37)

Woolson's language here implies a moral obligation to fight depression. It also implies that her family offered more than one model for breaking down—Charlie certainly; possibly her mother, though I suspect her mother was careful not to "overtax" herself; and even, perhaps, her father, whose sudden death she may have attributed to some kind of obstinate persistence in activity when a particular cycle of depression demanded more care. Words like "overtax" and "overdo" and phrases about "go[ing] without sleep" even point to manic depression, which could explain Charlie's erratic employment. The intensity of Woolson's *cannot*s and *must not*s indicates how aware she was of her susceptibility to depression, of the consequences she knew possible, and of the prevention she could employ. The open discussion also reflects society's increased awareness of the nature of mental illness. By midcentury, alienists, the nineteenth-century term for psychiatrists, had begun making an impact on the medical profession and the public consciousness. With the alienists' ability to diagnose mental conditions came the ability to treat conditions like depression.[12] Only in this environment could Woolson define herself and her family as susceptible to depression and self-prescribe a coping strategy.

We will never know if Woolson succeeded in fighting off depression or if she succumbed to it. We do know that on January 24, 1894, she fell or jumped to her death from her window in the Casa Semitecolo, Venice. She had written the sketch of her father sometime in late 1892 or in 1893, which must have had an impact on her sense of exile. She had also just completed *Horace Chase* and had been writing letters from Venice for several months about feeling depressed. Yet, this was her pattern after she completed any major literary project. It is a pattern one expects after the letdown in intensity of the creative process and that may be more prevalent in women who produce books but do not produce children and who, like Woolson, felt pressure from the publishing establishment to write according to the public's expectations for women. Throughout her life she shared her feelings of depression with friends. Compare, for example, a letter written on Christmas Day 1893 to her friend Arabella Carter Washburn with a letter dated February 12, 1882, to Henry James.[13] To Washburn she says that "if at any time you should hear that I have gone, I want you to know beforehand that my end was peace, and even joy at the release." Similarly, she writes to James, "Death is not terrible to me. . . . To me it is only a release; and if, at any time, you should hear that I had died, always be sure that I was quite willing, and even glad, to go. I do'nt think this is a morbid feeling, because it is accompanied by a very strong belief, that, while we *are* here, we should do our very best, and be as courageous and work as hard, as we possibly can." Yet Woolson's letters do not indicate suicidal depression as much as they reflect that she wrote about her feelings to friends as a way of coping with them. Both of these letters show her looking forward to death as fulfillment and escape, but their tone is not despairing, and the one to James emphasizes the courage to live. Because Woolson consciously fought and talked about depression, she was able to face life squarely, aware that it was a struggle but not self-pitying about her share in that struggle. Indeed, in her last letters to Sam Mather, she sounds as if she is recovering her psychological strength, feeling "more cheerful and serene" in Venice than in England and taking delight in the acquisition of a new dog (WRHS, 20 Nov. 1893).

At the end of 1893, Woolson's psychological health may have been improving, but her physical health was not. At the time of her death, she was battling influenza, an illness that fulfilled an early fear that she expressed to Henry James about feeling "a horror of being ill—ill a long time, over here all alone."[14] Joan Weimer has discovered a letter written to Sam Mather by a woman named Marie Holas, a companion hired to attend Woolson in the last two weeks of her life. Drawing on internal evidence from the letter, Weimer concludes that Woolson knew she had something worse than influenza—perhaps gallstones or pancreatitis that would have precipitated a slow and painful death—and that this led to a conscious decision for suicide.[15] Other evidence within the letter supports the suicide theory. According to Holas, Woolson had expressed her wished that she not be "buried in the cemetery of Venice, as she hated the place," but that she be buried in Rome, "the only place where she could rest in peace." She had instructed Holas to cable her relations "if she were to die" and to have her "house closed & put under seals" until Mather and Clara Benedict arrived to "dispose" of her things "according to her will." On January 22, she had Holas cable her friend Grace Carter to come, and on the morning of January 23, she told Holas that "if I sleep today, I shall be quite well tomorrow, but if I don't sleep, I shall be dead." That evening Woolson requested more morphine, but her physician denied it because more would make him "responsible for her death." On Woolson's request, Holas then closed the "door, windows, shutters, & curtains" to the room and, after Woolson told her "I am so comfortable, please let me alone," Holas went out, leaving everything in order so that the nurse would "not have to leave the patient for one moment." The nurse, however, did leave around 12:15. For explanation, the nurse reported to Holas that Woolson had been "very quiet" and called for some milk, but refusing "to drink it in the cup she handed to her," she sent the nurse "to the dining room to take another of pink china. She wanted that one & no other." When the nurse returned, "she found the window opened, & the bed empty," Woolson having fallen or jumped from her window to the pavement below. As overwhelming as the evidence appears that Woolson committed suicide—it would, after all, be difficult to fall accidentally if the windows had remained closed—Holas rejects this view. She writes that "nothing gave [me] ever to suppose that she had such a sad purpose in her mind, nor can I think she had it, as she sent for Miss Carter, & was going to make her will, that same day. Many people speak of death when ill, & Miss Woolson's illness was not such as to give any kind of anxiety." Holas, of course, is protecting herself from any blame involving Woolson's death, and we have no way of judging the accuracy of her letter. In fact, a letter written on the same day—January 31, 1894—by Clara Hay to Sam Mather's wife, Flora,[16] indicates that Holas "was not to be trusted" and that Grace Carter "found that though Miss Holas had only been [with] Miss Woolson about ten days, Miss Woolson had handed over keys, money, & everything to her, & had the greatest confidence in her." Carter was also depending on Holas's efficiency, but a suspicion had been cast by a Mrs. Bronson, who was involved in a "feud" with Holas. Hay goes on to say that one of Woolson's brooches appears to be missing. Although Carter "does not know but what it may have been lost or may be with some things somewhere else," the innuendo against Holas is clear.

Woolson's improving psychological condition prior to her last illness, accompanied by her deteriorating physical condition, supports an interpretation that she died as she lived—courageously and deliberately, not overcome by delirium as her friends believed. Woolson also would have had several models for suicide. Besides her brother Charlie's possible suicide, she knew that in 1885 Henry Adams's wife Clover had killed herself by swallowing photographic chemicals. She may also have known that Alice James had struggled with suicidal feelings, to the point that her father granted his permission for her suicide, his belief being that once she felt she had permission, she would not take her life. Whether or not Woolson discussed the justifiability of suicide with Alice, she did mark her personal copy of Epictetus at a passage that justifies suicide.[17] And she would have known that Alice's friend Rebecca Hunter had apparently thrown herself into the sea in 1888; that Ellen Gurney, Clover Adams's sister, had thrown herself in front of a train in 1887; that George Eliot's husband, John Cross, had fallen from a window in Venice in 1880; and that Amasa Stone, the father-in-law of both Sam Mather and John Hay, had committed suicide in 1883. There are, as well, two late works that prefigure how she died. In "Dorothy," the narrator thinks of the title character, who is standing on a precipice: "But one could never think of Dorothy as falling; her supple figure conveyed the idea that she could fly—almost—so lightly was it poised upon her little feet; in any case one felt sure that even if she should take the fancy to throw herself off she would float to the lower slope as lightly as thistle-down."[18] In *Horace Chase,* a male character almost falls to his death from a hotel room where he had been suffering from depression and fever resulting from inflammation of the brain. Although he is rescued, he dies from the brain fever, and his sister says he was not afraid to commit suicide, suggesting that his near fall had been deliberate. These fictional events reflect death as the joyful release from life Woolson spoke of in her letters, not the violent accident others interpret such a death to be.

Whether or not Woolson committed suicide at the last, she was not by nature suicidal, but rather a woman committed to the struggle of life, no matter how painful it became. Her legacy to us is a body of fiction that can add significantly to our understanding of the latter half of the nineteenth century. Like most of the fiction of her day, it was written for magazine audiences that expected novels with cliffhangers and stories with happy endings. Woolson knew that happy endings were rare and, early, wanted to try Hawthornian romance writing that allowed open-ended and ambiguous plots; however, her region was not Hawthorne's "neutral territory" but the landscapes she traveled through so extensively. She could paint a landscape and plot a story in such a way that one wonders if she might have been a film director in the twentieth century. Her knowledge of region and character enabled her to look at ethnic and class concerns that remained outside the range of Hawthorne or, later, even of James and Howells. Like James, she usurped many of the themes current in popular fiction by women, but her range is fuller than most of her predecessors or contemporaries. Rather than focusing on death, she looked at the problems of life: at alcoholism, child abuse, and poverty; at ethnocentricity and prejudice; at the freedom and bondage of marriage; at modes of parenting and gender expectations in parent-child relationships; at the advantages of widowhood over spinsterhood; at the marginalization of women who pursue education or art. Her themes are complex, her style highly textured and nuanced, her humor understated and very funny.

Constance Woolson spent her life searching for a home. Not only was she bound to home, to the past she remembered fondly and whose loss she felt so deeply and to the few people she cared about but could not seem to live with, but she also was bound by home and the nineteenth-century value placed on domesticity, which she could reject only by being an aberration in her society, an itinerant, solitary, single woman. Throughout her life she searched for a home—"a home of [her] own, no matter how small and plain," whether this were a villa in Florence or a cottage in Florida.[19] She could say to James that his work was her "true country," her "real home," because her love for literature remained one of the constants in a life continually shaken and uprooted. The other constant was her sense of beauty, her openness to the landscape that remained with her through all her travels. And so it is appropriate that she wrote on Christmas Eve, 1893, just before the attack of influenza that led to her death: "I should like to turn into a peak when I die; to be a beautiful purple mountain, which would please the tired, sad eyes of thousands of human beings for ages."[20] Her burial on a hillside in Rome in a grave bound by violets brought her to a fitting home.

2

Eden and the Anxiety of Influence
♣

Because she never ran a household, Woolson was not at home in the domestic realism of antebellum women writers. She used the marriage plot of the domestic realists in her novels, but her vision of human relationships and the possibility of happiness was darker than theirs and her characters were as likely not to marry as to marry. In this, her writing was more akin to that of antebellum romance writers, who created windows into an idealized or historical past as a way of coming to terms with the difficulties of the present. But Woolson was no more successful at invoking the past than she was at imagining a domesticated present. In an 1875 letter to Paul Hayne, she writes that her story "Castle Nowhere" is "something of an ideal, instead of a real tale. . . . But then I had been abused so for writing such deadly 'real' stories, that I did branch out, in that one, into the realm of imagination" (Hubbell, 15 June 1875). At this point in her career, she was still struggling to find a literary home suitable to her talents and to the demands of the marketplace.

Woolson reveals her sense of the conflict between romance and realism as early as 1871 in "A Day of Mystery." In that story, two women seize a day to go rowing on a lake, an excursion they turn into a melodramatic adventure. The lake itself, a discovered boat, a log shanty, an obscured grave, a mystery woman, a discovered ring, a phantom flame—all these are explained away in the end by a male who believes only in "prosaic reality" because "the increase of knowledge had banished romance, which was only another name for ignorance, from the world forever" (292). *Romance,* here, does not mean the love plot, which is at bottom the stuff of "prosaic reality": we fall in love, we marry or fail to marry, we are fulfilled or disillusioned in love. Rather, *romance* suggests the ability to imagine, to transform the ordinary, to confront the stuff of mystery. "A Day of Mystery" sounds a note of regret that female writers were discouraged from romance writing, but this was a regret that Woolson quickly moved beyond, for it is through a realism that extends beyond the domestic, not romance, that she learned to transcend the prosaic. Unlike her male predecessors, she was not successful on the rare occasions that she tried romance writing. In a story titled "Keller Hill," for example, she tried to rework the Hawthornian theme of sin and retribution into a new model in which the sinner is protected by the brother of the man he murdered, but also forced by this brother to atone for his sin by using his money to educate the friendless. In order to capture the imagined past of romance, Woolson writes "Keller Hill" in the format of a diary entry to establish the voice of an early Virginia settler. But her structural inversions and *-st/-th* endings are more annoying than historically convincing, so that the theme of sin and retribution gets lost in a tortured and unnatural style.

One of the major origins for Woolson's connection to romance writing was her life in the vanishing wilderness that her great-uncle, James Fenimore Cooper, wrote about. Her childhood in Ohio gave her the means of seeing beneath the myth of a free and idyllic state of nature that her great-uncle had popularized and that the westward movement tried to recapture and preserve. Eric Sundquist has studied Cooper in the light of this myth, arguing that the tension in Cooper rests in his almost erotic attachment to a wilderness that is being destroyed by the very forces that seek to transform it into a garden. Sundquist's Cooper is haunted by the idea that if we move "too far outside of society," we find "lawlessness and anarchy," but if we remain too much in society, we find a "denial of freedom if not outright suffocation" (8). Cooper's *Home as Found,* which centers around battles about land acquisition, ends, in Sundquist's view, by maintaining the connection between names and property in the quest for building a lasting home. The Garden of Eden, in other words, comes deeded to Adam and Eve, domesticated and boundaried.

Home as Woolson found it owes more to this Cooper than to the Cooper of the Leatherstocking Tales. By Woolson's day, westward expansion had moved well beyond the Mississippi River. Annette Kolodny has described this expansion in terms of exploring vast, unsettled lands coupled with the dream of building oases within the wilderness. For her, the male dream of discovery and adventure, represented in the

Natty Bumppo figure, clashes with the female dream of a domesticated garden. As Sundquist describes it, the dream of nature and family paradoxically fragmented the family by pushing it in too many directions and by destroying the land in clearing for the garden. This process of destruction was well under way by midcentury. With victories in the Revolutionary War and the War of 1812, the opening of the Northwest Passage by Lewis and Clark in 1804, and the expansionist mentality solidified by the Louisiana Purchase in 1803, the United States government began to establish a system of forts that would insure its physical possession of the land and maintain order among the various constituencies: British, French, and mixed-blood fur traders; Indians, missionaries, and immigrant settlers, including those of Swiss, Scottish, German, and Jewish origins. By 1819, Fort Snelling was established in Minnesota and travel continued to be made easier by steamboats (1811), the Erie Canal (1825), and the expansion of railroads that allowed transcontinental travel by midcentury. Annette Kolodny has summed up the rapid settlement: by the 1830s, a thousand immigrants per day were pouring into Detroit; by the 1840s, when Woolson's parents settled in Cleveland, one-third of the population lived west of the Appalachians and the United States had gained California and much of the Pacific Northwest as its territory; by the 1850s quantities of promotional literature and western domestic novels had been written. The American Indian population had been "controlled" and the fear of becoming Indianized lessened; communities had begun to see themselves as less isolated, and, in Kolodny's words, as places where men as well as women could be "governed by the values of hearth and home" (223).

During Woolson's childhood, the West may still have been a place where a new Eden might be found, at least in the imaginations of many of those who faced the challenge of settlement. The female version of the new Eden is represented in numerous stories about the process of domesticating the garden, such as Carolyn Kirkland's *A New Home—Who'll Follow* (1839) and Alice Cary's two-volume collection of short stories, *Clovernook* (1851, 1853), works, though published early, Woolson may have read because of their midwestern focus. She would have had access to large numbers of books because her childhood coincided with the rapid rise of book publishing and selling made possible by new printing techniques and by the railroads.[1] Throughout her life, her reading habits were more literary than popular, but as late as 1890, she wrote that she had read Susan Warner's *Wide, Wide World* and also claims to have read all the "popular ladies."[2] In addition to Kirkland and Cary, the popular ladies might have included New England writers Lydia Maria Child and Catherine Maria Sedgwick, whose *Hobomok* (1824) and *Hope Leslie* (1827) explored Indian-white relations in the historical past.

Woolson combined the literary traditions she was familiar with and her own considerable powers of observation as she wrote her first stories about the regions around the Great Lakes that she knew so well. But her West had turned into a series of cities with the largest proportions of the population living clustered together in increasingly urban environments. Cleveland, which had a population of six thousand in 1840, had become so industrialized by 1878 that Hannah Woolson complained of the "density of the Cleveland atmosphere, from the chemicals & coal fires" that veiled the "Forest-City" she had first settled in.[3] Woolson's interest in nature led her away from urban into rural settings. Because she began to see that the wilderness was becoming all too settled, she sought her literary home outside of the myth of domesticating the garden. Victoria Brehm believes that she used rural landscapes to create an imaginative, free space for unconventional female characters and has noticed that her most unconventional females live in areas protected by cliffs or labyrinthine waters; the closer her landscapes come to established communities, the more difficult life is for these characters (172–86).

By centering her fiction around sparsely populated landscapes, Woolson may be seen as subscribing to the romantic myth of nostalgia for the vanishing wilderness more than its optimistic corollary, the myth of the domesticated garden. But rather than embracing the myth, she exposes it. Whether of wilderness or garden, whether romance or domestic realism, these myths represent false Edens, available only to those willing to find homes within fortified boundaries. Woolson's fiction exposes three types of Edenic myths: a prelapsarian Eden where Adam is the keeper of the home, a postlapsarian Eden where the patriarchal church is the keeper of home, and a postlapsarian Eden where the female reenvisions the boundaries. These are imagined spaces that help Woolson early in her career move away from the mythic emphasis of romance literature. They are also realistic places that Woolson connects to people she observed within geographical rather than literary places. As places, Woolson felt attracted to them, but when she enters their borders through her imagination, she undercuts the attraction by seeing how constricting these real borders would be for her.

Woolson's early story "Castle Nowhere" best illustrates her version of a prelapsarian Eden and is especially interesting because it shows her reenvisioning the myth of the vanishing wilderness that her great-uncle treated in *The Deerslayer.* "Castle Nowhere" tells the story of a man raising a child, now grown, on an ark built from salvaged parts of swamped boats. The ark is hidden in an isolated portion of Lake Michigan, which is fogged in most of the time. The man, who calls himself Fog after the surrounding weather, has rescued the child, Silver, from an orphanage and has raised her in order to expiate a crime he committed as a young man. Jarvis Waring, a Natty Bumppo figure who is more like a weekend warrior than an authentic woodsman, stumbles across the ark and, of course, falls in love with Silver. He fights this love because he recognizes that part of his fascination with Silver is her splendid isolation and that he does not want to give up civilization for the girl.

Woolson was no dreamy-eyed idealist craving isolation in a wilderness closer to her great-uncle's novels than her personal observations. Not only does she make Waring aware that to love Silver's isolation is to be infatuated with a dream, she also makes it clear that a girl like Silver can exist only in a prelapsarian world, one isolated not just from evil but also from sexuality and from the concepts of life and death. Woolson would not have articulated Eric Sundquist's version of her great-uncle's Eden as erotic, even incestuous, but we can read this version in Waring's attraction to Silver. By equating Silver with her surroundings, Waring purifies her much as Natty tried to purify Judith Hutter. Woolson understood the falseness of such purity, writing in a memoir on Cooper that she thought Natty overly severe in his judgment of Judith.[4] Joan Weimer pursues this notion of sexual purity further when she discusses "Castle Nowhere" in relation both to *The Deerslayer* and to Hawthorne's "Rappaccini's Daughter." These works portray father figures imposing isolation on their daughters in order to expiate their own crimes, creating female characters who, like Silver, are "even more innocent than the unfallen Eve." She accurately sees "Castle Nowhere" as a commentary on patriarchal systems that mate "men with grown-up children," that keep women innocent by keeping them ignorant, and that imagine sexuality beneath a surface purity (*MG* xxviii–xxix).

Woolson's Eden is rife with patriarchy. Despite his attempt to recapture Eden, Fog lives in a postlapsarian world, where he has assumed responsibility for, and control over, Silver. The only way he can support Silver is by murder—he lures ships to wreckage by using a false light and then uses the booty to build and maintain his ark. On the one hand, the ark represents salvation, the place Fog can survive as he expiates his guilt, but it also represents punishment because it is a confining home that is a necessary protection from an outside, hostile world. Fog takes control of the ark, trying to transform it to a prelapsarian Eden, but he can do this only by eliminating all references to religion. The Judeo-Christian tradition moves immediately from the creation story to the fall and the fall is refigured in the story of Noah and his ark. To introduce Silver to the concept of Eden would also mean introducing her to the expulsion from Eden and into the concept of death. Fog literally conceals the existence of death from Silver. In doing so, he creates the problem of how Silver will care for herself when he dies. His way out of the fog he has surrounded Silver with is Jarvis Waring. But the screw turns again: to introduce Silver to death, he must also introduce her to life, which includes sexuality.

In choosing the name Jarvis, Woolson referenced her father, Charles Jarvis Woolson, who reminded her of both love and death and who helped shape her into a woman who valued home, but found her own freedom only outside the boundaries of home. Because of his susceptibility to depression, Jarvis Woolson was a reminder of the death of the spirit. But, even more important, he was a man whom Woolson saw as vitally alive. He introduced her to her love for nature, for physical activity, and for travel, activities that moved her outside the physical confines of home. By referencing her father in Jarvis Waring's name, Woolson neither excludes women, like Cooper's Natty does, nor controls them within limited boundaries, like Hawthorne's Rappaccini. Like Hawthorne, Woolson envisions a patriarchy that suggests what she and her father both knew: that life involves death and that Eden cannot exist. Even as Waring is attracted to Silver, he sees her as "shut up" (*CN* 35), something that Jarvis Woolson taught his daughter not to be. Waring is attracted by the simplicity and naturalness of Silver's beauty and prefers the white she wears to the artifice of a Titian portrait that he carries with him and that represents the civilizing power of a culture that has had centuries to define the beautiful in terms of art. But Waring also asks Silver to put up her hair, to braid it like a crown instead of allowing it to fall like a veil around her shoulders. He wants to widen Silver's horizons. Although he does not need the beauty of a Titian portrait, he still needs to tame the primitive, to civilize it through an artful conception of idealized beauty. He also needs to tame it with the sanctity of religion, thus he sends for the Presbyterian minister to marry him and Silver. Placing limits on his journey into the primitive, he is reminiscent of Cooper's Natty Bumppo, who, for all his attraction to the noble American Indian, persists in seeing a savageness in Indian cultures from which his own contact with white Christianity has saved him. He also represents Woolson's double vision of the charm and limitation of the natural but isolated existence.

In "Castle Nowhere," Woolson reenvisions Cooper by juxtaposing his Edenic nature with Hawthorne's darker view of the sinister patriarchy that controls the isolated garden in both "Rappaccini's Daughter" and *The Blithedale Romance*. Her own real encounters with the wilderness show her that only a prelapsarian Eden has no social class, no ethnic prejudices, no doctrinal religion, no art. It is a "Castle Nowhere," bought with ignorance and maintained for women only by the protection of a man who knows about death and, therefore, about sin, the origin of death. "Castle Nowhere" shows that Eden is no better a home for women than the world, for, if women have knowledge of the world, they also can develop ways to subvert it. The story's plot is not one of women's subversion—Silver dutifully passes from the protection of Fog to the protection of Waring—but Woolson's own subversion is clear. The narrator tells us that the Presbyterian minister who marries Waring and Silver lives among the Mormons. Joan Weimer interprets this as Woolson's suggestion that the name Silver references the Mormon use of women as exchange (*MG* xxviii). But the narrator of the story also says that even under polygamy "the evil tempers of men . . . are made endurable by a system of co-operation [among the women]; one reed bends, and breaks, and dies, but ten reeds together can endure" (*CN* 88). With her marriage to Waring, Silver may find other reeds and eventually discover a sense of life that does not depend on isolation and male protection.

Because of its depiction in the fiction and promotional literature of the nineteenth century, the West is an ideal setting through which Woolson could examine the quest for home and the myth of an Eden in the wilderness. However, as her echoes of Hawthorne's more imagined settings indicate, she does not confine her examination of the Edenic myth to a geographical place. Her southern story "Sister St. Luke" looks at how the institution of Catholicism creates an Eden as artificial as the one in "Castle Nowhere." Woolson saw Catholicism in both the French societies of Mackinac Island and the Spanish ones of Florida. The idea of a cloistered life attracted her, but she also saw it as an artificial creation of home. Sister St. Luke does not create her home in her convent, but has it created for her by a male hierarchy. Where the Eden in "Castle Nowhere" is one in which the female is sheltered by the male in an artificially created prelapsarian ark, the Eden in "Sister St. Luke" is one imbued with the patriarchy of an artificially created postlapsarian convent.

Not a Catholic herself, Woolson had no experience with convents, but she provides a spokesperson for her problem with the patriarchy of the system in Melvyna Sawyer, who has taken in Sister St. Luke while she recuperates from an illness. Melvyna complains that the nun has been expelled from the convent by the men who control it because, ill, she is "useless" (*Rodman* 46). She has been taught to fear men, though no men reside at the convent, and has listened to other nuns who have shaped their views according to what Catholicism has taught them. As Melvyna puts it, "She believes every word of all that rubbish those old nuns have told her. She thinks it's beautiful to be the bride of heaven; and, as far as that goes, I don't know but she's right: 'tain't much the other kind is worth" (*Rodman* 47). Woolson, of course, does not hold the same views as all her characters and, in fact, complains in a letter to her friend from childhood Arabella Carter Washburn about being "held personally responsible for the theology and morality" of them (Benedict 2:20). Still, Melvyna's comment suggests that the convent system offers a home that is unnatural for women. Nowhere in the story does Woolson suggest that the convent offers even the little bit of subversiveness that the Mormon system offers. Woolson encodes her belief in its unnaturalness in the image of the convent's garden, where Sister St. Luke walks from a tamed lime tree to a cultivated rose bush. Anything wilder is too fearful for this timid nun. In the course of the story, Sister St. Luke befriends two men who try to teach her to walk confidently and to love rather than fear the wild nature of the sea. They want her to discard the veil and "shroud" (*Rodman* 58) that imprison her in the attitudes of the convent and, ultimately, she does this by rescuing one of the men during a storm.

The veil imprisons Sister St. Luke because it allows her to be protected rather than challenged by faith. Unlike Woolson, who had been taught in the natural science environment of the Cleveland Female Seminary that was informed by speculations about the age and origins of the earth, Sister St. Luke has not had to wrestle with challenges to biblical authority. Woolson is quite clear that Sister St. Luke believes rather than thinks. She carries a "bead of a rosary that had belonged to some saint who lived somewhere some time, a little faded prayer copied in the handwriting of a young nun who had died some years before, and whom she had dearly loved, and a list of her own most vicious faults, to be read over and lamented daily" (*Rodman* 62). These faults include such serious things as sharp words to a nun who has a sharp tongue, coveting someone else's cell for its view, and wanting more marmalade. Woolson also implies that this type of naïve belief results from accepting whatever men say: when one of the men, in jest, offers Sister St. Luke a sea-bean that has washed on shore and tells her she must not lose it or evil will befall her, she does not get the joke. Although she shows independent courage in her dramatic sea rescue, she ends up relying on the help of male friends to return her to the convent from which other men had evicted her. To find Eden within a Catholic convent, she needs the help and the permission of men; she must adopt a male name; and she must believe, not think.

Woolson's vision of Catholicism, like her vision of western settlement, owes much to literary paradigms. Charlotte Brontë's *Villette,* for example, uses the image of a ghost-nun to show how the Catholic church provides a refuge for women whose role was defined by marriage whether she chose marriage or not. At the same time, however, the refuge is a cell for the nun, a room that is solitary and closed off, unacceptable for the novel's Protestant heroine. Where Brontë's nun was forced into her role by a family who wanted to prevent her marriage, Woolson's nun has been socialized to believe in the beauty of this role. Because Sister St. Luke, at one point, does make a choice for humanity in the sea rescue and for the life, with all its dangers and passions, that men and nature represent to her, she seems to have greater freedom than Brontë's nun. It is this kind of freedom to choose one's own prison that Mary Wilkins Freeman stressed a decade after the publication of "Sister St. Luke" in her story "A New England Nun." Freeman's Louisa Ellis chooses the fastidiousness of a nunlike cell over marriage, but where Louisa represents a woman choosing her own life, Sister St. Luke chooses between two life-styles defined largely by men. Her choice is thus limited as Eden is limited and represents a home that Woolson would have found impossible for herself even without her Protestantism.

Because Woolson mingled at least on the edges of Catholic cultures and even felt attracted to the convent structure, her writing contrasts that of many anti-Catholic sensation writers who were popular in the first half of the century and who relished portraying nuns as lustful and sadistic, given to alcoholism, prostitution, and infanticide.

This is myth degenerated into stereotype, the element of universal truth that informs myth turned to rumor and innuendo, the fear in the presence of the mystery of life turned to fear of the different. David Reynolds has unearthed a number of these stories, among them Maria Monk's *Awful Disclosures of . . . the Hotel Dieu Nunnery at Montreal* (1836), a work that is the earliest piece of American "pornography" housed at the library of the Kinsey Institute. The book sold more than three hundred thousand copies, and Maria Monk, who had billed herself as a former nun, was eventually arrested for picking the pocket of her customer in a New York brothel.[5] Quite unlike near-pornographic exploiters of anti-Catholicism, Woolson did not fear or denigrate Catholicism. She was drawn to the convent ideal enough that she once wrote to Henry Mills Alden, "If I could go into a convent (where I didn't have to confess, nor rise before daylight for icy matins), I think I could write three or four novels better than I have yet done. But there are no worldly convents."[6] Although, for Woolson, a convent is a route to happiness made possible by a male hierarchy, it can offer peace; although it represents a false Eden, it is an attractive place for those with the naïveté of Sister St. Luke to call home.

Woolson's lack of belief in the myth of the Edenic home, whether in an ark in the wilderness modeled after Cooper or in a convent modeled after Brontë, is more complex in "St. Clair Flats," one of her favorite stories, perhaps because it is the one in which the female exerts the most control. Where Silver leaves what has been for her a prelapsarian Eden and Sister St. Luke returns to her Eden having seen the postlapsarian world, the woman is this story lives in an Eden that is postlapsarian, doing what Joan Weimer calls "her best to realize Eden in the present" (*MG* xxx). In this story, Woolson again examines how the notion of a Cooper-like primitivism is attractive only up to a point and is more viable for men than for women. The narrator, a male, returns to a place he and a hunting companion had visited fifteen years earlier, in 1855. In the marshes of Lake Erie, before a canal had opened the area to civilization, they discovered a tiny island with a lone house, occupied by a man who calls himself Waiting Samuel and his wife, Maria Ann, whom he has renamed Roxana. Roxana had refused to marry a farm boy from Maine, choosing, instead, Samuel, an outsider to her village. Samuel is prone to religious visions and, eventually, he stops working and wanders as his visions dictate, until he settles with Roxana in St. Clair Flats.

The narrator and his friend see the charm of this couple's existence, but it is a charm permeated by a romantic rather than a realistic vision. They value the landscape, the fishing, the good food, the picturesqueness of the scene. The narrator's friend, Raymond, loves the allure of being lost and is attracted by the spiritual atmosphere of the place and by Samuel's religious madness, believing that religion needs madness rather than doctrine to maintain the allure of mystery. Here again, Woolson undercuts the dangerous and naïve myth that an idealized or spiritualized landscape can offer a viable home. When she does this, she draws on the literary landscape of Hawthorne's *The Scarlet Letter*. Like Hawthorne's narrator in the novel's Custom-House section, Raymond writes a poem about the place and maligns critics who have too much power in declaring what constitutes art. But unlike Hawthorne's narrator, he ignores anything that is grounded in reality, in this case not a scarlet letter but a brooch that he sees only as a "brass breastpin" (*CN* 331). The narrator of "St. Clair Flats" gives the Hawthornian twist to Raymond. Accepting rather than dismissing the brooch, he weaves a love story around it. The brooch itself, like the scarlet letter, serves as a link to the past: it had been a wedding gift from Roxana's sister and represents Samuel's and Roxana's past, with all the social obligations the past carries just as the scarlet letter represents Hester's past and its social obligations.

In "St. Clair Flats," Woolson is wrestling with the question of what will constitute her literary home, of where on the continuum between the real and the imagined she will place herself. The narrator can romanticize an imagined story from a brooch, but the real brooch must inform that story. He wants a real and reliable host, not a madman obsessed by religious visions. His art depends on his belief that a true work of art exists and will rise to prominence no matter what the literary critic says about it. In other words, he believes that the true work of art is definable apart from its context and that it will always surface as a work of art because art and its inspiration are real and concrete. His conception of art may be naïve, but it is not narrow. It includes a wide perspective—for example, the way St. Clair Flats must have appeared before the European invasion of America—but the perspective must have its origins in the actual. Woolson captures the allure of the St. Clair Eden in the power of the setting for the narrator: "The word 'marsh,'" he says, "does not bring up a beautiful picture to the mind, and yet the reality was as beautiful as anything I have ever seen,—an enchanted land, whose memory haunts me as an idea unwritten, a melody unsung, a picture unpainted, haunts the artist, and will not away" (*CN* 306). The allure of the Flats is an inspiration for the artist, who, in this narrator's view, will ultimately find a home in the real world where his work will rise if it is any good.

In the narrator and Raymond, Woolson shows two possible literary homes: one that will ground her art in reality and artistic productivity so that recognition becomes possible in the present, and one that sees it as purely a mysterious, spiritual construct that can never be arrested in a permanent truth. The two also serve as glosses on the search for a physical home represented in Roxana and Waiting Samuel. Waiting Samuel is like Raymond, willing to give himself up to his visions, to lose himself in an Edenic wilderness that has no connection to other people's lives. Roxana, like the narrator, tries to construct an Eden out of the reality of a postlapsarian world. That world includes a husband who does not allow her to eat with him, who forces her to stand behind him while he prays to voices only he can hear. Again, this Eden is patriarchal, but in it Woolson creates a space where a woman can subvert the dominance of a male and redirect her version of Eden. Roxana's Eden is grounded in a postlapsarian world because she has known the loss of her home in Maine and the loss of a child who was born there. Like the Mormon wives in "Castle Nowhere," she can accommodate to the Eden Samuel defines for her and redefine it in subtle ways for herself. Because Samuel ignores her for God and because no community judges her behavior, she enjoys almost complete freedom away from Samuel. She has freedom to come and go as she pleases in order to buy provisions for the household. She can cook what she wants, plant what she likes, work with the autonomy of a man. Although she admits that "the winters *are* long" (*CN* 345), during the summers she finds companionship with a lighthouse keeper and his wife. Society, not Samuel, causes her to lose her ability to shape this Eden. The canals intrude and when the narrator returns, Roxana is gone. But this does not mean that she is defeated. If we catch Woolson's references to the Ariadne myth in her descriptions of the labyrinthine flats, we are reminded of the conflicting versions of Ariadne's fate. In one, Ariadne is left on an island by Theseus after he follows her clue on how to kill the minotaur and dies before his return. In the other, she is abandoned by Theseus but then rescued by Dionysus, whose children she bares, and then, in death, she is transformed to a star. Whether Roxana dies or leaves with Waiting Samuel, she has demonstrated her ability to transform her labyrinth into something other than a prison. If she has died, she has done so having known freedom; if she has left with Samuel instead of a freeing Dionysian god, she has done so having learned how to tame the minotaur.[7]

Because Woolson claimed Cooper and Hawthorne more than the antebellum domestic novelists as her literary forebears, she constructs many of her early pieces around the metaphoric search for, and disillusionment with, an Edenic home rather than around a realistic portrayal of the details of domesticating that new home. She knew that for the colonists, America was a new land, one where the persecutions of the Old World could be left behind and life begun anew in an imagined garden that, despite all its harshness, possessed vast resources created by God for mankind's use. It became a land where people could free themselves from the shackles of oppression and create a government that imposed the least strictures on its people that seemed possible in a world that was fallen and imperfect, but still capable of striving for perfection. Even as it emerged from its own taint of slavery, the United States was a land where people could always find a new place to pursue the myth of Eden, albeit at the expense of its indigenous people. But Woolson also came of age in a country racked by civil war, which forced her to reread their versions of romance, thus enabling her to escape the anxiety of their influence. She did not need to turn Hawthorne's dark vision of oppression to the remote and the imagined, nor did she idealize the vanishing wilderness to the extent that Cooper did. She saw that the pursuit of the wilderness was carried out by Fogs and Waiting Samuels, who recreated the oppressions from which they were fleeing. She saw that women were no better off in the domesticated garden than they were expelled from Eden and might even have applauded Eve for first eating of the fruit of knowledge so that she not be kept dependent, like Silver or Sister St. Luke, or subservient, like Roxana. With her love of solitude and her love of nature, convent and wilderness Edens attracted Woolson, but she knew they existed only in the imagination and in the literature she had read and that half-Edens, where men still had power over women, were places she did not wish to go.

3

Regionalism and the Bonds of Place

❧

Woolson's nomadic life was a double-edged sword. On the one hand, it severed her from the comfort of family and a sense of place, so that she spent much of her life searching for a permanent home to which she could feel bound; on the other, it helped her to sever ties that would have bound her to the provincial and the ordinary. Because she developed the habit of travel early, she needed wider boundaries to nourish her imagination than did someone like Emily Dickinson, who could see all the world in the confines of her Amherst home. From the start of her career, Woolson turned her penchant for travel into sketches that allowed her to support herself, but, just as she moved away from imitating romantic modes of fiction, she also moved beyond the conventional boundaries of travel writing. Dennis Berthold has begun the task of recovering Woolson's travel sketches, which he numbers at sixteen, most about her early travels through the Great Lakes and Ohio River Valley districts of the United States and through the post–Civil War South, and has shown that they reveal her ability to make something new of a well-established genre.[1]

The typical nineteenth-century travel sketch employed a gender-neutral narrator who used the occasion of travel to comment on history and the natural landscape. Woolson expanded the genre, particularly in her later sketches, placing more emphasis on narrative by creating two character types, the detached spinster and the detached male professor. Berthold argues that through the spinster's commentary on the flirtations and interactions among tourist-travelers, Woolson exploited her expertise in social satire. I would argue, as well, that she found in this character a way of coping with the social situations her increasingly asocial nature shunned. Berthold sees the professor character as expanding Woolson's satirical eye to the authoritarian male who intimidates female travelers but, at the same time, gives her an avenue for providing historical and geological information about a place. I would add that through him, Woolson is also able to use the geological and natural science background she was trained in at the Cleveland Female Seminary.

In her later sketches, Woolson may be satirizing Clarence King, a geologist to whom her friend John Hay tried to marry her. King is remembered in today's geology community as its first head and as the first white man to chart the sequoia forest of the Sierra Nevadas, though he exaggerated his account of his experiences. He was a golden boy, a man who managed to keep his marriage to a black woman a secret and, until just before his death, to keep his profession a secret from his wife, telling her that he worked for the railroad.[2] John O'Grady's portrait of King helps us to see that Woolson might be drawn to the type of person he represented. Although she would not have known about his wife, she might have known that he had been attracted to an Indian woman named Luciana, whom he told John Hay he "escaped from . . . by a miracle of self control" (O'Grady 108). Not only had King the courage to break social boundaries, he also expanded the boundaries imposed on women by exploring California, a state Woolson's brother Charlie had moved to and one that she might well have wished to explore herself. King's connection to the landscape was as poetic as it was scientific. Like Woolson, he had written about the landscape and, like her when she moved to Europe, he had given up that connection. By the time she met him, King had turned his energies toward making money, but since this included acquiring art objects, Woolson might also have been drawn to him for this mutual interest. Henry James's biographer, Fred Kaplan, characterizes King as "sexually adventuresome and personally flamboyant" (252), so that despite any attraction that may have existed between the two, King would have been an easy target for Woolson's increasingly sharp satirical eye.

In his discussion of the travel sketches, Berthold emphasizes the intersection Woolson saw between the social and the geographical. This intersection also implies a tension that marks her fiction: the traveler through a geographical place who profiles regional characters and satirizes the tourist whose culture is tied only to the transient travel-vehicle becomes a double-outsider, barred from both the permanent and the transient community. The person who lives as this kind of outsider may become particularly susceptible to myths about regional charm. Just over the next mountain may rise the destination she longs to call home. Toward the end of her life, Woolson's longing for home takes on some of this idealization. It looks backward rather than forward, to the warm Florida climate she had passed through during the decade of the1870s. But although intellectually and artistically, she felt drawn to the idealized past, she found her literary home in more realistic modes, at first within the rising popularity of local-color fiction.

Woolson's stories in *Castle Nowhere* tend to be nostalgic for a place and time unpolluted by the technology of canals and railroads and by the factionalism of religious sects and competing ethnic groups. However much she looked backward for a place to call home, she was never naïve about the regions in which she had lived. If, indeed, an idyllic wilderness ever existed, it had disappeared after the Revolutionary War when the new country tried to form policies that would maintain peaceful relations among diverse groups and to develop U.S. trade priorities. As early as 1786, United States citizenship was required for Indian trade, so as the country expanded westward, the expansion intensified the factionalism between the primarily British and French traders and the United States' Indian agencies, which were commanded by government appointees. Policies that encouraged Indian education and integration into white society only complicated matters by encouraging competition for particular brands of Christian conversion.[3] Woolson's stories are often told by narrators who return to a once remote place only to see changes and to remember a past that, violent and uncultured, they believe was free of the social expectations that confine and limit people living within communities. The tension in these stories between civilization and the wilderness mirrors the tension that increased with every new group come to plant its garden or factory. When, for example, in *Jupiter Lights,* Hollis Clay, a member of a community developing on Lake Superior, becomes one of those men who move farther and farther west and is never heard from again, he is pursuing a chimera. He leaves not because he dislikes the civilization that women like the novel's heroine, Eve Bruce, might bring to the wilderness, but because Eve does not return his love. In *Jupiter Lights,* the wilderness moves farther west, a place to escape from whatever demons haunt one.

"Castle Nowhere," "Sister St. Luke," and "St. Clair Flats" illustrate how well Woolson understood the illusion of Edenic possibilities in a fallen world and how well she read the patriarchy inherent in the entire

notion of Eden as Eden was constructed in a male-dominated literature. Had she been born male like her brother Charlie or her character Hollis Clay, she, too, would like to have wandered safely through
the unsettled territories. But often, the closest her females get to the
wilderness is a rural garden. Her first published story, "An October
Idyll," establishes the mode. The October idyll consists of five days of
harvesting and wine making. A man and woman, outsiders to the rural
community, who meet there but do not name themselves to each other,
join the harvest. At the end of the story, the woman identifies herself
as Katherine Van Schoonoven, a twenty-eight-year-old, cynical, world-
weary person, who is about to marry a sixty-year-old judge and to
ornament his house. The male outsider, called Hazel Eyes throughout
the story, identifies himself at the end as a married man named James
Tracy Chillingworth. The reference is, of course, to Hawthorne's cold
observer who represents the kind of world that Hazel Eyes returns to
and that Katherine is about to marry into (and, as a female, be excluded
from). By choosing the name Chillingworth instead of Dimmesdale,
Woolson de-emphasizes the couple's brief union in nature and its sexual
overtones. The tactic is clever: it allows Woolson to write a story that
caresses the land and the harvest while not threatening a conservative
reading public, reflecting, in the process, Woolson's own perceptions
of the social constraints placed on women.

Woolson was drawn to the rural because it offered women autonomy and because, like her travel sketches, it allowed her to look at
the natural environment her schooling had taught her to appreciate.
Caroline Gebhard has argued that Woolson modeled herself on Bret
Harte in order to use the wilderness to declare herself a writer different from the sentimental women writers whose work was so popular
in the nineteenth century. But we should remember that the local-color
tradition arose out of those domestic novelists, not in separation from
them. Elizabeth Ammons has argued that Rose Terry Cooke (1827–
92), especially, used the close observation of her New England region
to create sketches that the next generation might have labeled local
color. Ammons believes that this kind of sketch became particularly
attractive to women, perhaps because they could be written in the short
snatches of time available to them, but also because they reflect women's
ways of knowing as described by Nancy Chodorow and Carol Gilligan:
these sketches allow women to relate to the specifics of environment
and relations within an environment more than to abstract concepts.[4]
Interestingly, Cooke, Woolson, and Sarah Orne Jewett all had fathers

who taught them to love the outdoors. Jewett began publishing toward the end of the 1870s, and Mary Wilkins Freeman a decade later, so that Woolson must, like Cooke and Harte, be seen as among the first to develop the local-color genre. Just four years older than she and writing out of the California western experience, Harte represents someone Woolson could—and did—read as her own contemporary.

By looking at Woolson in relation to Harte, we see her moving beyond the anxiety of influence of past writers into a more contemporary mode whose parameters she could help to shape. For Caroline Gebhard, "The Lady of Little Fishing" reshapes Bret Harte's "The Luck of Roaring Camp," transforming a silenced female narrator into the true center of the tale and the equal of men in passion and desire. But in reading Woolson's local-color fiction, we should not limit it to a dialogue with Harte. Where Gebhard sees Woolson rewriting Harte to emphasize autonomy for women, Joan Weimer sees her creating isolated settings as a metaphor for women's exile "from themselves, from their society, from their art—and for Woolson's sense of herself as a homeless outcast" (*MG* xiv–xv). Actually, both these views apply. In a story like "The Lady of Little Fishing," the woman finds only a temporary voice in a wilderness setting and this voice is removed from us by the narrative method of the story. We learn about her from a narrator who has heard her story from a man named Reuban Mitchell, whom he met when he stumbled across the ruins of a small town hidden far from civilization. Mitchell is Woolson's Natty Bumppo figure, a true isolato, and the narrator one of Woolson's city-men who play at the wilderness experience. For about a week, the two use the town's ruined houses as firewood and agree to part company when that wood, a symbol of community, is gone. The narrator is talkative but not communicative; that is, he talks to himself or anyone who comes in his path but rarely listens in return. But when Reuban tells him about the lady of Little Fishing, he listens intently to a story that represents a communal experience. This woman has stumbled across Little Fishing and its band of men from various social and ethnic backgrounds. She civilizes and democratizes them, coaxing them to build her a church from which to preach and a house, and to build themselves houses that are all the same, not competing structures in a bid for her affections.

"The Lady of Little Fishing" represents the lost melting-pot communities of fish and fur traders that began to disintegrate with western expansion and Indian removal policies. It does this by becoming an example of the dream of community that Annette Kolodny has traced as the woman's dream for western expansion. But with its perfect democracy of identical houses, it also undermines the notion of freedom that allows one to choose how to build and decorate a home. It places a woman at the center of the community and gives her power to preach, but it does this only temporarily. As a preacher, this woman is like the Universalist and Unitarian ministers who began to populate rural western communities in the 1870s until even this liberal church hierarchy began to direct women to subordinate roles advocating social causes and performing social services.[5] The idyllic time when women find voice and power is, after all, only a dream that destroys one community without building a viable other. Even the female ministerial voice becomes suspect if it is too consumed by the missionary spirit.

We see Woolson's suspicion of religiously imposed homes and her dislike of missionary zeal more explicitly in the story "Mission Endeavor," which opens with an outer circle of Indians and an inner circle of whites watching the trial of a white man for murder. This mission has not been allied with the American Board of Missions, perhaps to indicate the fanatical zeal of its elder, Ephraim Danvers, or its willingness to admit a female teacher, named Miriam, who is so positive an influence on both the Indians and the missionaries that Ephraim "counted [her] as almost on a level with men, so far above the weaknesses of her sex she seemed to him" (889). Not only is Miriam a saint-in-the-wilderness like the lady of Little Fishing, she has come to the wilderness in the first place because, stifled in her English home, she followed voices that told her to come to America. But rather than succumb to fanatical white voices like those of Waiting Samuel or Ephraim Danvers, Miriam finds her power when she adopts habits more associated with Indian women outside of the missionary structure. As a way of saving her from the danger that Mission Endeavor will stifle her as much as her English home had done, Woolson has Miriam follow an Indian custom of purchasing the murderer's life by joining him in exile. Outside the community, she learns that this man loves another woman and releases him by telling him she is married. Now, freed of men and the strictures of a Puritanical mission outpost, Miriam once again moves through the frontier, alone but on her own terms.

The role of women in civilizing the wilderness serves as a theme again in "Peter the Parson," a local-color story about the social climate of a remote western town, and one that is a good example of male vs. female roles in creating a home out of the wilderness. Rather than a spiritualized woman coming to tame the mining town on Lake Superior, an Anglican parson tries to tame it. He is the male version of the lady, but being male, he is not idealized and has little success. Through the parson, Woolson shows how impossible it is for the nonmanly man to have an effect on civilizing a place as rough as a mining town. Indeed, what church there is for him to be parson of was erected by the influence of a woman who adopted it, complete with artificial flowers and candles and embroidered altar cloth, as a long-distance charitable project. Peter bears the brunt of the town jokes and even deserves them for his nervous, finicky ways and his celibacy that is based not on religious conviction but on his belief that he is too pure for a woman. The plot of the story has one of the women in the town fall in love with Peter and try to woo him with the domesticating enticements of a warm fire and delicate food, rather than the greasy fare he gets at his boardinghouse. She is not successful, and Peter is killed by a rival for her affections.

Once again, Woolson has captured the tension that is part of the western experience for women. She does not subscribe to the belief in a wilderness garden nor does she posit a wilderness unsullied by upper-class comforts. Woolson's version runs this way: The woman who has been uprooted from a civilized home tries to bring civilized comforts into a new and more democratic community. To avoid becoming masculinized into a roughneck democracy, she chooses to love the nonmasculine man. Rather than finding freedom, she becomes bound by two choices: men with missionary zeal who consider themselves too pure for carnal touch or men so rough they can readily commit murder. Neither equation brings female autonomy. Woolson's audiences missed this nuance in "Peter the Parson" and tried to locate an ideal in the parson, expressing their anger that she allowed him to be killed. Her audience's preferences aside, Woolson knew, as she wrote to Sam Mather, that "both in an artistic and truthful-to-life point of view, my ending of the story was better than the conversion of the miners, the plenty to eat, and the happy marriage proposed by my critics."[6] The real wilderness, as attractive as it is in its naturalness, is no more fulfilling a place for women, or, for that matter, men, than the idealized Eden.

Woolson wrote most of her lake country short fiction while she traveled throughout the post–Civil War South with her mother. The 1870s confirmed her sense of herself as a woman without a home not only because she was removed geographically from the place she had lived for most of her thirty years, but also because the move was precipitated by the death of her father. Woolson and her mother traveled to St. Augustine, Florida, to escape their grief, to ease Hannah's rheumatism with a warmer climate, and to live more economically, a factor that became even more important for them as the country plunged into a major depression mid-decade. From Florida they visited much of the South, including the Carolinas, Tennessee, and Georgia, where Woolson saw firsthand what the Civil War had done to the concept of permanent and stable homes. Her success in this fiction about a particular time and place indicates, as does her lake country fiction, that she found her literary home in new forms rather than the antebellum romantic or domestic traditions. Henry James praised her especially for her success in showing southern Reconstruction, her unique achievement in a nation still wounded by a divisive war:

> Miss Woolson has done nothing better than the best pages in this succession of careful, strenuous studies of certain aspects of life, after the war, in Florida, Georgia and the Carolinas. As the fruit of a remarkable minuteness of observation and tenderness of feeling on the part of one who evidently did not glance and pass, but lingered and analyzed, they have a high value, especially when regarded in the light of the *voicelessness* of the conquered and reconstructed South. Miss Woolson strikes the reader as having a compassionate sense of this pathetic dumbness—having perceived that no social revolution of equal magnitude had ever reflected itself so little in literature, remained so unrecorded and unsung. She has attempted to give an impression of this circumstance, among others, and a sympathy altogether feminine has guided her pen. She loves the whole region, and no daughter of the land could have handled its peculiarities more indulgently, or communicated to us more of the sense of close observation and intimate knowledge.[7]

John Kern also praised Woolson for understanding the South during Reconstruction:

> Miss Woolson thoroughly understood the bitterness that was in the hearts of the southern people during that period when short-sighted northern statesmanship was rubbing salt into the old wounds. She knew the facts and she has the artistry to dramatize them. No student of American history during this troubled era can afford to neglect this and the other stories of hers which reveal so poignantly the effect of the war and of Reconstruction on individual southerners. (74)

James's and Kern's praise may overlook the colonialist implications in Woolson's position as a representative of the victorious North, but if we want to level this charge against her, we should tread lightly. In terms of its victory, its industrialism, and its literary traditions, the North was clearly the dominant culture, but Woolson was never a part of the eastern establishment tradition. Aware of her position as an outsider, a single woman who has lost her home, she was sensitive to southern loss; aware of the newness of western communities, she quickly perceived the age and tradition of southern ones; at home in nature, she looked closely at the varied landscapes through which she traveled. This, of course, does not mean that she was free from bias. She implies that the South will never adopt the democratic openness she located as part of the hope for western settlement. Where the West moved at least temporarily toward social leveling, she imaged a South far more likely to be immersed in social stratification or locked in the enmity that is the legacy of the Civil War. But even as she reflected these biases, she was able to expose the biases of more colonial-minded northerners. Her character Horace Chase from the novel of that title serves as a good example. He is the northerner come south, who envisions Asheville, North Carolina, as a vacation resort modeled on European resorts like those in Switzerland, where the locals do not trust to the mountains alone to bring tourists. "[T]hey don't leave people to sit and stare at 'em all day," says Horace; "they add other attractions" (350). He wants things like period costumes, lighted waterfalls, local trinkets, casino gambling and dancing, restaurants, music, shopping, and a "museum of curiosities, stuffed animals, and mummies, and such things" (351). Where Woolson sees most of the South locked in the past with devastating consequences for reconstruction, she sees Horace locked in the future with just as devastating consequences likely.

Woolson may have been drawn to the South's sense of the past because it represented the continuity of home and ancestry that was taken from her when her parents left New Hampshire. But she also was quick to see the social stratification this sense of ancestry perpetuates. Her novella *For the Major,* for example, takes place in Far Edgerley, a town that is actually close to Edgerley, both being in the same rural part of North Carolina, fifty-five hours from the capital. Edgerley has two thousand people, whereas Far Edgerley has only a thousand, but more important than size difference is a difference in ambience that represents the conflict between the old and the new South. Like Asheville to Horace Chase, Edgerley represents the future, but where Asheville's attraction is the possibility of resort building, Edgerley's is the possibility of industrialization. Far Edgerley, on the other hand, represents the past, a preindustrialized South with "an aroma of an undoubted aristocracy" (*Major* 260). Although the year is 1868 and the Civil War has made the existence of an aristocracy with summer homes in places like Far Edgerley an anachronism, the residents of this town weave heroic stories around their local Major whose southern army predated the Civil War. Numerous details of the story emphasize this clinging to the past: the Major's wife is called Madame rather than Mrs. and wears youthful clothes and makeup to disguise her age, their son Scar is dressed in aristocratic, effeminate clothes and is educated with old sayings from old books, and when the Major becomes senile, he is honored by the townspeople for whom he represents the glorious days of the past.

When Woolson captures the pain of Reconstruction in the southerner's tendency to fixate on the past, she writes out of a tradition that David Madden and Peggy Bach have identified as southern. Their survey of fiction written about the war and Reconstruction indicates that whereas northern writers have tended to move quickly into battle scenes and moral victory, southern ones have focused on how the Civil War impacted on families and the traditions of the aristocratic way of life. Unfortunately, they omitted Woolson in their survey and have even said that no northern woman wrote about the Civil War and its aftermath. Woolson, in fact, provides a valuable perspective on Reconstruction, and, in doing so, expands the traditional notion of local color to include not just close observation of the social mores within established environments but also the way changing circumstances reenforce established mores. She sees the impact of the war on a way of life and looks at the way enmities continue to be harbored between South and North as these regions struggle to maintain their identity in a rapidly changing environment. Enmity is so strong that the characters in *Jupiter Lights* who are fond of the northerner Eve Bruce persist in seeing her as British, thus embracing her, as they may have done Woolson, as a member their defeated culture.

Where Woolson's lake country stories are permeated with a sense of homelessness engendered by hope and disappointment, the southern stories are permeated with lost homes and the hatred engendered by loss. Woolson's southern women, especially, project their hatred onto the North that caused their suffering. The stories, however, indicate that Woolson understood rather than merely judged this hatred.

Because she was neither a northerner from the eastern establishment nor a southerner, she could keep a distance that enabled her to reveal a living and complex region. She exposes the kinds of extremism, both northern and southern, that led to the Civil War and that blocked Reconstruction, and she reflects her concern about women's tendency to perpetuate their limited role in society, which makes them so vulnerable when their homes are threatened. Quick to see the havoc the war has played on the southern way of life and the inefficiency and unwillingness of both northerners and southerners during Reconstruction to accommodate, she never looks with a blaming eye on either side. Rather, aware of how much her personal life circumstances forced her to accommodate change, she criticizes people's inability to change more than their hatred and anger. She captures both northern and southern rigidity in "Up in the Blue Ridge." Northerner Stephen Wainwright writes so that his "letters carried themselves crookedly, and never twice alike; but owing to their extreme smallness, and the careful way in which they stood on the line, rigidly particular as to their feet, although their spines were misshapen, they looked not unlike a regiment of little humpbacked men, marching with extreme precision, and daring you to say that they were crooked" (*Rodman* 276). The southern woman in this story is just as rigid as she works diligently on a composition called "Reflections on the Book of Job," complete with references to "authorities" and "dictionaries" (*Rodman* 290). Whether male or female, both northerners and southerners may represent extreme forms of behavior. As strangers to the South, northerners like Woolson must necessarily play the part of foreigners; in turn, as soon as they come in contact with a northerner, southerners adopt the role of conquered but still proud enemy. Colonial dominance, Woolson knew, cuts in both directions.

One of the things that Woolson became keenly aware of when she moved south was the extent to which women had been affected by the loss of homes and family. The story "In the Cotton Country" also suggests that she saw how loss sometimes immobilized women, a perception that would have made her all the more determined not to become immobilized by her personal losses. Joan Weimer reads the story, which she judges as one of Woolson's best, as the narrator's, and Woolson's, search for a "way out of her own isolation" by hearing and retelling the story told to her (*MG* xxxiii). Unlike Weimer, I see the story as a failure because its language, which I find maudlin, traps Woolson in the southern past and a romantic technique that tries unsuccessfully to recreate an imagined place. In the story, Woolson describes a young/old woman and her massive sadness, the fruit of losses in the war. When she has the woman tell her own version of the cruelty of war, which takes up the majority of the story, the language is untypical of any of her other pieces. It has no humor and is unconvincingly sentimental, enough different from the rest of the collection that one must wonder if Woolson was registering her disapproval of self-pity.

Woolson was much better at registering the cruelty of war in stories that exploit the tensions within changing local communities. "Crowder's Cove," for example, explores the problems faced by northern women who gave up their regional homes to marry southerners. Published in *Appletons'* just a month before "In the Cotton Country," "Crowder's Cove" can be read in counterpoint to that story. In it, a southern mountain farmer and his northern wife honor their marriage by trying to remain politically neutral during the Civil War. Both Confederate and Union soldiers confiscate their harvest and their livestock, leaving them nothing because each side abhors neutrality. Living in the household are two younger women, representing the South and the North. The southerner cares little for the war but falls in love with a Confederate soldier whose troops she saves by warning them of the Union army. Her allegiance is marginal, but she is celebrated as a savior while the northern woman has suffered a great deal more, not just because she fails to warn the Union troops, but because she has been forced to live away from the North so that she cannot help its cause. Despite her failure to save the Union troops, this woman does not give up her allegiance and eventually finds her way north, where she can help the Union cause. We do not learn what happens to the neutral couple, but, through their suffering, we understand that neutrality is impossible in a civil war.

"Crowder's Cove," though never anthologized, succeeds as "In the Cotton Country" does not because Woolson draws on her skills with realism. She was always better at putting characters in real rather than imagined landscapes. One of the central images of the real landscape is that of the house, an image that many scholars have associated with women's fiction. Judith Fryer has studied the image in relation to Cather and Wharton, examining the contrasts between Cather's open and Wharton's closed spaces and the way they use space to empower women, and Ann Romines has traced the image of housekeeping to Stowe and to the post–Civil War fiction of Jewett and Freeman, seeing it as transforming the domestic to the ritualistic. More helpful for a study of Woolson is Marilyn Chandler's discussion of how the centrality of the image of the house in American fiction represents the tension between material and spiritual/natural values and between the desire for civilization and the desire for unconfined freedom (1–3). By applying her general discussion to Woolson's southern fiction, we realize that what happens in the South as a result of the Civil War undermines both the choice for and the choice against a house: material houses have been destroyed and the value of a way of life dependent on cultivation of the land has been thrown into question by the inclusion of African Americans as legitimate participants in the American dream; the civilized plantation has been exposed as a prison, freedom from slavery has been forced upon the white population and given in name only to the black, and membership in the Union has told the South that it cannot construct itself as it wishes.

Lori Askeland's discussion of *Uncle Tom's Cabin* in an article on that novel and Toni Morrison's *Beloved* offers still more helpful commentary for thinking about Woolson. Noting that Stowe and her sister Catharine Beecher had written a homemakers' guidebook in 1869, Askeland argues that by advocating remuneration and recognition for homemaking, they wanted to increase women's power. They broadened women's influence within the domain of home, but, despite their efforts, women still remained vulnerable because men still owned their homes. In fact, the housing reform movements in the second half of the nineteenth century imposed order on the potential female subversiveness of home-power. Thus, even with more domestic control, women still had to imagine houses where they would find true power.[8] Like Stowe's cabin, Woolson's imagined houses serve as metaphors for both women's power and their powerlessness. In discussing her use of the house as metaphor, we need to remember the differences she would have seen between the houses of her Cleveland youth and those of the South. In Cleveland, the houses were new and proliferating with the influx of settlers. They connected her to the dream of democracy inscribed in the identical houses in "The Lady of Little Fishing," but, as the later need for housing reform suggests, they never resulted in equal power for all, including women. Whereas the idea of the house in the West connects to the new, the idea of the house in the South connects to southern pride in an ancestry that includes the Spanish and French as well as the British. Because so many houses were destroyed during the Civil War, Woolson finds in the house image a metaphor for loss rather than a metaphor for women's power.

Woolson uses the image of the ruined house most prominently in "Rodman the Keeper" and "Old Gardiston." Much of "Rodman the Keeper" centers as well on the loss of ancestral homes and the way of life this loss represents, thus it transforms the local image to the national and even the archetypal. In the story, Rodman comes across a wreck of a house, inhabited by a wreck of a Confederate soldier, whom he slowly nurses to a peaceful death, over the objections of the soldier's embittered female cousin. Only when the old soldier dies and the woman refuses to sign her name in the cemetery's visitors' book does Rodman connect to what the woman says about southern loss:

> Shall I, Betinna Ward, set my name down in black and white as a visitor to this cemetery, where lie fourteen thousand of the soldiers who killed my father, my three brothers, my cousins; who brought desolation upon all our house, and ruin upon all our neighborhood, all our State, and all our country?—for the South *is* our country, and not your North. Shall I forget these things? Never! Sooner let my right hand wither by my side! I was but a child; yet I remember the tears of my mother, and the grief of all around us. There was not a house where there was not one dead. (*Rodman* 40)

Rodman's awakened vision toward this southern woman's loss of home and family prompts him to accept the South, so that his final act of moving a vine from the house to his cemetery connects southern and northern losses. This gesture reinscribes the house, with its doors barred and windows blinded, its "clapboards . . . gray and mossy," its piazza floor "fallen in here and there from decay" into a cemetery monument even more poignant than the one that Rodman tends (*Rodman* 17).

Woolson extends the symbol of the fallen house into an essentially female image in "Old Gardiston" by showing how loyalty to a fallen home perpetuates unnecessary sacrifice from women whose sense of honor perpetuates their victimization. Old Gardiston is a "manor-house down in the rice-lands, six miles from a Southern seaport" (*Rodman* 105) that dates back to colonial days. The church that was once part of the house is gone, the road to it overgrown, and the ancestral members of the family are all buried in the churchyard. The house still has its latticed windows and Chinese ornamental vases and "spindle-legged sideboard, covered with dark-colored plates and platters ornamented with dark-blue dragons going out to walk, and crocodiles circling around fantastically roofed temples as though they were waiting for the worshippers to come out in order to make a meal of them" (*Rodman* 106). These cannot mask the house's decay, its "sunken and defaced" (*Rodman* 106) marble floor, its dampness, its hearth fireless because wood is too expensive.

Woolson fills her story with marvelous details of the faded South, none better than the portrait of the mistress of the house who one day is forced to entertain Union soldiers and who serves them using the four forks that are left of the family silver. For the occasion, she wears an old-fashioned gown and mildewed, blue kid slippers that she has "bravely" (*Rodman* 121) mended. As her name suggests, the mistress of the house, Gardis Duke, is guardian of the noble southern past, joined in her endeavors by her cousin whose life's work has been to keep a genealogy. But it is the house that is the main character of the story. The denouement of "Old Gardiston" involves the burning of the house, complete with the footnoted and red-inked genealogy. In the process of invoking this loss, Woolson is gentle, understanding, and very funny. Her meaning is clear, and one that only someone who remains distant from the southern pain could voice. This past, she implies, cannot be guarded but it can be loved, and in loving it, it should not be transformed, as was the house in "Rodman the Keeper" by social-climbing northerners. Better to burn than to sell. Further, only when there is a true union between North and South, when the old South symbolized by the cousin and the genealogy is dead, can a new South be formed. That South is symbolized here in, for Woolson, a rare happy ending in which Gardis, finally refusing victimization, accepts the offer of marriage to a Union soldier.

Just how far ahead of her time Woolson was in her portrayal of the South is represented in a review article in the July 1880 edition of *The Atlantic*. Here, Thomas Sergeant Perry represents what Rayburn Moore has called the typical Boston attitude against the South:

> The cantrips of Miss Gardis Duke . . . read like what one finds oftener in poor novels than in real life. This young person, Miss Duke, is a little chit, who, in extreme poverty, imitates the splendours of her former opulence, and gives the rough edge of her saucy tongue to two lovers, Union officers, who just after the late war are stationed near her house. She invites them to dinner, and then, when they are gone, she burns up the shabby finery in which she received them. . . . Certainly, this little cat is not a very impressive person, and it is not easy to interest one's self in such a lump of affectation; but Miss Woolson seems to take her at her own pompous valuation, and to see heroism in her imi-

tation of tawdry novels. Finally, she steps down from her pinnacle of conceit, and marries one of the officers, and we have no doubt that by this time she has satisfactorily taken vengeance for everything that happened during the war.[9]

Perry's inability to read about women aside, what he has failed to notice is Woolson's critique of the very things he complains about in Gardis. He has missed entirely Woolson's point that southern women have been twice victimized, once by the destruction of their homes and once by their socialization into martyrdom. Because the South of Woolson's day, more than the West, was a social construct with a long history, it needed to be reconstructed if its women, like its former slaves, were to find even a modicum of freedom.

Rather than showing women gaining control within the home, Woolson uses the southern house to intensify her vision of women's losses. However, in her novel *Anne,* about a woman who moves in milieus similar to her own, she uses the image in ways more in keeping with the traditions scholars have defined; that is, to show how women can gain personal space within houses. Thus Anne dreams of having her own house and furnishing all its rooms "according to a plan of her own" (11); she lives temporarily in the "half-house" (186) of a teacher who has gone to Europe, questions the wisdom of furnishing a temporary home, but is overwhelmed when her friend Gregory Dexter furnishes it for her. The need for home is strong enough that Woolson even describes how a murderer in the novel has furnished his cabin with "a gaudy picture of the Virgin and the Holy Child" (510). When Anne returns to her birthplace on Mackinac Island at the end of the novel, choosing marriage on her own terms, Woolson suggests that she is also choosing her own home, one which she will furnish according to her own tastes.

Woolson also uses the image of the house in *Anne* to show personal freedom in her portrait of Anne's friend on Mackinac Island, Miss Lois, a transplanted New Englander. A stereotypical old maid, Miss Lois drapes her curtains meticulously, cooks meals regimented by the day of the week, and keeps a perfectly dusted and arranged house. Miss Lois never loses her New England heritage, never finds a true sense of home on the island, or enough sense of liberality to abandon her chagrin that Anne's siblings are raised as Catholics. Had she no ties to Anne, via Anne's father whom she probably loves, she would be like all the "moneyless forlorn females left by steamers, belonging to that strange floating population that goes forever travelling up and down the land, without apparent motive save a vague El-Dorado hope whose very conception would be impossible in any other country save this" (42). Still, these ties, plus her spinsterhood, actually work to her advantage. She has power over the house she keeps and she is freer than the wives of the officers of the island's fort, who are left alone with families when their husbands are called away, or forced to follow those husbands in their transient lives.

Woolson's close observation of regional societies and her use of the house image in connection with regional issues show her defining the parameters of the local-color tradition. Another image that links her to that tradition and that connects the tradition to her use of travel writing is that of the land. In her novel *Anne,* the title character appropriately chooses Mackinac Island as her married home because she has been most at home in nature. When she is living with her Aunt Katherine Vanhorn among vacationers in an eastern waterhole, she alone dares to save a young woman who has been showing off on a precipice and is about to fall to her death. She gathers plants and, like Woolson herself, studies botany and feels the stirrings of genuine love in a cave during a storm. Cheryl Torsney discusses Anne's awakening to herself and her passion through her relationship to nature in terms of Annis Pratt's treatment of the archetypes of the green-world epiphany and the green-world lover, and she sees that this archetype connects Woolson to a larger tradition of women's writing. Nature in women's traditions is not a metaphoric representation in the Emersonian tradition of transcendentalism, but a real place in which women can come to maturity, independence, and passion.[10]

Even more, this relationship to nature connects Woolson to the tradition of Thoreau the naturalist and to the environmental movements of the nineteenth century. She explicitly references her sense of environmentalism when she excoriates the domestication of the West in a narrative comment about how the West has carved a college out of the wilderness: "Young America always cuts down all his trees as a first step toward civilization; then, after an interregnum, when all the kings of the forest have been laid low, he sets out small saplings in whitewashed tree-boxes, and watches and tends them with fervor" (*Anne* 99). By the end of the nineteenth century, the East and the South had been plagued by soil erosion and fires generated by indiscriminate logging. Lumber barons were becoming wealthy at the expense of the environment. Woolson must have been encouraged when

Mackinac Island was named in 1875 as the second national park in the United States, the first being Yellowstone, though she may not have liked its corresponding growth as a Victorian resort. She would also have been discouraged by the continued problem with deforestation, which her great-uncle had lamented a generation earlier in the Leatherstocking Tales. In fact, deforestation was most severe in her father's native New Hampshire and in the North Carolina she traveled through because in these states the quality of the wood was high and railroads had created easy access for trade. Deforestation began to be reversed only in 1911 when John W. Weeks, a native of northern New Hampshire, who had made a fortune in banking and had become a representative from Massachusetts, initiated the Weeks Act to form and protect national forests. Just how aware of the problem Woolson was is apparent in her novel *Horace Chase,* in which a North Carolinian fears the coming of the railroad to the Asheville area. Horace Chase is drawn to the area for its resort possibilities, but this native North Carolinian knows only too well that instead of a resort the lumber barons may descend until the "last acre of primitive forest is forever gone" (17).

Woolson knew and loved both the western and southern wooded landscapes and saw that landscape rather than society could generate the value of rootedness for her. Even more than to the forest, she seems to have been drawn to the Florida swamps. These are central to the atmosphere of her story "The South Devil" and to her novel *East Angels.* In both, Woolson uses the swamp to create a realistic atmosphere but, as with her use of the house image, she adds a metaphoric, though not what I would call an abstract or transcendental, level. The swamp attracts the artistic or rebellious aspects of human nature and represents a beauty that carries both challenge and danger. In "The South Devil," Mark Deal is a workaholic northerner who has brought his stepbrother Carl Brenner to recuperate on an old Spanish plantation. While Carl lies under a majestic, symmetrical live-oak tree listening to the call of the swamp and even sneaking away to its unhealthy depths, Mark energetically cleans up its overgrown orange grove. Woolson uses Mark and Carl to locate contrasting responses to the South. Carl can respond to the artistic mystery of the swamp because he can accept the South as it is. However, Woolson recognizes that Carl's response is not necessarily "better" than Mark's. It is he who gambles away Mark's money and who instigates Mark's marriage to a northern woman who will be the final cold insurance that Mark will never learn a more genuine artistic appreciation.

Woolson is also clear that the southern swamp represents something stifling and sinister, a spur to the exploitative, nonproductive side of Carl's character. This danger, Woolson implies, must be courted. The artist must be open to beauty and seduction and terror. These may paralyze, but without them the artist can never get his or her art right. Woolson develops this concept in analogous experiences of Mark and Carl. Before coming south, Mark had nearly died on an ice island in the Arctic, where he had spent a whole day and night drifting among dead bodies. Carl had a similar experience alone, without the dead bodies, in the Florida swamp. Mark's experience does not enrich him. Only for a fleeting moment, before he accepts his northern wife, does he feel the power of the swamp, the aloneness and mystery and threat that is the lot of the artist. Carl, on the other hand, takes his experience and finally produces from it; his rootedness is not permanent, but it is deep. He not only hears music in the swamp, but he gets the music right, though it is too late for him to write it down. And so on his last journey, when dead, he rides through the swamp with his eyes open to a South that Woolson knows can touch the soul. His is the kind of response that Woolson had herself and that, during her years in Europe, made her long to return to a state that had helped her develop into an artist.

When Woolson develops a scene in the Florida swamps in her novel *East Angels,* she sees much the same power, but here she equates it with sexuality more than with art. The heroine, Margaret Harold, becomes lost in the swamp while she is with the man she loves, looking for the man she is married to. The atmosphere is one of heat, fertility, danger, fear, passion. The swamp, with its dense vegetation, hanging moss and vines, twisting trees and branches both above and below, is labyrinthine, claustrophobic, a place where one can feel "strangled" and "suffocated" (469) by its "witchery flowers" (468) and "miasma of scent" (472). Margaret's response to the swamp signifies her deeper nature; her refusal of the passion it represents signifies how much she has been socialized in her attitudes toward constancy in marriage. In Florida, as in the West, nature can entice one to behave in natural ways, unhampered by social definitions of marriage and sexuality that were being debated in Woolson's day. But for Margaret, the rootedness of socialization has triumphed over the deep, sexual rootedness of the swamp. These are alternative values, and Margaret, finally, honors her socialization because she has found a sense of place in the Florida orange plantation she owns.

Woolson was always as much interested in landscape as she was in character, and I suspect that she found a more satisfying home in the geographical places she came to love than with the people she met in these places. Her subtitles *Lake Country Sketches* and *Southern Sketches* reflect this interest in landscape, and many of her uncollected stories are excuses to sketch the landscapes she knew and loved. For example, "The Story of Huron Grand Island" develops a stereotypical broken engagement and the discovery of a more appropriate love, but is most interesting for its portrayal of a lone hotel built at Grand Harbor by someone whose dreams of domesticating the West include a bustling city that never materializes. "The Waldenburg Road" also develops around a delayed love affair but highlights the landscape of a German farm in Ohio that has the allure of the Brontës' moors, and "The Old Five," a title that refers to an abandoned mine, exposes the hypocrisies of an eastern woman who tries to tame the wilderness with a piano, muslin curtains, and a rose garden and causes someone's death because she pretends to want a fern whose botanic significance she does not really understand. "Barnaby Pass" portrays the landscape of the southern mountains, incorporating the daily journey of a lone stage coach into that landscape and using a flood, again ostensibly to effect a marriage, but more significantly to describe the wildness and beauty that integrates with the havoc a mountain flood creates. Woolson titled her short fiction according to whether she wanted to emphasize character or landscape, and we need to pay attention to these titles in order to make some of her uncollected stories seem more than formulaic pieces written to please a popular audience. Her best fiction about the diverse regions of the United States, if we attend to it closely, never deserves a charge of being formulaic, but is filled with complexity and richness.

Woolson's regional fiction gains strength from the personal and literary tensions that generate it. We can infer much of the personal simply by noticing what regions she chose to write about. She never wrote about the diverse and rapidly growing Cleveland, though, as the next chapter will show, she valued diversity and was perceptive about the issues that surround diversity. Rather, she wrote about the isolated communities in regions that she visited. Put off by travelers likely to share her heritage, she was drawn to those communities to which she remained an outsider. This asocial quality joins with her love for nature, so that her regionalism is particularly successful for its painterly qualities. Not only did she add, as Berthold has shown, the element of narrative to her travel sketches, she also added the travel writer's attention to the natural landscape to her fiction.

Woolson's painterly quality arose from a tension with two distinct literary traditions. Attracted to the dark side of the Hawthornian romance, she emphasizes the destructive manipulation of rather than the domestication of the garden and what this manipulation does to women. But American romance was steeped in the past and in the imaginary, akin to the imagined landscapes of the sublime school of artists who painted scenes from places like Niagara Falls and the western Rockies. Trained in close and accurate observation, Woolson draws her connections to the past and her imaginary scenes from the real scenes she knew. We can see this nicely illustrated in the story "Jeannette" from the *Castle Nowhere* collection. The story takes place on Mackinac Island, which was well known in the nineteenth century for its botanical and geological interest and had been visited, in 1810, by the botanist Thomas Nuttall and, in 1820, by the geologist Lewis Cass. The story is filled with descriptions of the cliffs and caves of the island, including this one of the island's famous Arch Rock:[11]

> The Arch is a natural bridge over a chasm one hundred and fifty feet above the lake,—a fissure in the cliff which has fallen away in a hollow, leaving the bridge by itself far out over the water. This bridge springs upward in the shape of an arch; it is fifty feet long, and its width is in some places two feet, in others only a few inches,—a narrow, dizzy pathway hanging between sky and water. (*CN* 156)

Woolson breathed the air, felt the fog, walked the beaches that she writes about. I like to think that she navigated Florida's swamps and crossed Mackinac's famous arch. The homes or communities that she imagines in so much of her writing may represent a "castle nowhere," but the regions that serve as their backgrounds are a somewhere she named as home.

4

Regional Bias and Ethnic Diversity
♣

Woolson's relation to the literary landscape shows her moving toward a realism that foregrounds the natural contours of the places she called home. Once she left the United States, she began to yearn for a home in its southern climates. But memory is creative: for Woolson, it envisions a home in a comfortable landscape and forgets that the landscape frames a culture that directed her fiction toward the tensions and hostilities created by diversity. Woolson grew up in a diverse culture made up of settlers who moved west to work in farms or factories or forests. Although these diverse groups shared the status of outsider to a West that had no insiders, Woolson saw their differences as much as their commonalities. By the time she began to write fiction, she had moved south, become aware of herself as an outsider, and seen how diversity, instead of being valued, had shaped a system that had erupted in injustice and eventually war.

Woolson did not need the South to introduce her to this lesson. She had summered on an island that represented the competing interests of European cultures and a policy of friendly relations with Indians that aimed more at control and annihilation than respect and support. By the 1830s, the Indian Removal Act had begun to clear desirable lands for white settlers and to push American Indians into reservation systems. Its underlying message, like that of the American Colonization Society, established in 1816: send Indians west; send blacks to Liberia; keep the United States for white Europeans. Between western resettlement and southern slavery, Woolson saw the horrible effects of America's battles over diversity. We know that she supported the North during the Civil War, but we do not know how she felt about the policies of Indian removal or about the American Colonization

Society. We know that many of the magazines and schoolbooks of the nineteenth century predicted the extinction of races considered less endowed. Essentially, this meant all but the white races, which "scientific" phrenological studies and later the arguments of Social Darwinism had shown to be superior.[1] Much of the fiction also supported the idea of white supremacy. Louise Barnett, for example, has uncovered dozens of antebellum novels that examine Indian-white relations, and she argues that most mourn the loss of the noble savage—the good Indians who die or produce no heirs. These are comfortable stereotypes because, writes Barnett, the good Indians "could helpfully initiate whites into the wilderness milieu before falling victims to their inherent inferiority" and because the bad Indians "deserved the fate actively meted out to them by the conquering race" (96). Jane Tompkins has also read Cooper in these terms, seeing his novels as a warning not to cross ethnic or race barriers lest this lead to anarchy. Even the "little woman who made the great war," Harriet Beecher Stowe, ends *Uncle Tom's Cabin* with her fictional black family looking toward Liberia.

What we cannot know, of course, is whether or not Woolson perceived these messages that we have become so sensitive to in our re-readings of nineteenth-century literature. Did she share the fears of most of her contemporaries in the early 1860s when the Dakota Sioux rose against a government that was both ignoring and exploiting them or did she see the frenzy of Indian-hating that resulted from fear? Did she read Sarah Wakefield's narrative, published and widely circulated in 1863, that defends the Dakotas who captured her for six weeks but treated her well? Did she share Wakefield's outrage that the government hung a Dakota man for murder whose innocence Wakefield had substantiated?[2] How might she have felt about George Copley, the Canadian Ojibwa who had been expelled from the Canadian Methodist Conference but accepted in the United States, with his white wife, as a missionary to Wisconsin and Minnesota tribes? She would likely have known his work: he had met her great-uncle, had served as a United States representative to the World Peace Conference in Germany in 1850–51, had fought in the Civil War, and, in 1847, had published his autobiography, which went through six editions. Was he an example of successful assimilation into a higher culture or a threat to racial purity? And did Woolson recognize the racism inherent in both these statements? In a study of Thoreau and the Indian, Robert Sayre argues that Thoreau wanted to write a book about the Indian, but, once he started, quickly saw that the task was impossible because there was no single Indian culture, but rather an infinitely complex mixture of cultures. I suspect that Woolson always knew this and that, adding her observations in the South to what she had internalized in her youth in the Midwest, she became particularly sensitive to attitudes about ethnicity.

Ethnicity is shaped by many factors. Race, nationality, religion, and culture are all listed as broad categories in the general definition I employ. Although controversies deepen nowadays about the biological sources of ethnicity, it is clear that attitudes about ethnicity are socially constructed and that the home is immensely important in shaping these attitudes. Perhaps the largest issue concerning ethnicity during the mid-nineteenth century was that of assimilation and miscegenation. Indian policies all pointed toward solving the "Indian problem" by assimilating surviving Indians into white society. Assimilation of blacks was a more difficult issue, for until the Civil War assimilation would negate the possibility of slavery and after the Civil War there was no myth of cultural extinction to tame the level of fear as it had with Indian populations. The issue of assimilation via miscegenation of black and white became prominent in the 1863 campaign for Lincoln's re-election and illustrates the level of fear involved. A hoax pamphlet that advocated miscegenation as part of Lincoln's platform had been circulated during the campaign. Using trumped-up scientific data, the authors—who hoped to effect Lincoln's defeat by raising voter fears—argued that the ideal of the melting pot was necessary to keep races strong and that "all that is needed to make us [Anglo-whites] the finest race on earth is to engraft upon our stock the negro element."[3] Many white abolitionists, including Lucretia Mott and the Grimké sisters, wrote in support of the idea. They couched their support, however, in concerns that the country was not ready for such a platform. What they miss is the attitude that the "negro element" is used for the benefit of whites, who will, via miscegenation, bring a lesser race into a higher one.

Lest we feel superior in our ability to decode racist attitudes, we might remember the recent controversy over *The Education of Little Tree,* a veneration of American Indian culture disrupted and eventually destroyed by government intervention. The author, Forrest Carter, has been exposed as the segregationist Asa Carver, who created George Wallace's campaign slogan "Segregation Now, Segregation Tomorrow, Segregation Forever" and who had been a member of a particularly violent branch of the Ku Klux Klan. Those who adopted the text as an example of a model American Indian culture have ended up having to abandon it or to argue that even a racist can write a sympathetic portrait of another culture. Ian Marshall has found a scholarly angle into the book by arguing that Carter/Carver's villain is government intervention and that the book is a veiled protest against forced integration.[4] The races, *The Education of Little Tree* ends up suggesting, will do fine as long as the United States stays a segregated stew pot.

Like those who take the moral high ground against *The Education of Little Tree,* now that its author has been identified, we use a bit of the same hindsight to emphasize the racism of people in the nineteenth century who failed to see the implications beneath arguments for miscegenation or, in cases when race is not an issue, to see ethnic bias rampant in nineteenth-century texts. I am uncomfortable, for example, when Sybil Weir criticizes the following description of northern Protestants in Florida as representative of Woolson's cultural bias: these Protestants are "the pioneers of that busy, practical American majority . . . which turns its imagination (for it has imagination) towards objects more veracious than the pious old titles bestowed by an age and race that murdered, and tortured, and reddened these fair waters with blood, for sweet religion's sake" (Weir 145; *East Angels* 54–55). While the second half of the quote, which refers to Spanish settlers, is culturally biased, it is difficult to refute, nor is there any evidence that Woolson fails to see the same problem with northern Protestant settlers and their treatment of American Indians. Perhaps Weir's ethnic perspective causes her to miss the irony of the first part of Woolson's comment. Or perhaps my own northern background has allowed me to emphasize the irony of the first part of Woolson's sentence over her criticism of southern colonization.

Whenever I read or write about Woolson's South, I am conscious that I, like she, am looking at it as an outsider. The remarkable thing is that Woolson is so willing to recognize the inevitable cultural bias we all have. She knew that when she responded to issues of ethnicity and bias that she did so as a white, Yankee Protestant transplanted to the Midwest and then become a wanderer. Whatever its region, her fiction reveals a woman who deplores the divisiveness that turned diversity to hatred and war and who sees that cross-cultural understanding is both desirable and impossible and so can treat less insidious forms of bias with gentle satire. The fiction also reveals a woman who felt attracted to homogeneous groups that might have provided her a simple home free from the tensions of diversity, but who sees beneath this attraction that to be bound to such a home represents yet another form of bondage.

Although Woolson recognizes the inevitability of cultural bias and can often laugh at it, she never lets it off, even if it is not injurious to others but merely reflects ignorance. She becomes particularly annoyed at the northern ignorance of Florida, a state she grew quickly to love. In *East Angels,* for example, one northerner is "ashamed" of himself "for staring about and applying adjectives in this way to the people and scenery here, as though it were a foreign country; it ought to be as much a part of [him] . . . as though it was Massachusetts Bay" (83), while another is content that the difference between North and South be as sharp as the difference between the South and Japan. In "The South Devil," she writes that Spanish plantations in Florida were settled "fifty years before the first settlement was made in Virginia, and sixty-three before the Mayflower touched the shores of the New World." Then she proceeds to criticize explicitly: "The belief is imbedded in all our Northern hearts that, because the narrow, sun-bathed State is far away and wild and empty, it is also new and virgin, like the lands of the West; whereas it is old—the only gray-haired corner our country holds" (*Rodman* 142). Woolson recognized northern bias even if she could not fully escape it herself. Her awareness of bias also becomes a corollary to her ability to examine the qualities of different places that fostered rootedness. What she imagined for herself if she returned to the United States was a particular locale, but her fiction suggests that she both longed for and struggled against a sense of rootedness.

To relate to a particular locale requires attention to landscape; to struggle with rootedness requires attention to people within the landscape. Both landscape and inhabitants of a landscape are crucial elements in local-color fiction that attends so closely to regional social mores. What distinguishes Woolson is the frequency with which she often shows herself aware of how much ethnicity impacts on one's sense of place. Her story "Jeannette" from the *Castle Nowhere* collection illustrates nicely. The setting of the story is an idyllic place, Mackinac Island after the United States had secured possession of its fort from the British during the War of 1812, after its soldiers had been called to fight the Mexican War, and before they were called away again to the Civil War.[5] The story, in fact, opens on Woolson's observation of the idyll: "Before the war for the Union, in the times of the old army, there had been peace throughout the country for thirteen years" (*CN* 136). The narrator, Sarah Corlyne, lives on Mackinac Island with her nephew Archie. Sarah observes a "half-breed" island girl, Jeannette, and finds it endlessly fascinating to weave a poignant love story around her and Rodney Prescott, who is the island surgeon and a proper Bostonian. Jeannette epitomizes one of the things Woolson liked about both the West and the South—its racial diversity. John Kern describes this as an interest in "girls of a hybrid race," whom she finds "strange, unpredictable, and to a certain extent untrustworthy," though sometimes capable of "nobility and sacrifice" and suggestive of passion, complexity, and mystery (27, 61). Kern also believes that Woolson could not bring herself to allow successful cross-cultural marriages, especially when they involved upper-class Anglo women, and that however much she admired the virtues of common people she rarely married them to the higher social classes. When Woolson writes a sketch of Mackinac Island titled "Fairy Island," one could certainly argue that her fascination with its "mongrel children," "many-featured, many-hued, and many-charactered" (Benedict 2:283) smacks of condescension toward a group she sees as "other." In "Jeannette," as well, Aunt Sarah finds Rodney's fascination with Jeannette viable only on the island and only as a poignant, temporary liaison.

But Woolson has more going on in the story than Aunt Sarah's biases, and her writing often reveals her own recognition of bias. Aunt Sarah is taken aback when she discovers that her fantasy about Rodney and Jeannette is not farfetched, that Rodney really does love her. We should read the outcome of the romance—a refused marriage proposal—more in terms of issues of home than in terms of Woolson's ethnic bias. This becomes apparent when the soldiers at the fort have been ordered to Florida but their families are to remain behind, thus setting a backdrop for the breaking up of homes that occurred at the outset of the Civil War. Rodney, who has been giving Jeannette money that he criticizes her for taking, declares his love for her. Wishing to marry her, saying, "I accept you as you are" (*CN* 171), he claims he is willing to take her to concerts in fancy dress even though she is not and does not want to become culturally "educated." Aunt Sarah sees cultural education as the obvious and lucky path for Jeannette, who lives in an impoverished home. The triumph of the story and of Jeannette herself is that she refuses Rodney, declaring to Aunt Sarah that she will not be bullied because she is "not a child" (*CN* 174) and making it clear that she loves someone else. Woolson had emphasized her delight in this kind of female triumph in a comic version of "Jeannette," published two years earlier. The story is titled "One *Versus* Two," "one" referring to a Scottish "girl" who finds revenge on "two" men who think they can flirt with her though they would not stoop to marry her. We never see this woman in the story, but we applaud her treatment of the men, whom she has lured to her wedding, and, unlike the male narrator, we recognize that the rivalry in the story is not between the two males, but between male and female and between shallow high culture and regionally based low culture.

Where the center of "One *Versus* Two" is on gender battles and attitudes toward a cross-cultural marriage, the center of "Jeannette" is about the rootedness to home, in this case a rootedness that is shaped by Jeannette's ethnicity. Woolson captures this issue in the metaphor of Mackinac's Arch Rock, the limestone bridge Jeannette can easily cross without danger, but from which Rodney feels he must save her: he rushes to "save her,—to save her, poised on her native rocks, where every inch was familiar from childhood!" He catches her and she struggles "as an imprisoned animal might struggle" (*CN* 168–69). Woolson may be drawing here on a legend about another of Mackinac's rock formations, a cliff called Robertson's Folly. According to this legend, an English officer falls to his death when he pursues a beautiful woman onto the cliff. The woman turns out to be an "*ignis fatuus* of his own excited imagination," and death is the price he pays for loving outside his social class (Kelton 108). When Woolson changes the location of the legend and makes the woman more real, she changes the message and moves the focus away from the would-be savior. The point, of course, is that Jeannette does not need saving. She is culturally and naturally bound to her home on Mackinac Island and there is no reason why she should not remain so. It is true that Woolson manages to avoid a cross-cultural marriage here, but she also manages to put our sympathies on Jeannette rather than Rodney. She does not present Jeannette's point of view except through brief dialogue and action: she never developed even omniscient descriptions of the thoughts of characters whom she could observe only from the outside because of her own cultural background. But she clearly applauds Jeannette's choice not to be bullied into accepting a home that other characters in the story have seen as inferior.

Many passages in Woolson's fiction support the view that she understood how people form ethnocentric judgments based on their relationships to regional homes and their perceptions of others' regional homes. She reflects her sense of the different regions and their relation to ethnicity in her novel *Jupiter Lights* through the character Judge Abercrombie, who feels out of place in the West:

> [T]he rough forest was fit only for rough-living pioneers; the Indians were but another species of nigger; the virgin air was thin and raw,— he preferred something more thick, more civilized; the great fresh-water sea was abominably tame, no one could possibly admire it; Port aux Pins itself was simply hideous; it was a place composed entirely of beginnings and mud, talk and ambition, the sort of place which Yankees produced wherever they went, and which they loved; that in itself described it; how could a Southern gentleman like what they loved? (139)

Judge Abercrombie ignores racial and cultural diversity, lumping American Indians, African Americans, and Yankees simply as other and lesser than himself as southern gentleman. It is unlikely that Woolson read racism into the way the judge equates Indian and "nigger" as a "species" that seems other than human. The passage satirizes gently rather than maligns, precisely because she knew that region shaped ethnic attitudes.

In contrast to Judge Abercrombie's fixation on southern class and culture, Woolson's early story "Margaret Morris" contains a perfect, though predictable, statement about western classlessness. Traveling by boat to visit her sister, the easterner Margaret Morris scorns fellow travelers and settlers, whom she considers low class, ignorant, and dirty until they save her when their ship collides with another. Margaret represents the kind of attitude Beth Lueck has found many nineteenth-century travel writers adopting as they held themselves apart from or condescended to lower classes and that others, like Fanny Fern, satirized for their refusal to value the leveling of the social classes.[6] But Woolson also saw that the West would not remain immune to the class and ethnic judgments of the East. When, for example, the narrator of "Jeannette," Sarah Corlyne, returns to Mackinac Island after the Civil War, she meets someone who shows a more negative attitude toward Jeannette than even she had. This person tells her that Jeannette has married and had many children and that they are all happy "after their fashion; I don't know much about them. In my opinion, they are a shiftless set, those French half-breeds round the point" (*CN* 175). As the West is becoming more settled, Woolson implies, the ethnocentric biases are becoming worse instead of better. Thus when Sarah returns to Fort Mackinac in the story "The Old Agency," Woolson reveals how much doctrinal and cultural divisions have moved westward. The story focuses on an old Napoleonic soldier, Jacques, who as a youth blindly obeyed the French leader and hated the English and who now treasures a sprig from a tree that Napoleon once touched. He comes from an old order—an old divisiveness—that is a European order and that is now creeping into the post–Civil War United States. Aunt Sarah and the priest Piret, who wears American Indian rather than priestly clothing, represent The Old Agency, the old order that predates the divisiveness of European and eastern United States prejudices and the even worse divisiveness of a Civil War that has been fought and has taken the life of Sarah's nephew Archie.

Woolson's vision that the newer the region, the less bothered by issues of ethnicity, frequently centers on issues of religion. Like Crèvecoeur writing a hundred years before her, she saw how the westward movement gradually brought with it greater religious tolerance. The Catholic is neighbor to the Lutheran who is neighbor to the Presbyterian, and all live peaceably, plowing and clearing the land and becoming good citizens. Eventually, Crèvecoeur says, their

> children will . . . grow up less zealous and more indifferent in matters of religion than their parents. The foolish vanity, or rather the fury of making Proselytes, is unknown here; they have no time, the seasons call for all their attention, and thus in a few years, this mixed neighborhood will exhibit a strange religious medley, that will be neither pure Catholicism nor pure Calvinism. . . . Thus all sects are mixed as well as all nations; thus religious indifference is imperceptibly disseminated from one end of the continent to the other, which is at present one of the strongest characteristics of the Americans. (50–51)

One by-product of the religious indifference Crèvecoeur describes is the loss of religion in providing a sense of home. Woolson writes about dying and finding peace as a "purple mountain," but rarely writes about God. Throughout her fiction, she displays a blend of tolerance and indifference to matters of religion. She was officially an Episcopalian, but one suspects that she, like William Douglas in *Anne,* actually "drifted away from all creeds, save in one article: he believed in a Creator" (28). Even if Woolson never doubted the existence of a creator, her training in geology and natural history would have introduced her to Charles Lyell's *Principles of Geology* (1830–33), a book that revolutionized thinking about human and geologic time and led in 1859 to

Darwin's *On the Origin of Species*. These theories have never negated faith, but just as today they continue to challenge certain kinds of biblical interpretation and God concepts, in the nineteenth century they generated hot debates over the possibility of reconciling science and religion.[7] Woolson was sympathetic enough to religious doubt that she makes one of the attractions between Anne and her lover Heathcote their ability to discuss something as intimate as religious doubt. In that novel, Fort Mackinac is a place where ecumenism can be practiced at a Christmas service: one Protestant minister serves all Protestant denominations, Catholics are readily welcomed and presided over by their priest, and William Douglas, the deist, can feel comfortable despite the ritual he participates in only out of habit, his own sense of spirituality coming through music.

In reality, without ecumenism on Mackinac Island, there would have been no Protestant church. The first minister there, whom Woolson knew, was the fort's chaplain, John O'Brien, an Irish Episcopalian who served from 1831 to 1861. A missionary record of the church in 1833 indicates that when O'Brien arrived, there "were but two decided Episcopalians belonging to the congregation. Now it consists of about two hundred and fifty." We should underscore, however, that only "between twenty-five and thirty" were "communicants" (Nicholas 15). Even in a more denomination affiliated South, Woolson shows the impact of new attitudes toward ecumenism, especially in rural areas away from established communities in the coastal states. Her character Horace Chase, in the novel of that title, for example, represents an entrepreneurial spirit brought to Asheville, North Carolina. Though himself raised a Baptist, he would like to build a church for the Episcopal minister, Rev. Malachi Hill, a church that "might be built so as to be suitable for all persuasions" (226). People of these varied persuasions, we should remember, are the ones likely to populate the resort Horace also plans to develop.

Because Woolson's religious attitudes tended to be those of a free-thinker, she was attracted to ecumenism. She extended ecumenism to Jews, writing to George A. Benedict, her sister Clara's father-in-law, that "Reformed Jews and the Unitarians are nearer together than they suspect." Wherever Woolson lived in her adult life, she was drawn to observing ethnic differences, thus she also writes to Benedict that the Jews of New York hold aloof from politics, "busying themselves with their own affairs, rolling up wealth, and gradually assuming a position in the city which money, intellect, obstinacy and sometimes beauty combined to render impregnable."[8] The comment reflects the stereotype of the smart, rich Jew and seems to take comfort in the idea that at least they keep to themselves. Woolson's literary portraits of Jews, though few, present even more problematic stereotypes. In "Cicely's Christmas," a thief is identified as a Hebrew. In "Raspberry Island," a Jewish entrepreneur runs a raspberry picking and canning business. He trusts his employees, but he is willing to protect an accused murderer because he is a good worker and turns him in when he learns he can collect a reward. Only in our current sensitized climate have we learned to read the anti-Semitism and racism beneath stereotypes. Although the Jew is as "other" to Woolson as the Indian or the African American, she is less prejudiced about Judaism than someone like Alice James, who wondered how one could live in New York and "lead a virtuous and reputable life amidst the Jews, the tawdry, flimsy houses and the ash-barrels."[9]

This is not to say that Woolson foresaw an amalgamation of religions into one happy family where she could feel at home. She knew that religions often bound people against rather than bonded them to one another. In her fiction, Protestants cling to their Protestantism: in "Castle Nowhere," Fog, who has kept all religion from Silver, still makes sure that she is married by an Episcopal minister; in "Misery Landing," the Protestant tries to convert the Jesuit; and in "Sister St. Luke," the Protestant Melvyna Sawyer is married by a Justice of the Peace in preference to being married by a priest. More tolerant than many of her characters, Woolson never displays their animosity or distrust toward religion, especially toward Catholicism, which so much sensational literature maligned. She pokes gentle fun at Melvyna, who says of Catholics: "I don't love 'em yet, and don't know as I ever shell; but Miss Luke, she's different" (*Rodman* 47). Except for Sister St. Luke, Melvyna sees all Catholics as alike, even though she has readily married a Catholic. Melvyna's negative vision of marriage may signal that Woolson thought religious difference a barrier that should not be crossed, but, on the whole, her portraits of Catholicism broke from rather than built barriers. In *Anne*, for example, she has Anne's half-sister Tita exploit her Catholicism as a way of revenging herself on Anne, but she also includes in this novel a fully realized portrait of a wise priest whom Anne has loved since childhood. It is only in New York—in a Protestant-socialized society—that characters show anti-Catholicism. In New York, the socialites mistrust a priest who looks after Anne's French teacher's half-house. Like Crèvecoeur, Woolson sensed that only in the wilderness could religious animosity be tempered, so much so that in the wilderness a woman can become a preacher, as in "The Lady of Little Fishing," or an Anglican parson can be tempted toward Catholicism, as in "Peter the Parson."

Woolson's letters and her fiction reveal that her religious prejudices were few, partly, I would contend, because she did not have a strong commitment to a denomination. She does, though, reserve some particular dislike for Irish Catholics. The Irish followed the canals and railroads west in the nineteenth century, and Woolson portrays them as ignorant and shiftless. Even Charlotte O'Brien, the wife of the Irish Episcopalian chaplain at Fort Mackinac, disliked Irish Catholic servant girls, writing of one she had employed that she "may as well try this specimen as it will save the passage of another, and yet, if an intelligent Protestant girl should come . . . , I should not hesitate to hire her in preference. [T]his girl is cousin to the O'Malleys, & Darkins, I could never expect to keep her out of that set, and how long will they suffer her to remain with me? probably just long enough for me to take all the trouble of teaching her, and then they will coax her away or marry her to some twentieth cousin" (Nicholas 49). This letter reflects class issues as much as religious ones; in fact, O'Brien was open-minded enough to allow her children to attend Catholic services on the pre dominantly French Catholic island.

Woolson was quick to see the social codes that elevated some groups on Mackinac Island, regardless of religion, over others. In her fiction about Mackinac, the French hold themselves higher than the Dutch, German, and Irish soldiers. The island was also populated by English officers, Scottish shopkeepers and fishermen, mixed-blood French and Indians, and unassimilated American Indians. She uses these latter groups most often when she wants to comment on the tensions inherent in diverse communities. Her sister Georgiana was quite hostile to people of mixed blood. In 1853, she wrote in her journal that such mixing "has destroyed all traces of their national characteristics," their "noble traits and the dignified bearing," and that "[t]here are great numbers of these Indians and half-breeds at the Sault Ste. Marie, and a more lazy, dirty set of men I never saw!" (Benedict 1:80). We must remember, however, that Georgiana wrote this when she was only twenty years old and when prevailing attitudes still saw American Indians dying out in part because of their inferior heredity. If Woolson shared this loss-of-the-less-than-noble savage view, she shared it as a thirteen year old. By the time she wrote *Anne,* she recognizes that she cannot as a white person fully understand Indian cultures. Thus one of her characters in that novel says that, with her Saxon blood,

Anne cannot understand her "half-breed" sister Tita. Nevertheless, that sister has been admitted to her home, the child of a man whom Woolson portrays with great respect.

The headnote to chapter 3 of *Anne* illustrates further Woolson's recognition of ethnic bias. It is taken from Massachusetts colonial records about Indians being Christianized and becoming happy not to work on the Sabbath because, as the colonists said to the English, "they have not much to do on any day, and can well take rest on that day as any other" (39). The chapter contains comments about the zeal of missionaries who want to convert the Indians but who find what Miss Lois with her New England missionary zeal finds: that "her class of promising squaws departed with their pappooses and their braves, and left her scholarless" (54) and the contrasting border attitude that the "only good Indian is a dead Indian" (53). A narrative comment within the chapter exposes both missionary hypocrisy and western violence: "New England having long ago chased out, shot down, and exterminated all her own Indians, had become peacefully pious, and did not agree with these Western carriers of shot-guns" (54).

American Indian studies have moved from the purview of historians and anthropologists to today's interest in literary studies that decode the ethnocentrism in colonial accounts of Indian cultures and study the Indian adoption and subversion of colonial paradigms in their culture and their oral and written literature. Without the benefit of twentieth-century theories, Woolson uses language that we would term ethnocentric, or even racist. She has Anne recognize the error about the Indian work ethic reflected in the chapter's headnote, but only as it applies to Indian women. Looking at some Indian women after her father's death, Anne denigrates the men as lazy, and believes that the "submissive, gentle-eyed squaws" are "[p]atient and uncomplaining by nature." They also "performed almost all the labor on their small farms, cooked for their lords and masters, and took care of the children, as their share of the duties of life, the husbands being warriors, and above common toil" (144). Woolson emphasizes the ineptitude of Indian men again in *Jupiter Lights* when they serve as camp guides to the whites but are generally incompetent and, at one point, become dangerous because of alcohol.

Mary Young's study of Cherokee cultures can help us understand Woolson's stereotyping. According to Young, nineteenth-century white settlers and government agents misread Indian women's and men's roles in agriculture and hunting. They emphasized the new role of cloth making for women, and in emphasizing the women's role in agriculture, as well, overlooked that they had always held the responsibility for farming. Women's industry was at once threatening, because it gave them economic freedom in the transition from hunting to agricultural societies, and useful, because it served as a role model for men. Whites still thought of the Indian cultures as hunting societies even if agriculture had always been practiced; they ignored the integration of men into agriculture when sources became depleted by excessive hunting and trading. Rather, they read lack of hunting and the converse pursuit of leisure as evidence of laziness. Like many of her contemporaries, Woolson readily approved Indian women's industry and dismissed Indian males as lazy and threatening. Alcoholism contributed to the stereotype and was enough of a problem that laws prohibited the sale of alcohol to Indians. But as troubling and culturally bound as Woolson's attitudes sometimes are, she still softens the stereotype of the drunken Indian by having the hero of *Jupiter Lights,* Paul Tennant, reason with the Chippewa men. He knows that if he captures the key abuser, the other men will not be dangerous. Woolson reads the Chippewa men as lazy, but she does not read them as violent and ignorant.

Recent scholarship on American Indian literature and culture has helped us to understand how Indians, particularly in their humor, have both incorporated and subverted white paradigms. Richard Slotkin has shown that early-nineteenth-century writers could develop a myth about the vanishing noble savage only when the threat of Indian warfare had been reduced. Taking the Indian perspective, Gerald Vizenor has shown how his people resisted actual and cultural extinction. Woolson gives an interesting perspective that lies between the two: she presents a white woman's view of the Indian *survivor.* Sometime between 1875 and 1878, when she was in her thirties, she wrote a letter to her sister Georgiana's husband about Apaches imprisoned at Fort San Marco in St. Augustine for various crimes, mostly murder. Though the comment is brief, it is particularly interesting because it represents the prevailing attitude of whites and one that Woolson moved beyond later in her life. Connie May Fowler uncovered a pointed example of this attitude, when she was tracing her own Indian ancestry, in a report written in 1877 by Harriet Beecher Stowe. The Indians, writes Stowe, were "untamable," "wild," "more like grim goblins than human beings." Instead of being appalled that they had to abandon their religion, their culture, even their language, Stowe advocates government policies of education and conversion, writing, "Might not the money now constantly spent on armies, forts and frontiers be better invested in educating young men who shall return and teach their people to live like civilized beings?" (Fowler 49). Col. John Hay was one of the men who worked toward Christianizing Indians, and Woolson tells Georgiana that, Christianized, they do not need to be guarded. She then cites an anecdote about an Apache praying and winking at an officer, the implication being that the Apache's Christianity is a pretense, and obviously apprehensive, she writes that she wishes Col. Hay would "take his *Christianized* Indians with him" (Benedict 1:249).

Woolson uses this experience nearly twenty years later in her novel *Horace Chase*. By this time, the threat invoked by the Sioux uprisings in 1862 and by Sitting Bull's victory over General George Custer at Little Big Horn in 1876 had past. In the novel, the major characters attend an Apache dance by the Christianized prisoners at Fort San Marco. As in the letter she wrote to Georgiana, these Apaches posture for the sake of the whites: "Their dark faces, either from their actual feelings or from the simulated ferocity appropriate to a war-dance, were very savage, and with their half-naked bodies, their whoops and yells, they made a picture that was terribly realistic to the whites who looked on from the ramparts above, for it needed but little imagination to fancy a *bona fide* attack" (176). In this section of the novel, Woolson recognizes the power structure enforced by Christianity. Essentially, she has turned the wink from a threat to a mode of survival: by posturing for the whites, these performers easily take them in and thus maintain their own superiority. Rather than being the dying noble savage, they are very much alive victors who have outwitted their would-be destroyers. Dolly Franklin, the character in *Horace Chase* most like Woolson, does not believe in the experiment of Christianization. She is not an idealist—she believes that Indians and forests are settlers' enemies and prefers villages with a man's name plus the suffix -*ville*. She prefers a domesticated wilderness, where she can imagine "the first log cabins in the little clearing; then a short, stump-bedecked street; then two or three streets and a court-house" (211). At the same time, however, she recognizes that there is something right about American Indians refusing to be Christianized and something very wrong about them being imprisoned for murder: "The crimes for which these poor creatures are imprisoned here are nothing but virtues upside down. . . . They killed white men? Of course they did. Haven't the white men stolen all their land?" (177).

Writing as a white woman a hundred years ago, Woolson recognized patterns that many of us are only now beginning to see. These patterns enabled American Indians who were expelled from their lands and seduced from their religions to survive by reconfiguring their physical and spiritual homes into traditions and stories that are adaptive and subversive. She also saw how the nineteenth century turned miscegenation of some mixed-blood women into a fad that championed ethnicity. From early in the nineteenth century, in novels like Cooper's *The Deerslayer,* Hawthorne's *The Blithedale Romance* and *The Marble Faun,* and Melville's *Pierre,* literature had juxtaposed two kinds of women—the light and the dark—with the light representing the socially acceptable, the pure, the ideal of the slightly neurasthenic heroine, and the dark representing the dangerous, the mysterious, the vital and somewhat evil. Such a description represents a simplistic compartmentalization that many literary scholars, myself included, have been questioning for more than twenty years. Cooper's Hetty Hutter, for example, has none of the attraction or ambiguity of Hawthorne's Zenobia. She would clearly taint Natty's and Cooper's Edenic wilderness and cannot read the injustice of social or natural laws that categorize women into the good and the bad. Zenobia, on the other hand, fully understands how society and the domesticated garden of Blithedale have conspired against women, and though Coverdale may never get the point, Hawthorne does.

Antebellum readers may have taken comfort in the fate that awaited most of the dark women—usually rejection or death—but, after the Civil War, many began to seek the dark lady for her novelty and, as some of the miscegenation arguments ran, even for her robust bloodlines. By the late nineteenth century, the fascination with the dark lady had been legitimized. Woolson set *Anne* during the Civil War, but she projects onto it this fascination that eventually became part of the vogue of a new Union, particularly in the East, where society was charmed by mixed-blood women who they could marry into their cultures. Tita in *Anne* would be "quite a sensation in New York" (104), and as Anne's aunt says of the southern Creoles, "It is a novelty . . . ; a reaction after the narrow-chested type which has so long in America held undisputed sway. We absolutely take a quadroon to get away from the consumptive, blue-eyed saint, of whom we are all desperately tired" (196). Like those who argued for miscegenation, Anne's aunt looks toward southern Creoles as a way of strengthening the group she really values. Through her, Woolson exposes the hypocrisy that lies beneath this fad and also exposes the fear that the dark and foreign might contain the dark and African.

Because Woolson came of age during the Civil War and because her travels allowed her to see firsthand the devastation the Civil War wrecked on the South, it is not surprising that the ethnic group outside of her own that she looked at most closely was the African American. Peter Caccavari has studied how outsiders to the post–Civil War South are unable to internalize the region because they have not been born to it. He believes that, as one of these outsiders, Woolson does not create convincing portraits of southerners, including of southern blacks.[10] Where he emphasizes that she does not get blacks right, I prefer to emphasize that she knows she cannot because she understands the way that home shapes ethnicity and ethnicity shapes perception. As early as the story "Jeannette," Woolson showed how aware she was of false northern liberalness: her character Rodney Prescott hopes that the rumor of the "taint" of black blood in Jeannette might be proven and he saved from loving her. To love a half-breed is one thing; to love a black quite another. The narrator, Sarah Corlyne, bluntly lambastes racial hypocrisy, the irony, of course, being that she is the one who considers blackness to be a "taint": theoretically, she says, the New England abolitionist "believed in the equality of the enslaved race, and stood ready to maintain the belief with his life, but practically he held himself entirely aloof from them; the southern creed and practice were the exact reverse" (*CN* 167). One of Woolson's most revealing stories about northern attitudes toward freed blacks is "King David," one of the few stories she wrote that centers almost exclusively on a male character, which makes me suspect that it was generated by the public debate about education for blacks. The debate that had raged before the Civil War around whether or not blacks could be taught to read had begun largely because southern slave owners feared educated blacks. After the Nat Turner uprising, laws against teaching slaves to read and write were more harshly enforced. As the Civil War approached, these laws caused northerners to increase their efforts toward educating blacks.[11] By the end of the Civil War, the debate had shifted from whether blacks could be educated to how and by whom they should be educated. Woolson would have been aware of the lines of the debate about black education from an 1874 lead article for *Harper's,* an issue in which her story "Duets" had appeared. The article, written and illustrated by Porte Crayon, describes black schools after the Civil War and the desire of blacks to become educated, with fellow blacks as their teachers. Despite condescending dialect and caricature illustrations, Crayon respects black intelligence—with limits. He fears that blacks will be exploited for the vote and will succumb to imitation of white gentility, and he ends up advocating education for trades rather than for professions. He believes that "the education most needed by the Negro is that which will most directly develop his capacity for self-maintenance and accumulation. We would suggest industrial schools, and leave to statesmen and philanthropists to provide the ways and means" (468).

When Woolson writes "King David," she embeds more than a touch of irony, suggesting that she could read the stereotypes about black education much as she could read the stereotype of the savage Apache. In the story, David King has come south to teach the freed slaves, his aim being to lay before his pupils that "their mission . . . was to go over to Africa, and wake out of their long sloth and slumber the thousands of souls there" (*Rodman* 254). Like those who read American Indian leisure games as signs of laziness, this liberal northerner implies that blacks are not only lazy but also ignorant. He fails to see that a race that has been kept servile, in part under the guise of Christianity, will once again be exiled from their home and shipped to a continent they may well wish to ignore. His is the ultimate colonialism, aimed at educating the vanquished to serve as ambassadors to what he conceives as an even more primitive culture. Nor are David's methods any better than his motives: he tries to teach blacks the alphabet instead of skills to help increase their pride and self-confidence; he finds the "rude plainness" of their language "a pain to his pedagogic ears" (*Rodman* 257). Such an observation does not imply that Woolson really heard the black vernacular herself or caught the degree to which, in Henry Louis Gates's phrase, it "talks about talking." What it does imply is that Woolson at least knew that she was an outsider and that she could read dangers inherent in people like David King, who, for all their idealism, displayed the same kind of missionary zeal that had sought to destroy Indian cultures in the name of education.

As representative of this kind of hegemonic policy, David, like the biblical king who enslaved the people he conquered and denied his son, must fail. He tries to teach his students to fear his learning instead of trying to earn his students' love and respect. He eventually realizes that he should have bought a plantation and taught the freed slaves, as Crayon advocated, by using what they know. But this, of course, creates the unspoken problem at the heart of so much talk of education in the nineteenth century (as well, I believe, as in our own).

Education that succeeds—whether of Indians, or blacks, or women—threatens the dominant culture. Woolson understood this fully in terms of women's education. In "King David," she understood, at least, that both the North and the South have failed the freed blacks: southerners because they have assumed blacks cannot be educated and northerners because they use inappropriate educational methods or, worse, pay for work that is such false work that the northern carpetbaggers suggest blacks simply be given money. In "King David," the point is captured in a telling image that forecasts the image in Faulkner's *The Bear,* in which Fonsiba's husband wears spectacles without lenses and pretends to read a book instead of tending to his farm. Like Faulkner, Woolson shows David King's students passing around a pair of spectacles as an "adjunct to the dignity of reading" (*Rodman* 259). Ornamental spectacles are not the tools that educate. Only when people are given the tools and a sense of self-worth to help themselves within their own cultural context and value system will they build rather than destroy their homes.

The worst part of the failure to help the freed slaves to help themselves takes its toll on the women. Jean Fagan Yellin has taught us to see that female abolitionists argued against slavery because it replicated their own victimization under patriarchal structures, though Elizabeth Fox-Genovese, in her monumental study of black and white women in the antebellum South, has rightly cautioned us not to apply this to southern slaveholding women who prospered under a patriarchal culture that reinforced their consciousness of and acceptance of themselves as privileged females (37–99). Like her abolitionist sisters, Woolson saw how black women, especially, had been victimized by the slave system. She also extends this to see that black men imitate white patriarchy by sometimes victimizing black women. As she does this, she sees in black women what she sees in the Indian women in *Anne;* that is, an immense capacity for work and survival. In "King David," the women continue to bring their children to school when their husbands have ceased coming and have taken to drinking and to beating their wives. In a poignant description of the black women, Woolson documents how much women bear the larger burden of suffering in communities that have not found a sense of communal dignity:

> Often now they were seen with bandaged heads and bruised bodies,
> the result of drunken blows from husband or brother; and left alone,

they were obliged to labor all day to get the poor food they ate, and to keep clothes on their children. Patient by nature, they lived along as best they could, and toiled in their small fields like horses; but the little prides, the vague, grotesque aspirations and hopes that had come to them with their freedom, gradually faded away. "A blue-painted front do'," "a black-silk apron with red ribbons," "to make a minister of little Job," and "a real crock'ry pitcher," were wishes unspoken now. The thing was only how to live from day to day, and keep the patched clothes together. In the mean while trashy finery was sold at the new store, and the younger girls wore gilt ear-rings. (*Rodman* 267)

This passage exhibits some condescension with its statements about "little prides" and "grotesque aspirations." Elsewhere, Woolson is not above calling a black child a "little darky" who stereotypically "showed his white teeth in a perpetual grin" (419). She generalizes about violent black men, and she does not assess why young girls would want to break from the culture in which they had been oppressed in order to wear the "finery" of the dominant culture. Still, she has a remarkably sharp eye, an understanding of white exploitation of blacks, and a respect for how black women held together their homes. Particularly in her novel *Jupiter Lights,* she presents insights on three important debates of the nineteenth century: the issue of whether or not blacks are childlike people who were better off under the protection of benevolent masters; the issue of white male power in the face of freed blacks; and the issue of southern vs. nonsouthern ease around black cultures. Rephrased in connection to Woolson's thinking about home, she is asking if black people are capable of securing their own homes, how they threaten white people's sense of their own homes, and to what extent black people are part of the white home environment. As she looks at all these issues, Woolson creates white characters who make overtly racist comments, and those who reveal subtle racist attitudes, and black characters whose dialect and culture she renders peripherally but convincingly, at least to the ears of her nineteenth-century readers.

Just how aware Woolson was about the degree to which both race and gender were associated with childlike dependence is seen in a comment by a minor female character in *Jupiter Lights* and the scenes that surround the comment. The statement concerns the death of Ferdinand Morrison, which turns out not to be a murder and which has been incorrectly blamed on blacks: Morrison's "valuable life has fallen a sacrifice (in my husband's opinion) to the present miserable condition of our poor State, where the blacks, our servants, who are like little children and need to be led as such,—where these poor ignorant creatures are put over us, their former masters; are rewarded with office; are intrusted with dangerous weapons—a liberty which in this case has proved fatal to one of the higher race" (226). With the parentheses, Woolson encodes the statement with female as well as black dependence. The scene comes shortly after the scene with the drunk Indians whom Paul Tennant refuses to treat as children. He wants to bring them under control in order that they may continue to serve him; however, to ask for service is not to enslave, murder, or treat like children. The scene in which the woman comments on her husband's view of freed slaves includes a young black maid who keeps disobeying orders. Although she is viewed as childlike and incompetent by her former masters, she is, in fact, revealing not stupidity or uselessness but freedom and rebellion.

Woolson is no starry-eyed idealist who believes that suddenly freed slaves should be "intrusted with dangerous weapons." She shows the complexity of the problem in a scene in which a carriage holding most of the novel's main characters meets a cart driven by a young black. The driver of the carriage, Judge Abercrombie, yells at the youth, who, from the standard of safety, should yield the right of way, "Hey! what are you about there, boy? Turn out!" and the youth replies, "Turn out yourself" (62). The judge flies into a rage and wants to fight the youth but cannot because he is physically weaker. Instead, he speaks "with the imperious manner which only a lifetime of absolute authority can give" (63) and in a later scene laments, to the heroine Eve Bruce's chagrin, that "[i]n the old days we could have tracked them; but it's not so easy now. And even if we got them we couldn't string them up" (136). After the incident, the judge wants to hunt down the youth but is stopped by Eve's intervention.

Through the scene, Woolson raises questions that involve both women and blacks. If white authority is gone, does power automatically revert to the physically stronger, whether or not that person has any more right to such power? And if power goes to the physically strong, what does this say about the chances for women ever finding it? In fact, one of the problems Woolson sees in southern women is their willingness to give up domestic authority for the comfort of what slaves could provide. As Elizabeth Harrison has shown, the southern pastoral, created largely by male writers, defended the slave system as necessary for maintaining women's domestic comfort. After the Civil War, it moved to a nostalgic remembrance of this system and eventually to an even stronger defense of patriarchy as a hedge against black and female power. The problem, Harrison recognizes, is that women need to move away from this male pastoral into a version in which they will be seen in relation to the land rather than as symbolic of and dependent upon it (1–15). Woolson, too, recognizes that if women give up domestic power to a patriarchal slave system, they risk becoming like Cicely Tennant, the southern woman in *Jupiter Lights* who has been allowing Eve to do most of the caring for her child and has become so vulnerable that she is physically abused by her husband. Cicely is a victim because her socialization into love and marriage allows her to be a victim. This is the same kind of powerlessness displayed by Cicely's servant Porley. Cicely ties her up, and when Porley is asked why she allows this, she says that Cicely has conjured her. Because Porley could easily have resisted, we must read this as another case of being socialized into powerlessness and inferiority and as evidence that Woolson believed that blacks and females needed to see themselves as possessing dignity and power instead of seeing themselves as victims and victimizers.

As much as Eve the northerner seems to have enlightened attitudes toward race, Woolson does not make her an ally of blacks. Like David King, she remains more of an outsider to their culture than do her southern characters, even though these characters may insist on using the term "nigger" instead of the, at that time, politically correct "Negro." One is reminded of Harriet Beecher Stowe's portrait of Miss Ophelia in *Uncle Tom's Cabin,* a woman whose supposedly liberal views are sorely tested when she is given charge of the feisty Topsy. The southern Garda Thorne in *East Angels* puts the issue bluntly to that novel's northern woman, Margaret Harold:

> . . . you don't really like the negroes, personally, one bit. You would do anything in the world for them, give them all your money and all your time, teach school for them, make clothes for them, and I don't know what all; but you would never understand them though you should live among them all the rest of your life and never see a white face again. Now *I* wouldn't take one grain of trouble for them that you would, because I don't think it's in the least necessary. But, personally, I like them, I like to have them about, talk to them and hear them talk; I am really attached to all the old servants about here. And I venture to say, too, that

they would prefer me forever, though I didn't lift a finger for them, prefer me to you, no matter what sacrifices you might make to help them, because they would see and feel that *I* really liked them, whereas *you* didn't. (356)

Of course, the issue here is not so simple, for as much as she may "like the negroes" and respect the fact that they are self-sufficient, Garda still makes them seem like objects: to her, they are a collective group rather than individuals, fixtures that make her home more comfortable. She claims that it is not necessary to take trouble for them, but such an attitude allows her to use them for her convenience and entertainment. It is easy for Garda to read Margaret's unease as false sacrifice; easier still to lift no finger to help a people whose sole purpose is to serve her needs. In a letter to Paul Hayne, Woolson confirms that she sees the implications we read in Garda's attitude. At Madame Chegaray's School in New York, where she was one of the few northern students, she tells of a young southern woman who would call to a servant to shut the door, becoming impatient when the servant did not comply and never thinking to shut the door herself. She also tells Hayne that she made a public comment about southern women and incurred their wrath. She regrets this but is firm in her belief that southern women are still fighting the Civil War. She knows that, as much as the men may want northerners to come south to help with Reconstruction, these would be middle-class farmers and mechanics whose wives would not be accepted by southern women used to the leisure that slave culture brought them.[12]

This exchange and a similar one in *Jupiter Lights* reflect the relations between white and black women in the South that Minrose Gwin has traced in fiction about the old South. Whether written in the nineteenth or twentieth century, Gwin sees a pattern in this fiction that shows southern white women seeing black women "as servants, as children, as adjuncts, as sexual competition, as dark sides of their own sexual selves—as black Other. They beat black women, nurture them, sentimentalize them, despise them—but they seldom see them as individuals with selves commensurate to their own" (5). Woolson also fails to individualize black women—as she failed to individualize any women outside her ethnic profile, but the difference is that she recognizes her limitations. A scene in *Jupiter Lights* indicates this kind of recognition. In it, one of the southern women charges Eve with seeing blacks as a "novelty" (49) and proceeds to reveal her own concern for freed black women by thinking of them in terms of childbirth:

For they must be suffering in so many ways; take the one instance of
the poor women in their confinement; we used to go to them, and be
with them to cheer their time of trial. But now, separated from us, from
our care and oversight, what *can* they do? If the people who have been
so rash in freeing them had only thought of even that one thing! But I
suppose they did not think of it, and naturally, because the abolitionist
societies, we are told were composed principally of old maids. (49)

There are, Woolson knows, problems with this comment as well.
It is made in the presence of two who might qualify as old maids and
makes stereotypical assumptions about abolitionists. It fails to mention that a larger part of the motivation for caring for slaves who were
pregnant or capable of becoming pregnant was economic, the female
needing to be kept healthier in order to protect her childbearing ca-
pabilities.[13] It assumes that blacks are incapable of tending to their own
childbearing and that they would be cheered by the presence of their
white enslavers, who may be present in part to ascertain the racial
mix of the baby. Yet it also connects black and white women in the
most intimate way, one of the few areas on which they shared common ground. Eve, on the other hand, responds in a way that reveals
how little she understands the current situation of blacks—she believes
they can simply hire nurses for themselves, thinking nothing about
where they will get money to do this—or the nurses to tend them—
and not questioning the need for hired nurses.

    Just how much Woolson understood the degree to which one's
own ethnicity shaped social attitudes toward blacks is revealed in another way in the opening, comic scenes of *Jupiter Lights*. Here Eve
arrives from England with her maid Meadows, whom she cannot af-
ford and must therefore immediately send back to England even though
this means placing her back on a boat before she has time to get over
the seasickness she has incurred from her journey to the United States.
Cicely's black servants do not understand that this white woman can
also be a servant, and so they try to wrest Eve's bags from Meadows.
Meadows, equally ethnocentric, does not understand what the black
servant is doing and, taking him for a thief, fights for the bag. Cicely
laughs; Eve, on the other hand, does not because Meadows is her friend
as well as her servant. Such a scene reveals Woolson's attention to
issues of race, and it also gives a brief glimpse of her attention to issues of social class. As a southern woman, Cicely expects to have servants despite poverty; as a resident of England, Eve hires a servant

less because she needs one than because it is protocol and selects one she can consider an equal; as a reintegrated American, Eve can drop this financial burden though it means saying goodbye to the only friend she has.

Slave cultures, Woolson knew, allowed southern women to maintain a home structure that drew clear lines between servant and mistress and between servant and master, even when masters used slave women for sex. A large body of American literature, written by both blacks and whites, has helped us to understand the destructiveness of such a system for both servant and served. Another large body of literature has exposed the exploitation of immigrant groups that made up the working classes. Most of this, like Melville's "The Tartarus of Maids" (1855) or Rebecca Harding Davis's *Life in the Iron Mills* (1861), is focused on the exploitation of women—whether immigrant or farm women—in the industrial market place.[14]

Historical research by Faye Dudden has helped us to understand the dynamics of employer-servant relationships in the nineteenth century. Dudden has shown that as the United States moved into an urban-based industrial economy, the relationship between employer and servant changed dramatically. Early in the century most domestic service involved "hired girls" who came from within the community and enjoyed a close relationship with the family. These girls could be hired temporarily to help with births, illnesses, and deaths. Often they were hired for home tasks such as spinning or churning that added to the family income. By the middle of the century, this kind of work had moved into the industrialized cities. Those who hired themselves out as servants had followed, sometimes to earn money as a stepping stone for tuition to one of the new female academies, but more often as a means of finding survival wages. These new "domestics" no longer enjoyed a close relationship to the families they served, so much so that organizations such as the New York Society for the Encouragement of Faithful Domestic Servants were formed. The major immigrant group to enter domestic service were the Irish, which added another level of complication to domestic-employer relations. Although they enjoyed the advantage of sharing a common language with their employers, Irish girls had not been trained to do the kind of household tasks required in an environment that no longer depended on home production but instead used domestics for housecleaning that would allow leisure time for wealthier women. These wealthier women, often untrained themselves, had to train their Irish "Biddies," who might, as Charlotte O'Brien had feared on Mackinac Island, then leave for higher wages elsewhere because they depended upon their income to support relatives in Ireland. Religious difference added to the conflicts, with white employers fearing that their Catholic servants would try to convert their children. The distance between employer and servant was so great that jokes proliferated and one Boston employer was said to have provided the best excuse for a suicide note: "I *kept Irish domestics*" (Dudden 59).

Unless it is specifically reformist, nineteenth-century literature tends to ignore the lives and the poverty of servant classes. For example, as poor as the March family in *Little Women* are, they, like the Alcotts, keep a servant. Alcott's awareness of poverty is apparent in the family's support of the Hummel family, from whom Beth contracts scarlet fever, which eventually kills her. But even though she had herself spent time as a servant, she did so under the earlier tradition of the "hired girl." She never examines the lives of the domestic servant classes, so much so that we do not know what ethnic group the March's servant Hannah belongs to, though it seems likely that she is Irish, the immigrant group Alcott's mother worked with. Given the attitude toward Irish domestics, Alcott may have purposely withheld this information in order to portray Hannah as a loyal member of the March family, more in the tradition of the black "mammy" than the Irish "Biddy." In fact, as a child I assumed that Hannah is black. Half Irish myself, I was unable to think of an Irish woman in terms of a servant class. All I knew of servants were misreadings: Hannah, the slaves in *Uncle Tom's Cabin,* and Aunt Jemima, the latter made even more an "other" by being called *ant* rather than *änt*. The failure to individualize servants extends, as well, to literary studies. In a cursory look at biographies of Alcott, I find only one mention of the family's servants. Servants are invisible in literature and scholarship not aimed explicitly at exposing the conditions of the group. We do not know if the Woolsons had servants in Cleveland. It was a populated enough settlement with immigrants arriving regularly, and the Woolsons' economic status would have allowed them to hire at least some help. Even the chaplain on Mackinac Island kept a servant, as did the Alcotts, who considered themselves "'poor as rats,' nonetheless [they] had not yet sunk to the ignominy of a servantless house."[15]

Two writers who can help us position Woolson in her literary portraits of servants are Charlotte Perkins Gilman and Edith Wharton. As outspoken and polemical about women's economic needs as Gilman was, she, too, failed to look at servant classes, at times even dismissing them as unworthy of anyone's regard. Even the Swedish servant Gerta in her story "Turned" is primarily a prop to show how the male head of the house wrongs all women; the wife who protects her does so in solidarity of women against men, never considering Gerta as more than an ignorant immigrant. It also seems significant that the girl is Swedish, the Swedes being a maligned group in the Midwest, a region to which many of them had immigrated (Dudden 62), but never so maligned as the Irish—and conveniently not Catholic. Unlike Gilman, Edith Wharton became closely attached to her servants, especially, at the end of her life, to Catherine Gross. Gloria Erlich theorizes that this closeness to servants stemmed from Wharton's relationship with her childhood nursemaid, Nanny Doyley, whom she saw as the good mother figure in contrast to her distant biological mother, and that this pattern is consistent with research involving children raised with divided mother figures, such as those who have been raised by nannies.

Woolson did not divide her loyalties between mother figures, nor does she speak in her letters about any close relationship to servants. An early story, "A Merry Christmas" shows her unaware or unconcerned about the private lives of servants. The story centers on the breakdown of social barriers at a Christmas dinner, with the more elite characters managing in the course of the evening to befriend the less privileged. On the outskirts of this story hovers a servant named Tony, who does not know how to serve a dinner party of mixed-class guests. By the end of the story, one of the characters has pledged to take in a crippled child because she "like[s] the lassie, and will take her as [a] Christmas present" (231–36). Neither she nor Woolson think to ask if the child's guardians might miss her, even though they have ten children of their own. Nor does Woolson include the servant Tony within the class structure. He is a prop, a non-entity, a mere servant.

Once in Europe, we know that Woolson hired servants, particularly because she preferred to have her meals cooked for her than to dine out. Here, she wrote two stories that, along with the opening of *Jupiter Lights,* show her enlarging her vision of servants. In a story titled "A Christmas Party" (*FY*), which echoes the earlier title "A Merry Christmas," an American consul in Venice and his wife place a high value on their servants, but they really know nothing of their lives. The plot of the story has the family's gondolier, Ercole, dress as an acrobat-clown to entertain at a Christmas party. The American family had no idea that he could perform in this way—and in fact he cannot, for we eventually discover that the real Ercole has been beaten and tied up and that the performer is an imposter. So little do they know the real Ercole that when he tells what happened, the family do not believe him. The inside connection to the robbery turns out to be another servant, Carmela, whom the family has thought youthful but who is really a seventy-year-old woman who has been trying to support herself and her prodigal son. Although "A Christmas Party" is a kind of mini-detective story, Woolson's point is really about how blind people are to the lives of servant classes. She had little access herself to these lives from which to observe them and portray them in her fiction, but she does make it clear that such lives exist and deserve the attention of people like the American consul, who becomes so moved by Carmela's plight that he helps her to escape.

Woolson's commentary about employers' failure to look at the lives of their servants is again clear in her story "A Waitress," which is told through two male characters, the employer John Dennison and his guest Edward Gray. The story's title places the emphasis on the servant Modesta even though the main narration centers on the two men. Gray likes Modesta because she is "extraordinarily handsome," and Dennison likes her because "she is perfect as a servant" (89). Even the terminology places the servant apart from them—she is, as Gray says, "[a] waitress; that's what we call 'em now; we've given up 'help.' Is she married to your cook?" (89). She is not married to the cook and has a lover whom Dennison judges as lazy though he is himself an indolent man who thinks of little other than his own comfort, a man, in short, willing to let some "other" wait on him. Gray and Dennison are eventually awakened to Modesta's life when she nearly kills a Swedish servant who has been receiving the attention of her lover. Dennison saves the Swedish woman, but never sees her as someone other than a foreigner who is upsetting his peace, and so, like those in the United States who would expel the freed slaves to Africa, he "dispose[s]" (101) of her by shipping her back to Scandinavia so he can regain a more peaceable Modesta to keep his life in comfort.

"A Christmas Party" and "A Waitress" show that when Woolson began to live in Europe, she also began to write in a way that recognized servants as people. Ironically, it was in the great democratic United States that Woolson saw clear ethnic lines separating servant classes. In Europe, she was the foreigner. Could she have feared that if she failed as a writer, she might have to seek employment in the service of others, not as a house servant but as a companion or nurse?

Alice James deplored the English class system and championed the masses in her diary, but she insists on calling her nurse *Nurse* instead of dignifying her with a name, and she used her friend and companion Katharine Loring as if she were a cross between a private secretary and a housekeeper even though she knew that Loring belonged to a well-connected American family. Loring, in fact, had once been invited to a servants' ball where she interacted with those present, writes Alice, "as if they were friends and hosts." Alice goes on to report that Jennie, her housemaid, "said to Nurse, with delight, the next morning: 'fancy Miss Loring shaking hands with me before the whole room.'"[16]

Besides the James household, Woolson's neighbors in Florence, Francis Boott and his daughter Lizzie, provided a family model that included Lizzie's childhood nurse, Mary Ann Shenstone, who continued to live with them long after Lizzie was grown.[17] Francis Boott was a widower and amateur composer who lived on an income from a New England textile mill. Lizzie lived with him as a single woman until she was forty years old. At forty, she decided to marry Frank Duveneck, a German American from Cincinnati who had been her painting master. Many read Lizzie as stooping to marry Duveneck, but we can imagine Woolson reading the family differently. Here is a father-daughter bound together with the kind of closeness she had had with her own father. Instead of being the daughter in the scene, Woolson is closer to the painter, depending on a patron/publisher to support her, or to the nursemaid, with no visible means of support and no role save that of companion.

A final example of a hired or supported companion comes from the last two weeks of Woolson's life. Woolson had at least one maidservant at this time, and a trained nurse was called in to attend her during her severe illness. In addition to these, Marie Holas had been called in to serve as an untrained nurse-companion. We know nothing of the woman except that Woolson's friend Clara Hay mistrusted her and thought she had been stealing from Woolson. However, in the letter that exists from Miss Holas to Woolson's nephew, Sam Mather, describing the last weeks of Woolson's life, it is impossible to detect any dishonesty.[18] The letter is detailed and well written and leaves one asking, as with the case of Mary Ann Shenstone, what circumstances led this woman into service. The two are foreigners in Italy, reminders that without her writing Woolson, too, might have taken on the role of server.

Woolson lived in Europe at time when large numbers of Americans were settling or traveling there: wealthy nouveau riche who were being "finished" by Europe, poor pretenders who were economizing, appointees of a United States government that was taking its place in the international community, artists who were studying old world masters and—as the artist life often goes—economizing. Observing these people, Woolson saw the American tendency to label all that is not American as other. The Americans in her stories are often ugly Americans, ethnocentrically tied to their own language and comfort. In "A Waitress," for example, Dennison is especially upset with the Swedish servant after she is almost murdered because he thinks that "[n]one of them can speak *anything*" (101), and the American consul in "A Christmas Party" thinks that Italian is "gibberish" and that he is "patriotic not to understand" (*FY* 195). Another wonderful ethnocentric exchange occurs in "The Street of the Hyacinth" between an aspiring artist, Ethelinda Faith Macks, and an art critic, Raymond Noel. The conversation concerns a potential art teacher for Ettie:

> Ettie: "I am glad it isn't a foreigner. . . . I don't believe I should get on with a foreigner."
> Noel: "But it is a foreigner."
> Ettie: "Why, it's an English name, isn't it?—Jackson."
> Noel: "Yes, he is an Englishman. But isn't an Englishman a foreigner in Rome?"
> Ettie: "Oh, you take that view? Now, to me, America and—well, yes, perhaps England too, are the nations. Everything else is foreign."
> Noel: "The English would be very much obliged to you. . . ."
> Ettie: "Yes, I know I am more liberal than most Americans." (*FY* 147)

Aside from the humor in these exchanges about foreigners, they suggest that Woolson believed Americans never could be really at home in Europe, in Italy in particular. "A Christmas Party" and "A Waitress" place the blame on Americans who are too culture-bound to open themselves to other cultures. Two other stories in *The Front Yard* collection reveal different, more sympathetic, responses to the issues facing Americans in Europe. In "A Pink Villa," an American widow, Mrs. Churchill, is playing the role of elite American enjoying the charm of Italy and trying to marry her daughter to an Italian count. Her daughter, however, will have none of this. She does not feel particularly at home in Italy and rebels against her mother by marrying the American David Rod, who will settle with her in a new Florida, one devoid

of its Spanish history. Mrs. Churchill is especially annoyed by the newness of Rod's clothes, "[m]ade in Tampa, probably." She has "no doubt
but that he took pains with them—wanted to have them appropriate"
(*FY* 106). But one, of course, cannot buy appropriateness, and the
daughter's choice to marry a nouveau riche American is ultimately more
sympathetic than her mother's ambitions toward Old World aristocracy.

Much like Edith Wharton's "Roman Fever," written nearly fifty years
later, "A Pink Villa" (1888), represents how a new generation of Americans, unhampered by elitist attitudes, pursue homes they choose rather
than accept homes society dictates for them. In the case of "A Pink
Villa," the choice brings the woman back to a United States Woolson
dreamed of returning to. Another of her European stories, "The Front
Yard," leaves an American woman in an Italian nightmare. The story
reverses the plot of the wealthy American girl marrying an Italian aristocrat many years her senior by examining the fate of an American
who marries an Italian peasant eighteen years her junior. Antonio
Guadagni has charmed Prudence into being imprudent in accepting
his proposal. Immediately after the marriage, Prudence discovers that
not only does Tonio have no money, he also has the grandmother
and uncle of his first wife to care for and seven children of his own
plus an orphaned nephew. Worse still, Tonio dies within a year of the
marriage and Prudence is left to cope with a family who exploits her
New England work ethic and her generosity with what little money
she is able to save from her hard work and thrift. Every time she saves
nearly enough to build herself a front yard, a member of the family
asks for or simply takes that money. But this is not an anti-Italian story;
rather, it is a story about the clash of cultural expectations. Prudence
values the domestic, thus she works and gives money to the family
she believes she has become obligated to serve when she married.
She wants a front yard for herself because she can plant it with vegetation reminiscent of New England and can sit in it on special days.
Her sense of beauty is so narrow that she does not even realize that
she already has an unobstructed view of old Italy, antiquity being to
her merely "everything that was old and dirty" (*FY* 3). Conversely, her
Italian family exploits her because they do not understand her desire
for a front yard, being as they are, already at home in Italy. The story
represents Woolson's vision of how difficult it is to become encultured
into a society one is not born into. That she finally rewards Prudence
by having some wealthy Americans find her and build her her cov-

eted yard is a poignant reminder of Woolson's own longing for a home she could call her own.

As much as Woolson's fiction respects and encourages diversity, it still recognizes the tensions that diversity creates. Instead of Edenic gardens, she saw western territories that were being settled in ways that repeated exclusionary cultural patterns of the Old World, southern cultures that formed bonded communities through the bondage of others, and Old World cultures to which new world Americans had lost their ties. She recognized that people could choose from all the imperfect places a place to call home, but that they were shaped by cultural heritages over which they had no control and that the choice of a place to call home never erased the marks of this heritage. The splits between heritage and place that she portrays range from the poignant (a front yard or an Italian landscape) to the comic (a savage Apache or an Apache posturing savagery) to the dangerous and oppressive (blacks whom southerners genuinely like or blacks who support the southern life-style). Her life's journey moved her further from her personal sense of home into cultures to which she was increasingly an outsider and into a position from which she could look back at the tensions more than the rewards of diversity. By putting these tensions into context, she helps us to understand as well as judge them. Reading Woolson, we can learn much about our own attitudes toward our increasing diversity, so that in building our own front yards, we do not forget to admire the global vista.

5

Woolson's Ambivalent Love Affair with Europe
❖

Once Woolson left for Europe in 1879, she could only write about and dream of a home in her beloved Florida. Although her European letters reveal her as a woman intellectually alive, observant and caustic about the society around her, and enthralled with the varied landscapes of England and the Continent, they also sound a recurring theme of rootlessness.[1] Her letters to Sam Mather, her sister Georgiana's child, reveal her at her most melancholy. Because he represents family, she writes to him often about homesickness and illness and depression, and, because she had put him in charge of her financial affairs, she writes about her financial worries. Frequently she apologizes for not writing and expresses gratitude for some favor Sam may have performed. Her letters to Katharine Loring also sound the theme of homesickness. She writes, for example, at length about her roots in New England, about how Loring's mention of baked beans remind her of her father's love for this New England staple, and about how she has traced her father's ancestry to a pirate involved in the Mount Wollaston community in Massachusetts. She also talks about women's issues to Loring, particularly about her support of medical colleges for women.

Where the letters to Mather are family centered and the letters to Loring are women-centered, the letters to Edmund Clarence Stedman and Paul Hamilton Hayne, both writers she met during her years in the South, are less personal and more focused on literary matters. The letters to Col. John Hay, the diplomat and writer who is remembered for his biography of Lincoln, and his wife, Clara Stone of Cleveland, whose sister Flora married Sam Mather, reveal Woolson's openness to the natural and social landscape. They provide a full picture of the social milieu around which Woolson shaped much of her later fiction and a picture of the way American artists and writers moved in Europe. Woolson's circle overlapped with James's, and for a time she was content to expand her friendships into the artistic and literary, having complained to Hayne while in the American South that she never met any writers. The people she writes about to Hay include Francis Boott, Frank Duveneck, and Lizzie Boott Duveneck; William Dean Howells, whom she met often; Horatio Greenough, whose bust of Woolson is now part of the Rollins College archives; Clarence King, the geologist and art collector; McWalter Noyes, the United States consul in Venice; John Addington Symonds, the essayist and art critic who lived in the same Venetian palace in which she had rooms; Edward Poynter, a painter, and his sister Eleanor, a writer; J. J. Jarvis, an art collector; Mrs. Launt Thompson, an Irish sculptor; William Stillman, an American journalist and artist; and a variety of wealthy Clevelandites who flit in and out of the European scene. Many of these names are lost to us now, but they indicate that Woolson traveled with the intellectual elite—or pretenders to the elite. Her early letters to the Hays are energetic and gossipy, filled with a sense of newness, yet also with the ability to see through the initial charm to the social posturing she exposed so well in her European fiction.

Two of Woolson's letters to John Hay, one written from Venice on April 24, 1883, and the other on May 5, 1883, convey the complexity of Woolson's feelings about herself and her new world. That they are written so close together and that she also wrote to Stedman on April 30, 1883, indicate that she may have felt a bit lonely, needing to communicate with people to whom she felt close. However, the tone of all these letters is anything but lonely. The ones to Hay are long, written with a burst of energy that is interesting given the many letters later in her life in which she apologizes for not writing and complains of writer's cramp. The letter of the twenty-forth starts with a description of her delight in Venice, of the rooms she occupies and the views from her balcony. She then tells Hay how pleased she is to learn that Symonds is her neighbor and praises him as a preeminent art critic. She spends four paragraphs on a variety of mutual acquaintances, ending with the information that she bowed to Howells's insistence and allowed someone to do a medallion portrait of her. She is basking in Howells's praise and the implication that she will soon need to have a portrait to accompany her stories in *Harper's*. From here, Woolson proceeds to a gossipy story about the British writer Violet Paget, who wrote under the pseudonym Vernon Lee, delighting in the fact that she can use Paget's ten-day trip with another female writer and an American male to defend American girls against the charge of going about unchaperoned. After several more paragraphs about mutual friends, a new Emerson essay, and a living artist she has discovered, she ends with kisses for the children.

Though a bit shorter, Woolson's second letter to Hay has much the same tone. She even spends a paragraph indicating that she is much too enthralled with Europe to consider returning to the United States. But there is a strange turn. She ends the letter with "Oh yes, Venice IS enchanting," then adds a "P.S. Evening." The Howells have just left and she is feeling "a little downhearted to-night, even if I am in Venice. I should say I was a trifle homesick—only how can one be homesick who has'nt a 'home['l? Be thankful that you have one; & keep kindly thoughts for the less fortunate" (Petry 48, 5 May 1883). The tone of both these letters indicates that Woolson knew periods of joy and energy at the same time that the postscript reveals her susceptibility to mood swings. Her correspondence with the Hays and others also shows her enthusiasm for Europe wearing thin. When she is in Venice, she longs for Florence, in Florence, for England. It takes her long periods of time to muster the energy for travel, she has a burst of enthusiasm when she reaches her destination, then begins to long for some other place where she may feel more at home.

Woolson's letters reveal that, in Europe, she remains a fundamentally asocial person. Although she observes the social setting with the same trained eye she has turned to the American social landscape, she also finds herself gravitating to the nonsocial—long walks apart from the Venetian ladies who "sit up half the night; & never have any 'walking dresses' because they never walk" (Petry 54–55, 9 Aug. 1883), meals taken in her rooms so as to avoid society, and visits to the art galleries that substitute for the rural landscapes she had known in the United States. In Europe, Woolson became further divorced from her regional and family roots, but at the same time it is here that she found her true literary home. Unlike Hawthorne, she does not turn to the antiquity of Europe to develop a sense of the remote and imagined that inform his brand of romance, which she was never successful at imitating. Here, instead, she continues to develop her skills in realism, both by continuing to use local-color realism in the four novels and one novella she wrote while in Europe and by developing the social realism of her many short stories set in Europe. None of the short stories that she wrote in Europe has an American setting, yet all the novels and the novella do. As she tackles the longer form and copes with the pressures of serialization and publisher's deadlines, she stays with the locale she has become comfortable with, but as she tackles the new, she writes the stories that are her most complex and fully realized.

Two things happened that explain this new dimension in Woolson's writing: one, she has served her apprenticeship, moved away from imitative romantic modes, and committed herself to the modes of realism that she was involved in developing; and two, she has entered a community of writers and artists with whom she can exchange ideas. Her most important literary friendship developed with Henry James, whom she met in 1880 as a result of a letter of introduction she had from his cousin, Henrietta Pell-Clark, Minny Temple's sister. In his biography of Henry James, Leon Edel seriously misrepresents Woolson and the Woolson-James relationship, and Cheryl Torsney and Joan Weimer have both taken him sufficiently to task for this misrepresentation.[2] Still, it is worth looking at the relationship again because it can help us to see how Woolson blended her sense of homelessness with her intellectual and artistic friendship that helped her to find her literary home.

James did not look forward to his first meeting with Woolson, but once he carried it through, he immediately liked her. He accompanied her to art galleries in Florence in the spring of 1880, met her at various intervals and in various places for the remainder of Woolson's life, and even shared a villa with her in Florence for four months in 1887. Even though Woolson and James developed a friendship based on mutual affection, Edel's version of the relationship projects his own condescension toward women. He insists on calling Woolson an "authoress" and paints her as "serenely preparing" her collection of stories for *Rodman the Keeper* as she sails from Italy to London, where she misses meeting James the first time because he is in Paris. But Edel's comment on Woolson's serenity contradicts his more accurate version of her as lonely and depressed by nature.[3] With no firm evidence, Edel says that Woolson "had come to Europe half in love with James from her close reading of his works," that "we . . . know that she had to face her hopeless love for a man who had no thought of marriage," and that "Henry could not 'collaborate' with Fenimore in the one way in which she would have liked him to."[4] Even if Edel has found legitimate grounds for much of his psycho-biography of the

Woolson-James relationship, he undermines his argument with constant references of this kind that devalue Woolson and assume that she must have aspired to marriage.

Specifically, Edel misrepresents the extent of the contact between the two writers, including the written contact revealed in the surviving correspondence from Woolson to James, the quality of and motives behind Woolson's admiration for James, and the circumstances surrounding Woolson's death. In his version, Woolson followed James to England despite her dislike of the English climate, but this version ignores references in Woolson's letters to her need for the solitude she gained to write in England, even though she disliked where she was living. While Edel makes much of Woolson's movements in location toward James, he makes little of James's movements toward Woolson in Italy. He implies that James disguised his living arrangements in Woolson's Florentine Villa Brichieri, though a letter written by Clara Benedict in 1889 from that villa indicates that she had known about the arrangement and saw nothing clandestine about it, and one written in 1887 by Alice James to her sister-in-law indicates that she knows Henry will join Woolson in Florence.[5] Edel suggests that James met Woolson secretly, though two more letters from Alice James, one to her Aunt Kate and one to her brother William, indicate that Alice knew about meetings in Europe, where, she says to Aunt Kate, Henry is off with his "*she*-novelist" and, to William, that he is "somewhere on the continent flirting with Constance."[6] James himself is open—though perhaps defensively humorous—to William Dean Howells about the "discreet intervals" at which he sees Woolson.[7] And to Francis Boott, he wrote that he and Woolson were together in Switzerland, albeit in different housing arrangements.[8]

Edel comments on the inordinate length of Woolson's letters to James. They are longer than many of her letters, but all of her letters reveal a habit of writing that tended toward fullness, and some of the ones to John Hay rival their length. Woolson hated to leave a page of a letter unfilled and often squeezed in a last line over her salutation. She waited long periods between some letters, distracted by her professional writing and a neurological problem with her arm brought on by writing, so that when she felt she could write, she often made up for periods of noncorrespondence. If we remember that she suffered from increasing deafness, we also realize that letter writing was her way of communicating and that James was the person with whom she could most share her feelings about writing.

A good example of the ease with which Edel manipulates facts occurs in his interpretation of a reference Woolson made about Alice James. In a letter to Sam Mather, dated according to Edel April 29, 1893, Woolson says, "I don't know what made me tell you and Will that last message of his sister to me, that touched me so much." She believes it may have been "the relief of having some of my own family to talk to . . . without having to think whether it was safe or not, wise or not, prudent or not."[9] Edel refuses to state outright what he believes was in Alice's letter to Woolson or Woolson's reference to it in her letter to Sam, but his innuendo is that the reference involved Woolson's feelings toward James. However, the only substantive reference to Alice James I have found in a Woolson-Mather letter, dated February 8, 1892, just a month before Alice's death, suggests a far different interpretation. Here Woolson describes reading William James's *Principals of Psychology,* in which he writes that people should "'*express* an emotion of benevolence if it rises in them.'" Woolson goes on to give William James's examples, including one that refers to the need "to speak genially to one's aunt!!" She then

> sat down and scratched off a note to Alice James . . . demanding to know what that meant! We have been writing back & forth about it ever since; & though it is a joke (she is very witty), yet I have been astonished to find that she found her brother's illustration a perfectly good one! Heavens—is that the usual idea of aunts? Why—the only importance I have is that of an aunt; it is only through nephews & nieces, & new grandnephews & niece, if you please, that I keep in touch with the actual life of the day. (WRHS)

It might seem odd that this would be the "last message" of Alice to Woolson and that a reference to herself as aunt would elicit the kind of response from Mather that would cause her to write about the "relief" of talking to family. But this interpretation is supported in the rest of Woolson's February aunt letter, which lists a host of reasons for her current melancholy state. One can imagine Mather replying in a way that will reassure her about how much he values her role as aunt, that this is not merely an "emotion of benevolence" but one of genuine love, and imagine Woolson, coming out of her depression, replying about the impetus behind her reference to Alice's "last message" to her. While the reference does not read like a "last message," it would have impacted on Woolson because three days before she wrote her 1892 letter to Mather, she wrote Dr. William Wilberforce Baldwin, a physician she and Alice both saw, that "Alice lives, and even enjoys, for every now and then I get a witty message from her. If she had had any health, what a brilliant woman she would have been."[10] Alice James died just a month later, on March 6, 1892. I have not located the 1893 letter Edel refers to at the Western Reserve Historical Society, nor does Edel identify its location. The dating of Woolson's letters is often inaccurate because she did not always include the year. A more likely date for the April letter would be 1892, when Alice's death would be more recent. If Woolson were still writing to Mather about Alice well after Alice's death, the "last message" could have involved something other than benevolence and aunts. But rather than a message about Henry, it would more likely have been a message about depression or suicide, both subjects of Woolson's story "Dorothy," the last story Alice James was to hear, just two days before her death.

The best access we have concerning Woolson's relationship to James are the four letters that survived the help James gave Clara and Clare Benedict in sorting through Woolson's effects after her death. These letters were written in 1882 and 1883, and their full text is now available in Edel's edition of James's letters. Edel finds them full of "mocking and competitive challenge," the letters of someone who "plays the woman scorned and the woman pleading," who is "full of self-pity at her footloose state," who casts herself in the role of "rejected woman," and who, "under the guise of discussing and criticizing Henry's writings," implies that "he is cold, disinterested, does not understand women—does not understand how a woman—say Miss Woolson—feels."[11] My own reading of the letters infers quite a different picture, for, written early in their relationship, the letters are too open to suggest a woman in love with someone who remains disinterested. Although they are mildly flirtatious, and wonderfully flippant, such an attitude does not seem to me to mask the kind of suffering Woolson would have felt had she loved James in any sexual way. At one point, she even calls her relationship to him that of "a sort of—of admiring aunt."[12] James is a man she wants to marry off to some eligible young American. In her letters to James, Woolson mocks him as stiff, referencing a young lady who looks forward to a visit from him, so that, Woolson says, "now of course it will immediately become hilarious—he [James] is such a turbulently gay, eager, excitable person."[13] This tone is not reserved for her correspondence to James only. For example, in a much later letter to Katharine Loring, she says that she hopes "Mr. James has given a good account of me? If he mentions me as 'worthy,' let me know in private, that I may think of revenge. Curiously enough he considers it a complementary adjective, I believe!" (BHSM, 19 Sept. 1890).

The most provocative reference in Woolson's letters to James involves his decision to return for a period to America—where he received the letters that have survived. They were "'talking it over' (the going home) 'against an Italian church-wall'"; the quotation marks suggest that James had used this phrasing in a letter to Woolson. She then proceeds to say,

> Your letters are better than you are. You are never in Italy, but always America; just going; or there; or just returned. And as to a "church-wall," there has never been but that one short time (three years ago—in Florence) when you seem [*sic*] disposed for that sort of thing. How many times have I seen you, in the long months that make up three long years? I do'nt [*sic*] complain, for there is no reason in the world why I should expect to see you; only, don't put in these decorative sentences about "Italian church-walls."[14]

Something must have occurred between Woolson and James as early as these first weeks of their relationship that allowed her to feel free to write this way. This directness is not the language of a woman who masks feelings with flippancy, but it is the language of a woman becoming aware that she has lost her rootedness in America. Even when she was still in the United States, she wrote to Paul Hayne, "I have no real home, however. I shall never return to Cleveland, save for a visit. The death of my dear Father six years ago broke up my home there, and for the town I care nothing" (Hubbell 731, 14 May 1876). Only two days before she wrote to James, she had been writing to John Hay about the prospect of not returning to the United States, of spending, instead, many more years traveling through Europe. But a week earlier on April 30, she was telling E. C. Stedman, "I am so American! I didn't know it until I came over here. I see, now, that, though I should stay in Italy ten years longer, I should never be anything but American; should never write any but the most 'American' prose." The tone is positive, but it shows Woolson well aware of how influenced she had been by the "Lake Country & Mackinac, the beautiful South, the farming-country of Ohio." "[T]hese are the scenes that I belong to," she writes, "that I can never separate myself from—though

I should live years in Venice and Rome."[15] It is, then, not surprising that the letter to Hay is the same one in which Woolson adds the postscript lamenting her homelessness. Whatever occurred between the day and evening of May 5, 1883—we know there was a visit from the Howellses; might there also have been a letter from James?—Woolson has turned her thoughts toward the more melancholy longing for home that she had articulated as early as 1876 to Hayne. Quite likely, the church-wall discussion Woolson refers to centered on settling permanently near James in the United States, in order to continue the artistic friendship they were developing.

James's willingness to champion Woolson's fiction, especially in his article "Miss Woolson" for *Partial Portraits* and his use of some of her ideas for his own work, indicate that Woolson was a valuable critic for him.[16] She saw in him a soul mate and, because she was so blunt, he could use her as his ideal reader. Over half of one of Woolson's long letters to him represents an extraordinary reading of *The Portrait of a Lady*. In another letter, thinking over all his portraits of women, she tells James that he needs now to create a woman we can really love, who knows how to love; "If you will only care for her yourself as you describe her, the thing is done."[17] Edel wants to read this as Woolson's plea that James love her; however, it is too accurate a description of James's work to dismiss it in this way. If these letters are a valid indication of Woolson's tone with James, the mysterious ties that drew them to each other involved their perception of art. About such perceptions, Woolson once wrote to Sam Mather that

> [i]t is dangerous to ask a writer of novels about novels! . . . The truth is,
> that, to a writer, the subject is so vast,—really his whole life's interest—
> that if he is to tell you what he thinks, he will almost never get
> through. . . . This is the reason, I think, why writers like to be with
> writers, painters with painters, & so on; the subject of their art is to
> them really inexhaustible, & they never tire of it. But others do!
> (WRHS, 27 Feb. 1887[?])

Rather than pretending with James in order to mask her love, Woolson found in him one of the few people with whom she did not have to pretend, an artist–soul mate whose works she could, without embarrassment, tell him "are my true country, my real home," a phrase she took from John Hay's description of Clarence King.[18]

Leon Edel is not wrong when he reads an atypical intensity in the relationship between Woolson and James, but his version of her death as a suicide brought on by unrequited love has little support. Worse, he has delayed attention to Woolson by scholars who have accepted his dismissal of her. Fortunately, Fred Kaplan's new biography of James takes a far kinder view of Woolson as a woman and a writer, even going as far as calling "Miss Grief" and "The Street of the Hyacinth" "brilliant" (312). On the other hand, Edel has been quite convincing in his reading of James's rather extraordinary reaction to Woolson's death, interpreting it a result of James's guilt over failing in his attentiveness. In letters referencing Woolson's death, James insists, in language he repeats from letter to letter, on her melancholy disposition, though one has to ask if he overstates that melancholy both because of his own sorrow and because he held a male view of what constitutes a woman's happiness. His sorrow over Woolson's death is unmistakable—he could not even bring himself to attend her funeral when he learned that her death may have been a suicide. What is less clear is why he was so attracted to Woolson, aside from his sense of her qualities as a writer and reader. I suspect he saw in her capacity for bluntness and independence a mature version of his cousin Minny Temple, whose early death enshrined her in his memory and his fiction and whose sister was the impetus for his meeting Woolson. Edel has suggested the connection, especially in James's subsequent portrait of Milly Theale in *The Wings of the Dove*.[19] Woolson also was a healthier version of his sister Alice, and her death, which he believed a suicide, so soon after Alice's may have shocked him into seeing her response to the difficulty of living for women as being sadly close to Alice's.

With their capacity for caustic humor and sharp-eyed observation, Woolson and Alice might have been destined to be as close as Alice and Katharine Loring. In her biography of Alice, Jean Strouse reports that Woolson was one of the only people that Alice could have near Henry and near Katharine Loring without retreating into illness brought on by jealousy, an odd fact if there were any signals of love, rather than the flirtation Alice laughed at a bit, in Woolson's relationship to James.[20] They did correspond, but Woolson's life circumstances place her closer to Katharine than to Alice. Alice was the baby of the James family and had learned from infancy that as a female in a family with five brothers, she could not hope to compete. Although Woolson came to see the privileged position of males when her brother Charlie was born, she developed during her more formative years in a predominantly female family. Alice adopted the James family pattern of gaining affection through illness and regularly sought the aid of various physicians. She even went to the clinic of Dr. Frank Page, who advocated rest cures for hysterics, discipline and control for neurasthenics, and exercise and electric shock for melancholics. Under the care of a different physician, Dr. William B. Neftel, Alice tried a combination of electrical shock and exercise, but her general pattern tended toward inactivity. Katharine Loring, on the other hand, turned Alice toward exercise and the outdoor life for a brief period of time in 1879 and 1880. Sharing Woolson's belief in education, she also involved Alice in the Society to Encourage Studies at Home, an organization that tried to formalize women's education. By the time Woolson met the two women, they had aligned themselves in a Boston marriage that most biographers have read in terms of its lesbian overtones. We have no way of knowing if Woolson saw homosexual tendencies either in Alice or in Henry (who may have felt attracted to Woolson's neighbor, the homosexual John Addington Symonds), but, homosexuality aside, she must have seen the unhealthy qualities in the Katharine-Alice relationship, especially because Henry himself sometimes remarked on it.

The connections between her life and Loring's might well have given Woolson pause. Where Woolson was tied to caring for her mother in the American South and even in Europe sometimes felt hampered by her widowed sister Clara Benedict, Loring moved between caring for her invalid sister Louisa and the needy Alice. Although we see Loring moving about in society and traveling to America to be with her sister, we see Alice's power always pulling her back. We do not see Loring traveling for pleasure or reenacting the outdoor excursions on which she had once taken Alice. Instead, we see the two leading sedentary lives, with Alice exercising her intellect in letters and, in the last two years of her life, in a diary that reveals little about her emotional life with Loring. In a more ideal society, Loring might have turned her caregiving skills into the medical profession. We know that she discussed medical education for women with Woolson, and R. W. B. Lewis recently has argued that in *The Bostonians,* James used Loring not for his portrait of Olive Chancellor but for his portrait of Dr. Prance.[21] At one point, even Alice sees the kind of restrictions she had imposed on her companion: "Her existence must be a mild purgatory. Some day the rights of women will be respected, I suppose."[22] A biographical study of Katharine Loring would undoubtedly reveal much about how nineteenth-century attitudes shaped women's choices. Without it, we can only wonder what tied Loring to Alice James and regret that the biographers of the various Jameses drop Loring after they reference her return to the United States with Alice's ashes. Leon Edel even spelled her first name incorrectly as *Katherine,* an error replicated by Fred Kaplan, Cheryl Torsney, and Joan Weimer, but corrected by Jean Strouse and R. W. B. Lewis. Loring lived forty more years after Alice's death, dying in 1964 at the age of ninety-four. During her years with Alice James, Katharine Loring found her home, but it came with a cost to autonomy that Woolson would have found difficult and with little reward from those whose lives she made so much easier by caring for Alice.

Although Edel may overstate Henry James's cooling ties with Loring after Alice's death, it is clear that James feared Loring would publish Alice's diary. When she had four copies printed and sent him one, he never thanked her; he dissuaded her from sending a copy to his brother Robertson, and he eventually destroyed his own copy.[23] This same kind of fear governed his treatment of Woolson's papers after her death. He helped her sister Clara and niece Clare sort out Woolson's papers in order that he might retrieve anything that pertained to himself. He even went as far as erasing Woolson's name from a copy of his essays that he had inscribed to her.[24] At one point he wrote to Francis Boott that Clara and Clare were both "very futile and foolish, poor things."[25] But where he loosened ties with Katharine Loring, he continued his relationship with the Benedicts long past the time he needed to for politeness sake. It appears that he even projected onto Clare some of the feelings he had had for Woolson. In *Five Generations,* Clare included several portions of warm letters from James to her and her mother, letters often insisting that they visit him. The most interesting aspect of this continued friendship is that James felt a kind of ESP with Clare. The James family was accepting of psychic phenomena: Henry Sr., William, and Henry Jr. had all had psychic experiences and William founded the American branch of the London-based Society for Psychical Research. Hannah Woolson also described psychic experiences, one involving a ghost she felt in the Woolson house in Cleveland in the room where her daughter Emma died (Benedict 1:220).

Woolson was well-aware of her society's interest in psychic phenomena, and in a letter joked to Katharine Loring that she must have sensed her interest in medical colleges for women when she sent her a pamphlet about these, a psychic connection, she says, worthy of sharing with the Psychical Society (BHSM, 19 Sept. 1890). She felt an unusual closeness to her niece Clare and wrote about psychic experiences in *Horace Chase,* though it is impossible to tell from available

material what her position on the rising interest in psychic phenomena was. Nor do we know if Woolson discussed psychic phenomena
with James, but we do know that Clara Benedict believed that James
and Clare "had repeated proofs—from the earliest times until their last
meeting in 1913—of the existence of a strong telepathic sympathy between them." A letter from James to Clare about wanting to write just
when she writes confirms that he felt this kinship to at least some degree
(Benedict 3:84–85). If Constance Woolson was his mature Minny Temple,
might he have been projecting this image yet again onto her young
niece? But this, like so much of the relationship between these two
families, must remain speculative. We will never know the full story
of the mysterious attachment between James and Woolson, but we
do know enough to see that it was not a one-sided attachment.

What is most important about Woolson's friendship with James is
that she found in it a sense of permanence and an avenue through
which to cultivate her literary home. The relationship also worked in
tension with her search for a geographical place to call home. In a
letter to E. C. Stedman, written from Florence in 1887, she delights in
the home she is creating:

> After seventeen years of wandering, I have at last a home of my
> own—(though but a temporary one). Such joy as I take in my own
> tables & chairs, tea-cups & cushions, I don't believe you can imagine,
> but Mrs. Stedman can. . . . But the view, & the air, & the scene, & the
> flowers, & the sense of ownership (for a year)—the tranquility of spirit,
> the far-awayness—these to me, just now, seem infinite riches.[26]

Woolson's sense of well-being in this letter reflects not just her delight
in the Villa, but also her delight in James, who at this time was sharing the Villa Brichieri with her. However, her sense of well-being was
short lived, and she continued to wrestle with issues of home.

Robert White has read Woolson's ambivalence about home in terms
of her ambivalence about Italy, which he sees as akin to Hawthorne's
treatment of this country in *The Marble Faun*. But White's readings of
the Italian stories often unfairly equate Woolson with characters she
is creating as ironic. A more profitable avenue for reading Woolson's
attitude toward her Italian home would be to explore how she uses
her emerging comfort with social realism to develop ideas for stories
that she discussed with Henry James. Her story "A Transplanted Boy,"
probably the last she wrote, serves as an excellent example because it

is almost certain that she discussed it with James and because, at approximately the same time, he treated the germ idea in his own story "The Pupil."[27] In "A Transplanted Boy," Woolson transformed her need for a sense of place into a vision of the impact of rootlessness on Americans in Europe. She had watched James enjoy the freedom of travel to America to renew his roots and had seen herself shuttle around Europe, making do in a variety of temporary residences. Read with "The Pupil," "A Transplanted Boy" reveals some striking implications for how gender affected the way Americans with limited means found, or failed to find, homes abroad, for how this impacted on children, and for how children serve as a metaphor for displaced adult women.

Woolson, we know, visited with James in September of 1890, just after he had heard a story that generated "The Pupil." The story came to him from Dr. William Wilberforce Baldwin, physician to many Americans in Europe, including Alice James, whose cancer he diagnosed, and Woolson, at whose death he officiated.[28] Baldwin had told him of an itinerant American family who had been jumping hotel bills and who had a male child with a weak heart who judged them for their life-style. The story struck a chord in James, who had spent his teenage years traveling with his family in Europe, living in temporary residences and, except for a brief stay in a Swiss school, being educated informally and with governesses and tutors. While the James family were certainly not like the itinerant family of Baldwin's story, Henry's childhood in Europe was marked by the kind of transience Woolson was so troubled by in her own life. That James and Woolson discussed Baldwin's story or "The Pupil" is likely since Woolson's "A Transplanted Boy" is clearly derivative. The plight of a hotel child whose family had not quite enough money must have struck an equally powerful note in Woolson, for besides moving around Europe herself, she had watched her niece do the same until she reached her majority and inherited enough money so that she and her mother Clara Benedict could live without worry.

James's version of the itinerant American family in Europe includes two parents, four children, and a tutor. In straightened circumstances, they can carve a recognizable place for themselves in a region where they are outsiders: men, like Mr. Moreen and the oldest son Ulick, can carry off a show of well-being; married women, like Mrs. Moreen, can help complete the facade; and girls, like the daughters Paula and Amy, can be shaped into bargaining chips for marriage. Young, male, and sickly, only the youngest child, Morgan, has been out of place in the family unit and so must die in order that the family can rebound again. Even Morgan's tutor, Pemberton, manages abroad because of the advantages of his gender. Educated at Yale and Oxford, he has opportunities that no American woman could have had, but, even with his degrees he chooses service as a tutor. His error is to attach himself to a family to whom he considers himself superior and who fails to pay him. His great pretense has been that he is attached to Morgan, when it is the entire family that enables Pemberton to live off others, albeit without pay, and that gives him a way of surviving in a foreign land.

Unlike the traditional intact family of "The Pupil," the family in "A Transplanted Boy" consists only of a widowed mother, Violet Roscoe, and her thirteen-year-old son, Maso. When Violet becomes ill, Maso insists that she convalesce in Aix-les-Bains. Without adequate funds sent from a relative in America, who we infer is her brother-in-law, Violet cannot take Maso with her and, instead, hires a tutor to look after him. The tutor, however, is called away and Maso spends nearly five months deceiving his mother in his letters so that she will not know that he has been abandoned in the heat of the Italian summer. He manages poorly, unable to find work because his mother has taught him no skills and unable to find help from the American consul because his status as an American is suspect. In the end, Maso, bereft over the death of his dog, Mr. Tiber, and near death himself, is discovered by an acquaintance of his mother, the spinster Roberta Spring. Violet, who has extended her stay away from Maso in order to spend three weeks in Paris with a man she has met, is duly sent for. Maso does not die, but the implications are that he may. The story ends with a scene shift to Violet's relatives in America, who note that she has "made ducks and drakes of almost all her money" and that, though she is returning to America with Maso, it is "too late" for the boy (*Major* 258). Although the mother has clearly loved her son, she, like the Moreens and Pemberton in "The Pupil," has failed to provide him the well-being that connection to a place or to a sense of heritage offers. Like the Moreens, she has kept her son a transient and ignored his needs in the pursuit of her own and, like Pemberton from Morgan, she has stayed away too long.

Throughout "A Transplanted Boy," Woolson emphasizes issues of home and of the gender implications involved when one seeks a home. Maso's tutor, Benjamin Franklin Waterhouse, for example, is a minor character, but symbolic of Woolson's theme. He leaves Maso because he must go to England to see his sister, who has come from America to see him but has ruined her health in the journey and cannot make it as far as Italy. In other words, Waterhouse has had to curtail his temporary job, but his sister may well have given her life in order to see him. Furthermore, Waterhouse also has a strong sense of his American identity, possessing (like James) the name of a famous American, looking like Emerson, and even writing a life of Christopher Columbus. His means may be limited, but he has an identity as an American that his employer, Violet Roscoe, does not enjoy. She has lost whatever her maiden name was and has even given up trying to explain her married name, Mrs. Thomas Ross Coe, to her Italian acquaintances. Instead of connecting her to her heritage as an American, her appearance connects to her heritage as a female; that is, she uses it as something she must manipulate to survive. Where Waterhouse can write about an Italian who discovered a new world, Violet lives in an Old World, Italy, where her position as a woman is one of exile and dependence.

More than she uses Waterhouse, Woolson uses an Italian widow, Madame Corti, and an American spinster, Roberta Spring,[29] as foils to reveal how few options for finding a sense of place are open to Violet Roscoe, a single mother with no money under her own control. Unlike Violet, Madame Corti has no difficulty managing in Italy, and Woolson, much more than James, describes the physical qualities of the home, both house and landscape, she has found there. Though she has some English blood and has inherited the Casa Corti, a Pisan palace, from her English heritage, she is at home as an Italian. The palace has been in the same family for four generations and can house seventy guests. Madame Corti is not Old World, wealthy aristocracy, but she has the means and the status to carry off the show of being such. She has "guests" rather than "patron[s] or boarder[s]" and is a "proprietress" rather than a "landlady." She dresses elegantly, complete with "amber beads wound three times round the throat" (*Major* 219), for elegant dinners with her mostly English "guests," who are expected to treat her as an Italian aristocrat. She carries this off in the way the Moreens carry off their status, but without the precariousness of their position.

Madame Corti is a woman who has established herself in the Old World because she has property and family that connect her to it. Roberta Spring, on the other hand, would like to forge a new world for women but is unable to do so. She discards her femininity, refusing the feminine comforts Violet offers her: coffee, a chair, a footstool, calling herself "[n]ot superior; only bilious and long-legged" (*Major* 226). Although she manages to survive on her limited means—where she gets her money we never know—she has not found any place for herself. She is a woman much like Woolson herself, who prefers things to which her sex has given her limited access. She likes math and astronomy, has studied evolution and read Herbert Spencer, and, in an allusion to the Jameses, belongs to the Society for Psychical Research. She is a woman of reason, an "impartial investigator" (*Major* 230), more than a woman of feeling and, therefore, tries both art and music as a kind of scientific experiment, but does not find them satisfying. She is also a woman who does not find Pisa "an attractive place for a permanent residence" (*Major* 226), one who may well find her only refuge in becoming a nun despite her Protestant background. Above all, Roberta Spring holds true to her convictions and would not, like some of the American tourists in Italy, pretend to love Byron and Shelley but, if it were possible, refrain from visiting them or Mary Shelley because of these writers' unconventional life-styles. But this conviction brings her no fame, no money, no sense of personal satisfaction—no home. Roberta remains a woman whose personal tastes are defined as male and are, therefore, at odds with a society that allows her no sense of rootedness.

At one point in "A Transplanted Boy," Violet finishes reading a novel and declares to Miss Spring, "Women who write don't know much about love affairs. . . . And those of us who have love affairs don't write" (*Major* 232). Where Miss Spring is the woman who chooses to live without love affairs, Violet chooses the opposite. Although the extent of those affairs is never clear, and Woolson does not accuse Violet of any kind of sexual promiscuity, there still is little in her for us to admire. She accepts her femaleness, but the implication is that to do so is to accept a role of childlike dependence. For example, she loves Maso, but because she is like a child herself she allows him to behave in such a childlike way that he does not learn the skills that would enable him to survive. Much like Pemberton and Morgan in their scheme to live together, Violet and Maso "had been like two children together" (*Major* 239). Violet is sent money and will economize on her lodgings, which others can attribute to "American eccentricity" (*Major* 236), but she will also spend it on expensive clothes for herself, which enable her to create the facade that draws men to her. As the bank clerks recognize, "she goes it on her face" (*Major* 241), but without wisdom beneath that face she loses what little money she has when her bank fails. To some degree, Violet's relatives in America are right to withhold money from her, but had she been allowed to manage her own funds or not been a woman socialized to dislike arithmetic, she might have learned to behave more responsibly.

Woolson was keenly aware of the lack of dignity of having access only to money that is under someone else's control because she had to depend on Sam Mather's financial management and because her sister Clara had been unable to manage her daughter's estate, that estate being withheld until the child came of age. In her novella *For the Major*, Woolson specifies her awareness of the humiliation of such dependency. Here, a minister praises the major for giving his brother, who lost money in a bank failure, a lump sum, one-half of all his own money: "He didn't dole out help, keeping a close watch over its use, or grudgingly giving so much a year, with the constant accompaniment of good advice; he simply deeded a full half of all he had to his brother, and never spoke of it again" (*Major* 270).

Because of the irresponsibility of the adults around them, James's Morgan and Woolson's Maso are doomed to being victims who will never find a place to which they belong. Neither can make it as a potential man, Morgan because of his health and Maso because of his awkward, unattractive looks and his total lack of skills. Where Morgan is a victim of his family and Pemberton and their sycophantic lifestyles, Maso's victimization is deeper. Like Morgan, he is a victim of his mother's failure to love sufficiently, but he is also a victim of his own lack of roots and of a society that demands roots and fails to aid women and children or train them to better aid themselves. Numerous details in the story emphasize Maso's rootlessness: allowed to be neither Thomas nor Tommaso, he lacks a name that signals a nationality, so much so that he does not at first even know that his mother's name is not Roscoe but Mrs. Thomas Ross Coe; he knows little about his country or his heritage and does not recognize the oddity of visiting the American Consulate on the Fourth of July. He has not even the tenuous national connections of Benjamin Franklin Waterhouse or Madame Corti. He is an invisible child, one of the thousands of urchins who roam the streets, victims of a society that does not provide help or dignity for women or children. Yet for all his innocence and ineptitude, Maso is the one who has shown the greatest responsibility in the way he provides food and shelter and, finally, a burial for his dog, Mr. Tiber. Woolson, who loved dogs and had many throughout her life, often provides what few emotional ties a character has through a dog. She modeled Mr. Tiber on her own recently acquired dog Othello, or Tello, whom she spoke of in letters in mock babytalk and whom she had sleep in a basket like the one Maso has for Mr. Tiber.[30] Mr. Tiber dies having been educated (he's taught to do tricks), having been given a name, and having been loved adequately.

On an emotional level, Woolson's story is more powerful than James's. In it we see the dignity and beauty of the child, perhaps because in the child Woolson focused so much of her own sense of rootlessness and loneliness at the end of her life. At the end of her life, Woolson is like Miss Spring, who has faced Europe alone and found it lacking. In "A Transplanted Boy," Woolson writes out of a culture she sees sharply and fully. She sees the plight of women like Violet who are forced to choose between their own health and their children, of women like Roberta Spring who choose the unconventional and find no place for themselves except in a nunnery in a religion they do not believe in, and of children like Maso who cannot go it on "show." All of these people risk ending up not in third-rate hotels but in squalid single rooms in the damp, dirty alleys of streets ironically named the Street of the Lily. Maso finds his "bachelor quarters" (*Major* 243) in just such a room, content with his dog as companion, his nightly escape from the heat on a rooftop under the stars, and his anticipation of the return of a mother whose life he will have saved by his sacrifice. James's Morgan is a victim because the people around him have made bad choices, but Maso is a victim because the people around him have choices limited because of their sex.

In all probability, Woolson took the germ for "A Transplanted Boy" from Henry James, but where James emphasizes the psychology of Pemberton and how he deceives himself and betrays Morgan, Woolson works in a larger social arena. Most of Woolson's European stories represent this leap into social realism. Like the American stories, these continue to look closely at landscape, though the landscape is now based more in architecture than in nature. Woolson also continues to explore issues of ethnicity, but now, like James, in terms of nationality rather than race. Through her friendships within the Jamesian circle and through her discussions with James, she has found an arena to develop her skills of observation and exercise her sarcastic wit. The European stories are artistically complex, psychologically and sociologically perceptive, and emotionally moving. Because Woolson found herself farther and farther removed from her geographical home and because she came to see how much that removal had to do with her gender, she deepened her emotional and intellectual range in her fiction. She died longing for a home, feeling herself a transplanted and, as my subsequent chapters will show, a marginalized woman. Ironically, out of this tension, Woolson found her literary home.

6

The Marriage Question
❧

Using the different locations of her fiction, Woolson asks questions about the impact of region and ethnicity on the search for a home. Even more, she embeds all her work with questions about the impact of gender on this search. Woolson knew that to be born female in the nineteenth century meant that the boundaries of one's home would be limited—by access to property and education, by expectations within the family and the community, by socially defined cultural and artistic norms. Because her artistic temperament found its strongest voice in observation of the present rather than in an imagined past and because that present included both the boundaries placed on women and an increasingly vocal objection to those boundaries, Woolson could use her position as observer to its greatest advantage. When she wrote about isolated western communities, about the South, or about Europe, when she wrote about African Americans or American Indians or Spanish Americans, she wrote primarily from external observation. Even her emphasis on the geographical features of the landscape were, by definition, external observations. But when she wrote about women's issues, she could combine the external with the private struggles of one who knew what it felt like to be born female and to encounter the boundaries that limited the female's search for home.

Of all the gender questions Woolson raises, the one that most closely connects her to her sociocultural milieu is the marriage question. Woolson knew that most of her female contemporaries looked for the physical sanctuary of home in marriage. But when she turned her powers of observation onto the forces that pressured women to marry, she had to endure the criticism of the male literary establishment that defined these forces as a less than profound subject for fiction.

When, for example, Henry James wrote his generally favorable review of Woolson in the February 12, 1887, edition of *Harper's Weekly,* he criticized her for limiting women's choices by too often having them choose marriage: Miss Woolson, he says, "likes the unmarried . . . but she likes marriages even better." For him, Woolson was not revolutionary in her portraits of women: rather than adding further complications to women's lives, she was content to explore the complications that already existed for women "fenced in by the old disabilities and prejudices."[1]

James's criticism represents the dilemma of the female novelist. For a woman, to center on the marriage question is to write in ways that are not revolutionary; for a male, to center on the marriage question is to explore how society constructs the social and psychological reality of women's lives. What James defines as Woolson's weakness, others define as James's strength, for he, too, centered most of his novels about women around issues of marriage. In *Henry James and the "Woman Business,"* Alfred Habegger has ably demonstrated that many of James's plots were appropriated from nineteenth-century women's fiction and that these enabled him to develop his fantasy of orphaned girl and father-lover. Like James, whose father was deeply involved in the mid-nineteenth-century debate about the nature of marriage, Woolson came of age in an era that asked questions about what constituted the family home by examining the roles of husband and wife in marriage, by arguing about the legitimacy of divorce, and by experimenting with free-love communities. And like James, Woolson found her literary home by exploring the context of these debates.

Habegger's study of James provides ample historical background about the nineteenth-century debates on marriage that Henry James Sr. was so involved with and that serve as backdrop to the social realism of Henry Jr. and of Woolson. This was an age that drew on the doctrines of Charles Fourier, a figure lurking behind Hawthorne's Blithedale community. Fourier, a French socialist, believed that a variety of models were needed for sexual relationships among men and women, including models that allowed free love. Drawing on Fourier-like doctrines, a Vermonter named John Noyes founded, in 1848, the Oneida Community in New York. Noyes preached that monogamy was selfish and that men and women should be able to share sexual partners. The Oneida Community practiced free love until the confusion about children's paternity became too uncomfortable. Although the general public accommodated male infidelities, it feared sexual freedom within communal experiments like Oneida because these threatened to undermine established definitions of home and family by offering sexual freedom to both men and women. So, too, did the practice of birth control. Despite the support of birth control in infamous journals like *Woodhull and Claflin's Weekly,* in the larger society, authorities were prosecuting physicians and midwives not just for performing abortions but also for dispensing information about birth control—their fear being that immigrant populations were changing the ethnic profile of the family by outproducing white Anglo-Saxon Protestants.[2] At the same time that free-love experiments were flourishing and birth control was being used, Mormon communities with their advocacy of male polygamy were being established as another kind of threat to the traditional-marriage home. Woolson never portrayed free-love communities, but she did look at the way the Mormon and Zoarite communities impacted on women's lives and at the implications of a double-standard of sexual behavior. And although she never directly addressed the issue of birth control, she did often comment on attitudes that scorned large broods of immigrant or French or Hispanic children.

When Woolson began writing, she had decided that she would never marry and that she would not, therefore, have to make decisions about divorce should her husband prove unfaithful or her marriage unsatisfactory. Nor would she be pressured to increase the Anglo-American population. When she made her decision to pursue her home through writing rather than through marriage, Woolson freed herself to write about how marriage decisions impact on women's ways of finding home. She saw how in the West, the culture encouraged that people should be happy, free, able to pursue a new life, thus able freely to seek divorce.[3] Yet the more the West became socialized, the more it adopted eastern standards of marriage. Woolson depicts this most explicitly in a story titled "Lily and Diamond," which sounds as if it will be a Wild West adventure, but which instead shows the tension between those who want freedom in the West, saying that "[s]urely in a country-town . . . , we can do as we please," and those who want fashionable society, saying about the same resort, "[s]urely in a city of one hundred thousand inhabitants, or in a summer hotel containing more than a hundred people, we owe it to ourselves to preserve all social requirements intact" (477). Society wins the day in the story as its female protagonists engage in rivalry for a man. The diamond figure, an older woman who has been widowed, loses the man and marries as society believes she wants while the young lily figure wins him. He minimalizes her act of bravery in following him in a storm when he says, "And so she came out alone in her cockleshell skiff, with those soft little fists, to rescue a great, strong man like me, in a steady old sail-boat like the scud, did she?" (482). The West may offer the dream of freedom for women, but Woolson knew that its marriage norms too often imitated the East and imposed similar kinds of strictures on women that made the married home the expected one.

Just which pieces about marriage, divorce, and sexuality Woolson read is unknown, but given the currency of these debates in the context of debates about women's suffrage, including those conducted at women's conventions in Cleveland while Woolson was still living there, she would have been well-aware of the issues. It is likely that she also learned that Henry James Sr. had joined the debate about divorce. James argued that monogamy was really promiscuous when, as so often was the case, it forced sex with no love; sexuality without marriage, on the other hand, could be endorsed when love was involved. James, according to Habegger, came under public scrutiny when he was referenced in an 1852 book by Marx Edgeworth Lazurus called *Love vs. Marriage,* which argued for variety in sexual partners. James, who had had Lazurus to dinner, did not, in fact, endorse such practices, advocating instead a spiritualized sexuality. He countered Lazurus publicly in a *New York Tribune* article called "The Marriage Question," in which he defended monogamy. Men, he said, will always be disappointed in marriage because women cannot fulfill the idealized promise they held before marriage. Marriage binds men to less than what they dreamed of; at the same time, however, it is a disciplining institution through which men can ultimately transcend physical and selfish desire.[4]

When discussing Woolson's attitude toward marriage and divorce, it is important to note that even though figures say that nine of ten women in the nineteenth century married, both the westward movement and the Civil War made it more difficult in eastern and southern sections of the United States for them to do so: in 1850, for example, there were twenty thousand more women than men in the United States, by 1870 that number had risen to fifty thousand, and by 1880 to sixty-six thousand (Chambers-Schiller 334). When James criticized Woolson's attention to issues of marriage, he missed the crucial fact that much of Woolson's fiction involves an explanation of the expectations that women marry and the conscious decisions of women who subvert these expectations by choosing what Joan Weimer calls "homelessness and habitual solitude" over human relationships, particularly those involving marriage.[5] One of Woolson's first stories, "Cicely's Christmas," is almost allegorical in its recognition of the pressures on women to marry, presenting the plight of a single woman in the city who resists a suitor who prefers his inventions to her, only to find herself face to face on Christmas with the lot of an unmarried woman: she finds that women's restaurants are closed on Christmas Day and is forced to lunch in an overpriced restaurant, where she is stared at for being alone; she leaves the theater because the men on either side of her accost her; she has her purse stolen; she has supper alone in her room; and, as a final insult, she discovers a man who has been flirting with her flirting with someone else. When the inventor returns, it is no wonder that she accepts an unsuitable marriage over an equally unsuitable spinsterhood.

Woolson knew that it was difficult for women to find a home outside of marriage, and she often couches her anger at the expectation for marriage in satire. In one of her most satirical pieces, "Matches Morganatic," a suitor declares his love in overblown lines like "Idol of my life, give me a smile—no, not a smile, for I could not see it in the darkness [the man is so nearsighted he would not be able to see it in the light]; but give me your hand, your lily hand, that I may know I am not despised" (524). Another couple banter about a woman's obedience in marriage only to have the woman accept marriage when a Confederate commander kidnaps her and her suitor and forces them to marry as a condition for their release. Woolson uses this as a way to force marriage onto a couple who love each other and to satisfy audiences who love the marriage plot. But the satirical level is so high that she subverts that plot by having marriage becomes a metaphor for battle, surrender, and optionlessness. Given society's expectations, it is no wonder that so many of Woolson's characters fail to live up to their pledge that they "will never marry for a home" (9).

Woolson's treatment of marriage centers less on demographics than on how the search for marital relationships often results in betrayal, not only of men toward women, but also of women toward each other in the competition for suitable partners. Still, this does not imply that Woolson disliked marriage. In a letter to her nephew Sam Mather near the end of her life, she called it "the best thing in life; it's the only thing worth living for; this is the sincere belief—& the result of observations of one who has never had it."[6] One could easily read this as evidence that Woolson yearned for marriage, perhaps to Henry James; however, the attention she paid to observing society's attitudes about marriage and to observing individual marriages in order to write about women's decisions to marry more likely point simply to an increased awareness about the difficulties women who do not marry face. John Kern wonders if the sense of loss Woolson reveals in so many of her stories indicates a shattered love affair, but there is no evidence for this (34). Woolson made a conscious decision early in her life not to marry. She never expressed regret over her broken relationship with Col. Zeph Spaulding when she was in her early twenties and, later in her life, referenced him as a childhood friend, saying that the "glamor that the war threw over the young officers who left their homes to fight . . . made me fancy that I cared for him."[7] A letter to her friend Arabella Carter Washburn seems to be quashing a rumor about suitors, though it is unclear if they are suitors to herself or to her sister Clara, who, Woolson tells Washburn, she believes will never remarry, being contented with her life as it is (Kern 51).

Joan Weimer thinks that Woolson associated marriage and childbirth with death because of her family tragedies, but given the fact that she was nearly thirty before her father died and that her mother lived another ten years, this may be overstated. (*MG* x). Two stories can serve as better explanations on Woolson's decision not to marry. One, "Hepzibah's Story,"[8] probably written between 1871 and 1873 but never published, portrays a woman who nursed her family, especially her father, during the Civil War even though her caretaking duties prevented her from following Theodore, the man she loves, west. Finally released by the deaths of her father and mother, she joins Theodore, only to discover that he loves someone else when she overhears a conversation between the two lovers. Theodore is willing to fulfill his promise and marry Hepzibah, but Woolson avoids this through the device of a fire that causes a denouement that prevents the marriage. The other story, "Ballast Island,"[9] published in 1873 when Woolson was still tied to the caretaking of her mother, portrays two lovers who discover a solitary woman, Miss Jonah, on Ballast Island. Like Hepzibah, Miss Jonah had overheard her fiancé making love to another woman, in this case her sister. Miss Jonah releases her fiancé by feigning her drowning and then retreating to the island. Where Hepzibah's act is tied to self-sacrifice, Miss Jonah's is tied to independence, and the message it gives to the lovers is that they should seek in their marriage the kind of freedom she has found in solitude. Where Hepzibah is like Hawthorne's spinster who nurses Clifford and loses herself in the process, Miss Jonah, like her biblical namesake, defies authority and, in a subversion of the story, thrives.

Reading "Hepzibah's Story" psycho-biographically, we can argue that Woolson's ties to her own mother and father, her sense of obligation to care for them, plus her own tendencies toward melancholy and solitude made her decide not just to refuse marriage to her soldier friend (or readily accept his rejection of her), but also to build a wall around herself that would discourage other marriage proposals, and, after the death of both parents, allow her to build an independent life. If we knew Woolson's emotional attitudes toward potential marriage partners, we would know more about a particular woman in the nineteenth century. What we have, instead, is the evidence of her fiction that generalizes about the impact of marriage on women's lives in the nineteenth century. Three more of her short stories are of particular interest here, one for its exposure of sentimental views of marriage, one for its exploration of marriage in an experimental community, and one for its exploration of how marriage is often the result of sexual blackmail. Each helps us to understand Woolson's response to the tremendous pressures on women to find marital homes, whether or not these homes are likely to provide happiness.

In "Up in the Blue Ridge," collected in *Rodman the Keeper*, Woolson manipulates the melodramatic form so that this story of a glamorous lover saving a damsel in distress is filled with humor and irony that subverts the sentimental marriage plot. The damsel in question is Honor Dooris, a woman who has found her potential marriage partner in the hills where she used to vacation before the Civil War. The melodrama involves her protecting the man she loves from her bootlegging cousin, who is about to murder him. Honor ends up marrying this man, preferring him to the northerner Stephen Wainwright, who also is beginning to love her. Despite the intrigue, Woolson undercuts any notion of a great passionate love both in Honor's relationship and in Stephen's relationship to the widow Adelaide Kellinger, who has caused the melodrama in order to prevent Stephen from declaring his love for Honor. Honor's choice of husband

> ended well; that is, he married her after a while, took her away to the North, and was, on the whole, a good husband. But from first to last, he ruled her, and she never became quite the beauty that Mrs. Kellinger intended her to be, because she was too devoted to him, too absorbed in him, too dependent upon his fancies, to collect that repose and security of heart which are necessary to complete the beauty of even the most beautiful women. (*Rodman* 338)

With Honor married to her southern lover, Woolson implies that Stephen Wainwright will eventually, with no fanfare, marry Adelaide Kellinger. "This woman loved him," says the narrator; "the other [Honor] would never have given him more than gratitude" for saving her cousin from being murdered. "What would you have?" (*Rodman* 339). Neither, one would like to say, for although the settled, unpassionate premarital relationship between Stephen and Mrs. Kellinger seems natural, Woolson undercuts it, suggesting that social expectations hinder a natural relationship between an eligible woman and an eligible man. The omniscient narrator describes the "natural" relationship between Stephen and Mrs. Kellinger:

> If he asked a question, she answered with the plainest truth she could imagine; if he asked an opinion, she gave the one she would have given to her most intimate woman-friend (if she had had one); if she was tired, she did not conceal it; if she was out of temper, she said disagreeable, sharp-edged things. She was, therefore, perfectly natural? On the contrary, she was extremely unnatural. A charming woman does not go around at the present day in a state of nature mentally any more than physically; politeness has become a necessary clothing to her. Adelaide Kellinger never spoke to her cousin [Wainwright] without a little preceding pause, during which she thought over what she was going to say; and, as Stephen was slow to speak also, their conversations were ineffective, judged from a dramatic point of view. (*Rodman* 279)

From a dramatic point of view, Woolson finally says in "Up in the Blue Ridge," sentiment and melodrama are fine; in real life, steady, mature, rather dull marital relationships are the norm—perhaps to be preferred, but only as long as society expects men and women to marry.

Woolson was never so liberal a thinker—or so sure of her status with her publishers—that she examined open marriage systems or free love in her fiction, though there are undertones in many of her novels about the impulse toward sexual freedom. She did, however, look rather closely at the Zoarite system that disconnected marriage and human relations in general from sexuality. The German Zoarites settled in Ohio around 1819 and, soon realizing that it was not practical to ban sexual intercourse entirely, advocated it only for purposes of procreation. Woolson often visited this community with her father and, though she admired its peaceful ways, she realized, especially after the Civil War, that the community's young people would become rest-

less under its austerity. In a letter to Arabella Washburn, she is sad-
dened that the Zoarites objected to what she thought a respectful sketch
of them called "The Happy Valley" (Benedict 2:273).

The Zoarites would have found Woolson's story "Wilhelmina," in
the *Castle Nowhere* collection, even more disturbing because of its
exposure of the Zoarite's privacy and its focus on the restlessness of
their youth under a rigid marriage system. The story has Wilhelmina,
who has grown up in the community but is not German, wait for her
lover Gustav to return from the Civil War, where he has gone because
the Zoarites, though pacifist, were pressured into sending men. Gustav
gladly fought, but he returns now unwilling to accept Zoarite ways.
He rejects Wilhelmina and the community for a more worldly woman,
and Wilhelmina is bullied into marrying a widower with five children,
shortly after which she dies. The narrator has misread Wilhelmina by
believing her when she says she is "contented" in this charming but dull
life, for there is no evidence that she stops loving Gustav. The narrator
believes, "So were they taught from childhood, and I was about to say—
they knew no better; but, after all, is there anything better to know?" (*CN*
277). This is the sentimental view, and if the narrator thinks it so charming, we must ask why she wants to take Gustav and Wilhelmina out of
the community and educate them. She faults Gustav for his attraction
to a woman whose photograph she sees as frivolous. But the photograph also forces her to recognize that women do foolish things for
love and that she herself has done so: "If it had not been for this red-
cheeked Miss Martin in her gilt beads! 'Why is it that men will be such
fools?' I thought. Up sprung a memory of the curls and ponderous jet
necklace I sported at a certain period of my existence, when John—I
was silenced . . ." (*CN* 298). There is no evidence that the narrator has
made an ideal match herself, traveling without her husband as she does
when she visits the Zoarite community for its charm. What Woolson yearns
for is for Wilhelmina to be content within the Zoarite community, for her
to be able to be who she is and still to marry for love, and not to be
scorned for being uncultivated, as she is by both the narrator and Gustav.
At the same time, she sees how impossible this is. As Carolyn VanBergen
has demonstrated in an essay on "Wilhelmina" and "Solomon," another
Zoarite story, Woolson undercuts the nostalgia for the unity of the
Zoarite community by showing how it suffocates diversity and creates
disharmony rather than love.[10] These tightly controlled communal
homes—like Catholic nunneries—attracted Woolson, but she knew that,
with or without marriage, such a home would become her prison.

Even Woolson's early short fiction frequently portrays marriages that are unfulfilling whether because, like Honor's in "Up in the Blue Ridge," they do not reach their early promise or because, like Wilhelmina's, they are forced by social expectations that endorse marriages of convenience. Woolson reveals another very troubling aspect of marriage when she recognizes that it often occurs under circumstances of sexual or emotional blackmail. The pattern occurs in much of her fiction—for example, in "Jeannette" and "Peter the Parson" in *Castle Nowhere* and in the novels *Anne, East Angels,* and *Horace Chase.* The story "Misery Landing" from *Castle Nowhere* best illustrates the issue. It involves a narrator who finds letters of John Jay, an aristocrat, who escapes his unrequited love for a society woman by building an isolated hut on an island cliff in Lake Superior. A young man, George Bram, saves himself from a storm by climbing a ladder to John's house. Subsequently, John tries to educate him for a role in the larger world, but George has fallen in love with a local girl, Martha, and does not want to leave Misery Landing. Martha does not love George, however, but both John and George practice emotional blackmail so that she accepts George anyway. George's blackmail is perhaps subconscious, occurring when he is about to die because Martha has not accepted him. Woolson recognized that the loss of a loved one could hasten one's death—her sister Emma, who married someone her parents at first objected to because he was ill, died soon after her husband.[11] But there is no evidence that Emma married, like Martha, to save her husband from death because of unrequited love, and such a motive is one that Woolson would have disapproved of.

Woolson's life and fiction reflect a belief that one could and should face up to disappointment and live. Thus she makes John's sexual blackmail blatant and uses it to represent the worst aspects of male-female relationships. John takes it upon himself to find Martha and bring her back to George so that George will live. Then he leaves the two of them at Misery Landing and ends up himself marrying the woman who had refused him, the implication being that she accepts him for his money even though he originally wanted her love as well. Of course, this does not represent a triumph for him, but he has gotten vicarious revenge by forcing marriage onto Martha. John's view of women is decidedly sexist. They are frivolous and false, "an inferior race" (*CN* 223) who are "all alike" (*CN* 228) and who "cannot learn, or rather unlearn" (*CN* 223). Men have two choices: they can be tyrannized by women as George is because of his love, or they can enslave them, as John finally decides on doing. That John is an artist furthers the barb, for he has chosen to shape the lives of two people he does not respect. He is no Thoreauvian nature lover who prefers commoners to aristocrats. He loves Bret Harte but marvels that only "cultivated people . . . are taken with Bret" (*CN* 219), suggesting that Harte's readers condescend to these primitive character types. George is John's bit of local color, worthy to be shaped while Martha, without beauty, is not. John is one of Woolson's earliest versions of male attitudes toward unattractive women: "A homely woman is a complete mistake, always: a woman should always be beautiful, as a man should always be strong" (*CN* 215). Martha, with little choice, becomes Martha of the Bible, serving rather than loving.

Because Woolson saw so clearly and so satirically how real-life and fictional marriage plots manipulated women into false homes, her short fiction presents a decidedly bleak view of marriage. It is not, however, marriage that Woolson opposes, but only the pressure to marry. In some of her short fiction, there are glimmers of success in marriage. The settled marriage of Stephen Wainwright and the widow Mrs. Kellinger is dull, but stable, and there is hope within limited lifestyles for the unions in stories like "Castle Nowhere," "Jeannette," "Old Gardiston," and "Miss Elisabetha," to name just a few. Much of Woolson's uncollected short fiction ends in marriages that promise to be successful, but this fiction, written early in her career, tends to be formulaic and the marriages either unimpassioned ("Black Point") or between childlike women and older men ("Miss Vedder"). It is interesting, as well, that childlike women, whether they marry or not, are often less naïve about sexuality than their deeper counterparts, having, as the omniscient narrator says of a flirtatious girl in "A Flower of the Snow," "[t]en times more knowledge of the world, twenty times more coquetry . . . than . . . the educated woman of twenty-six," who eventually marries the story's hero (79).

Woolson's European short fiction continues to explore the marriage-plot in ways that show resistance to the idea of a happy ending, but in the novels written during the same period, the view of marriage is more complex and more positive. In them, Woolson, like most of her contemporary women writers, endorses women's role of holding together homes, particularly marital homes.[12] While in the short fiction, as Joan Weimer has shown,[13] Woolson's most interesting women, all artists, choose not to marry, in the novels, they almost always choose a home equated with marriage. Woolson is not abandoning the broader sphere of the female that Weimer sees her developing in her short fiction; rather, she is using the longer novel form to reconcile independence with the idea of a marital home.

Because she was also quite aware that "nine-tenths of the great mass of readers care *only* for the love story" (Benedict 2:103) and because she had to please these readers to maintain her financial independence, Woolson needed to reconcile her sense of the rewards of independence despite loneliness with the tastes of the audience of her day. As she wrestled in each of her novels with the expectations of her audience and her own conflicting needs for home and independence, Woolson broke out of what James called the "old disabilities and prejudices" by stepping back to observe the implications of the choice for a home that is equated with marriage. Because she continued to long for a home outside of marriage, she also asked, particularly in her last novel, how a woman can possess a home that is not equated with marriage.

Like so much of the fiction written by males canonized in American literature, each of Woolson's longer pieces of fiction juxtaposes naïve or shallow girl-women with women more aware of the ambiguities of life. The girl figures always choose marriage, and through them, Woolson reveals her ability to understand why women did not often exercise other kinds of choices. Woolson's niece Clare Benedict describes her aunt's capacity for understanding all types of women as an "intense sympathy with and understanding of all . . . moral and intellectual aspirations, that [enabled her] to draw out of people the best that was in them, while giving them in return the most inspiring and comforting comprehension" (Benedict 2:xiv). Such a capacity for comprehension is even more apparent in Woolson's portraits of complex women. While the girl-women in the novels are interesting but similar, each of the complex heroines provides a different focus on the issues involved when a woman desires or is expected by her society to desire a marital home. Woolson's character pairings show her observing closely how women compromise as they seek homes and show her struggling with issues involving kinship, sexuality, violence, and loneliness.

Woolson's novel *Anne* develops the marriage plot around intricate twists and turns that would keep its momentum in serialization. The title character is engaged to a childhood friend, Rast Pronando, on Mackinac Island and is relieved when he elopes with her sister, Tita. In New York, where she lives with an aunt and attends school, she rejects the proposal of another suitor, Gregory Dexter, and falls in love with Ward Heathcote, who marries her best friend, Helen Lorrington, but is reunited with Anne when his wife is murdered. Rather than being purely melodramatic, the plot allows Woolson to explore a society in which women exist for marriage or can find financial security only within marriage. Anne's long interlude at a private, but fashionable watering hole in New York gives Woolson ample opportunity to reveal the kinds of things that attract men to women: beauty, coyness, discreet rather than ostentatious fashion. Because the possibility of home is equated with marriage, Woolson reveals not only how women use these devices in their pursuit of a husband, but also how ruthless they can be in their pursuits. The novel's shallow, though hardly naïve, girl figure, Helen Lorrington, articulates the feelings that plague all of women's relationships: Helen befriends the title character Anne because "Anne admired her, and was at the same time neither envious nor jealous, and from her youth she [Helen] had been troubled by the sure development of these two feelings, sooner or later, in all her girl companions" (161).

Several plot complications suggest how often women's jealousy or fear leads them to betray one another if they equate home with marriage. Anne's aunt subverts Anne's engagement because her fiancé is the son of the man her aunt once loved and had hoped to make a home with, and Anne's half-sister, Tita [Angelique], is another shallow girl who like the island girl in "A Flower of the Snow" has "twenty times more coquetry" than Anne, so much so that she elopes with Anne's fiancé. An even worse betrayal comes from Helen, who tells Heathcote, the man both she and Anne have fallen in love with, that the Angelique whose marriage notice has appeared in the newspaper is really Anne and thereby wins Heathcote for her own husband. At the same time, however, Woolson seems loath to condemn any woman who manipulates for love, understanding as she does how much women's lives depend on marriage and how much better marriages are likely to be if they are based on love. She does, though, readily expose falseness, and it is interesting to note that all the admirable men in this novel prefer Anne's honesty and independence to the coquetry of the fashionable young women frequenting the New York resort. Woolson might have ended *Anne* with Helen Lorrington's marriage to the man Anne loves, thus being consistent with her versions of exiles from home in the short fiction. Instead, she reunites Anne and Helen. Believing Heathcote dead, they become honest with each other and share the bond of suffering. Through their bond, Woolson suggests that although women often betray each other in their search for the security of home, they also can be honest with each other. Although betrayal severs friendship, honesty redeems it and draws them into a closer relationship than they might otherwise have had.

Through more plot twists, including Helen's murder and Heathcote's arrest and acquittal for this, Woolson eventually manages to unite Anne and Heathcote in marriage. Joan Weimer objects to this union, finding Heathcote "a character who seems to exist only to give Anne opportunities to show her superior strength and character" (*MG* xli). But Gregory Dexter is no more appropriate a match for Anne. He is too much a father figure and represents Woolson's rejection of the older-man/younger-woman motif that was so current in the fiction of the day. In fact, one of the striking things about Woolson's fiction is how often she develops the opposite motif, that of the older woman/younger man, the best example being the marriage of Prudence Wilkins in her story "The Front Yard" to a man eighteen years her junior. Woolson was quite aware that older women could be attracted to younger men. Earlier in the century, there had been Margaret Fuller and the Marquis Angelo Ossoli, who was ten years younger than she. Woolson had arrived in Europe at the time that George Eliot was being much talked about for marrying John Cross, a man twenty-one years her junior. In Florence, she watched the novelist Ouida making a "goose of herself . . . by falling in love with a young Italian 20 years younger than herself."[14] Likewise, for Prudence, love for a younger man is disastrous but explicable by "her having already become the captive of this handsome, this irresistible, this wholly unexpected Tonio, who was serving as a waiter in the Perugian inn" (*FY* 5).[15]

Although Ward Heathcote is also older than Anne, in his early thirties compared to Dexter's late thirties and Anne's eighteen, Woolson chose his character type carefully. He is, as Weimer has noted, like Woolson's prodigal brother Charlie (*MG* xli) and, therefore, seems younger and in need himself of growing up before he can enter into an adult marriage. His marriage to Helen, a childhood friend, is much what Anne's marriage to Rast, her childhood friend, might have become, an exercise in duty rather than love. It is the kind of marriage that Woolson may have imagined for herself had she married Zeph Spaulding. Despite Heathcote's love for Anne, the novel presents him as faithful to Helen. At the same time, however, it suggests an undercurrent of a double standard. When people observe Anne at Heathcote's trial, they see her as evidence of Helen's obligation to endure her husband's infidelity: Anne represents "one of those concealed trials which wives of 'men of the world' were obliged to endure"; that is, the man's affair with "a girl of the lower class, beautiful, and perhaps in her way even respectable" (478). To underscore the inappropriateness of such a double standard, Woolson gives as the reason for Anne's aunt's refusal to marry Rast's father the fact that during their short engagement he ran around with a "common girl—a market gardener's daughter" (182).[16] Woolson is documenting not just the double standard here, but also how much the ideal of the true and virtuous woman was a social construct of the middle and upper classes. Elsewhere in her fiction, however, she does suggest that sexuality outside of wedlock is not confined to the exploitation of poor women, and even Anne is nearly seduced by Heathcote until his honor forces him to tell her that he has married Helen.

Woolson wants to provide Anne a relationship based on openness, freedom, sexuality, and maturity, thus in choosing Heathcote's name, she echoes Emily Brontë's name Heathcliff. She would also have known that Cooper had given the name Heathcote to the Puritan family in *The Wept of Wish-ton-Wish*. She echoes Cooper's background of Indian warfare in the background of the Civil War, and Mark Heathcote Jr., who falls in love with a woman who was saved from Indian capture instead of his sister, prefigures Ward Heathcote. But Cooper's Heathcote is a minor character only, and Woolson's Heathcote, though not as sinister as Heathcliff, is blasphemous rather than pious, a religious doubter, a man locked into an inappropriate marriage and haunted by a love associated with the natural—though not the supernatural—environment. Anne is attracted to Heathcote in the first place because with her he can discuss his deepest and most unorthodox feelings, represented in a discussion they have in which they question the nature of God. Like Brontë's Catherine Earnshaw to Heathcliff, she is also attracted to him because he has no family whose expectations he must fulfill. Heathcote and Anne, however, both must mature before they marry. Helen serves as the disciplining force for Heathcote, and their marriage represents what Henry James Sr. saw as the nature of marriage, a state in which a man's instincts are spiritualized by the care of a loving wife. Besides becoming freed from his marriage to Helen, Heathcote must learn to treat Anne as a woman, not a child, a word he often uses when wooing her and, indeed, Anne must become more than a child. The two encounter each other several times on a train and each encounter brings them a step further into maturity and equality until Heathcote, unlike Dexter, drops the word *child* in reference to her. An early scene in the novel has Anne in a tableaux vivant dressed as the Goddess of Liberty and Heathcote holding her up, when the ladder she is on nearly falls. What Woolson implies by the end of the novel is that Anne must find liberty before she finds connection, something she and Heathcote both finally do. Imprisoned at first by her engagement, Anne gains the freedom of temporary spinsterhood and is able to free Heathcote from the prison of his marriage that has been represented metaphorically in his literal imprisonment for a crime he did not commit.

Once Anne proves Heathcote's innocence, they join together in a marriage that is liberating rather than imprisoning. Anne's choice of Heathcote is similar to her half-sister Tita's elopement, a choice made despite what society defines as sensible. A significant difference in the choice, however, is that society would define Anne's choice as morally acceptable. It is important that the marriage takes place on Mackinac Island, Anne's girlhood home, one which would have been a limiting home had she married her girlhood fiancé. Because Anne has been independent and intelligent, hers is not the limiting fate that fulfills women like Helen and Tita; rather, it is one that combines freedom and responsibility at the same time that it satisfies a reader's desire for romantic adventure within or outside of marriage. As Cheryl Torsney has so ably pointed out in a discussion of *Anne* and Henry James's *The Portrait of a Lady*—novels the two were composing at the start of their friendship—Anne, unlike Isabel Archer, "assert[s] her identity in the real world": she names herself and uses the active voice to say, "I, Anne, take thee, Ward, to my wedded husband, to have and to hold, from this day forward" (539).[17]

Woolson presents a radical vision in *Anne* because she refuses to criticize Helen for betraying friendship and Tita for betraying kinship. However, she endorses Anne as the heroine who follows the conventionally moral path no matter the cost to herself, and she rewards her by providing her what we judge will become a mature, satisfactory, even romantic home within marriage. In *For the Major,* she continues to explore the kinds of choices women make to establish marital homes, but now with a heroine whose behavior might be considered less socially acceptable. Again, she juxtaposes the girl figure with a woman whose life circumstances are more complex. Sara Carroll is one of Woolson's least complex girl figures and her virtue is rewarded by marriage to the man she loves. Sara is of minor interest in the novella, far more conventional than Tita or Helen, but providing her with a home via marriage enables Woolson to validate her simplicity because it is accompanied by honesty. In her conventional morality, Sara is more like Anne than Helen or Tita, but this morality is never really tempted. Sara's stepmother, Madame Carroll, might be compared to Helen and Tita in the sense that she must compromise standards of behavior in order to gain a husband. However, because Woolson has focused on Madame Carroll, we see her not just following self-gratification but also weighing the consequences of her actions within both a social and familial context. Unlike Helen and Tita, Madame Carroll is honest with herself even though she is not truthful with those around her.

For the Major explores an interesting angle toward marriage and home because Madame Carroll articulates so explicitly the reasons why many women act the way they do. Through her, Woolson finds a voice that helps us to understand her own unwillingness to belittle any of the decisions her female characters make regarding marriage. Left with a sickly daughter to support, Madame Carroll teaches, working as hard as she can, but finding that she can do no more than feed her child. As she says to her stepdaughter Sara, "I had strained every nerve, made use of all my poor little knowledge and my trifling accomplishments; I had worked as hard as I possibly could; and the result of all my efforts was that I had barely succeeded in getting our bread from day to day, with nothing laid up for the future, and the end of my small strength near at hand" (*Major* 342). At this point in her life, she meets, through a friend, Major Carroll, in front of whom she pretends to be younger than she is. She also leads Major Carroll to believe she has had only one child, the daughter who dies shortly after her marriage to the major. In reality, she also has a son who finds her at Major Carroll's home in Far Edgerley. When the son dies and the major's ill-health deteriorates into senility, Madame Carroll reveals the truth to Sara. In a final plot twist, we learn that Madame Carroll has either never married the major or, more likely, married him not knowing her first husband was still alive. Woolson downplays the bigamy and the illegitimacy of her child by the major, reminding us of these only when Madame Carroll (re)marries the senile Major at a bedside ceremony.

Madame Carroll's actions have hardly been what we want to admire: living a lie based on feminine appearance to satisfy a man. Yet the portrait is sympathetic because Woolson has shown us that although loving has required Madame Carroll to be false, it has not required hypocrisy. Explaining her position to Sara, Madame Carroll displays the kind of integrity Woolson wanted us to see in her:

> [The major] saw in me a little blue-eyed, golden-haired girl-mother, un-acquainted with the dark side of life, trusting, sweet. It was this very youth and child-like look which had attracted him, man of the world as he was himself, and no longer young. I feared to shatter his dream. In addition, that part did not seem to me of any especial consequence; I knew that I should be able to live up to his ideal, to maintain it not only fully, but longer, probably, than as though I had been in reality the person he supposed me to be. (*Major* 341)

By having Madame Carroll become only superficially a child-wife, permanently youthful and beautiful but also fully aware of the implications of her pretense, Woolson has focused on her observations about the things that matter to the major's kind of world. It is the men in that world who, as Sybil Weir has noted, end up being the most deeply scarred, for where "the woman is aware that the sentimental disguise masks her actual self, the man is robbed of self-knowledge." For Weir, the major's son Scar, a shortening of Scarborough, "a sickly and effeminate child," serves as a metaphor for the perversity of relationships where men treat women as children (141). Given this demeaning social expectation, is it really so awful, Woolson suggests, to choose honest pretense and service as a more viable way of living than self-delusion or loneliness and poverty? Madame Carroll is not, at the core, false or childlike, for she knows that she is not a person who possesses a "lofty kind of vision which sees only the one path, and that the highest." Instead, she sees "all the shorter paths, lower down, that lead to the same place—the crosscuts." "[T]he great things, the wide view," says Madame Carroll, "are beyond me." She is not fitted for "struggle" but can "work and plan and accomplish . . . only when sheltered—sheltered in a home, no matter how plain, protected from actual contact with the crowd," where there is always "brutality" (*Major* 342–43). Some of Woolson's more limited characters may take a superficial kind of high road; Madame Carroll outdistances them because she understands how much societal expectations have shaped her own decisions in securing a home.

By the time she wrote her third novel, *East Angels,* Woolson had been in Europe long enough to observe the differences in American and European marriages, one of which was the extent to which European marriages served as avenues through which women could lead more-open and freer lives. One of the great themes of the nineteenth century, worked out most fully by Henry James, was what happened to innocent Americans faced with the darker experience of Europe. In a remarkably clear and candid letter to Mrs. Samuel Livingston Mather, her brother-in-law's second wife, Woolson suggests how this applies to females by talking about the differences between American and European attitudes toward marriage. Florence, she writes, "is no place for *young* young ladies; they have no liberty, and can hardly speak unless spoken to, can go nowhere alone, and flirtation is—for them—unknown; if they indulge in it, they lose their reputation; the only thing they can do is to marry and they generally do that at least once," provided, of course, that they have dowries. In Florence, Woolson continues, "the married women, and in fact all older women, whether married or not have a much better time" than those in America. The problem, however, is that no matter how old they are, if

> they have a little money, especially, they are never secure, but are considered proper subjects of discussion [for marriage] as long as they live! These, of course, are the widows and old maids; as to the married ladies, there is a great deal of flirtation going on. What our young ladies amuse themselves with at home, the married ladies amuse themselves with here. It is all very curious and, to a looker-on like me, amusing. (Benedict 2:26–27)

Embedded within Woolson's comments is her awareness that European marriages give women a license for sexuality, protection from unwanted advances, and freedom of choice and movement. One thinks especially of the European-style marriage of the Touchetts in James's *The Portrait of a Lady,* where Mrs. Touchett feels free to travel as she chooses, merely dropping in now and again to visit her husband.

For nineteenth-century American women, marriage carried expectations of women's fidelity and decorum even if husbands were unfaithful. Married women could not pursue freer life-styles than unmarried ones, nor could they resort to divorce if marriages were unsuccessful, unless they wanted to flout the prevailing social attitudes that condemned divorce. Henry James's Aunt Kate (Catherine Walsh), for example, had married at age forty but quickly separated from her husband, Capt. Charles Marshall, to rejoin the James family as a valued companion-nurse. The grounds for the separation are unknown, but one wonders if Marshall may have been abusive and if Woolson used this as background to *Jupiter Lights*. Whatever the grounds for separation, it was unusual for Walsh to leave her husband even though she never pursued a formal divorce.

The alternative to the quiet separation of Catherine Walsh and Charles Marshall is represented in the example of Harriet Beecher Stowe's brother Henry Ward Beecher, whose affair midcentury with his parishioner Libby Tilton triggered a highly publicized and scandalous trial, the kind of scandal a decorous family would want to avoid.[18] Even though society in the nineteenth century was debating the divorce question and Henry James Sr. for a time advocated divorce, the majority of society vehemently opposed it and avoided scandal. Nina Baym has noted the tendency of reviewers in the nineteenth century to respond negatively to books about divorce,[19] and Woolson herself documented in her notebook an idea for a story about society rejecting a divorced woman (Benedict 2:134). After the Civil War, Howells dared to treat divorce in *A Modern Instance* (1882), but even Kate Chopin's *The Awakening* (1899), which caused a furor among her contemporaries for its refusal to condemn a woman's adultery, avoids treating divorce. It was not until the turn of the century that divorce became a more open topic in fiction, with Edith Wharton, herself divorced in 1913, using it in such works as "The Other Two" (1904), *The Custom of the Country* (1913), and *The Age of Innocence* (1920).

Woolson knew that many marriages, whether European or American, were imperfect. Given this fact and the prohibitions against divorce, her fiction considers the compensations a marriage of convenience, like that of the Touchetts, can give a woman. Her story "A Florentine Experiment" illustrates some of the issues such marriages raise, issues she explores more fully later in her novel *East Angels*. Both works center on characters named Margaret, as if Woolson is consciously showing two avenues of responding to the notion of a marriage of convenience. The choice of name makes it tempting to speculate that Woolson was paying homage to Margaret Fuller, a woman whose life was similar to her own and whose life-style reflected many of her fictional concerns. Even more than Woolson, Fuller had been educated and shaped by a father. She was never interested in fiction and had more of a reputation as a conversationalist than a writer, but, like Woolson, she had been a journalist, had traveled to and written about the Great Lakes in *Summer on the Lakes* (1844), and had settled in Italy. Unlike Woolson, Fuller married, but only after she had borne her husband's child out of wedlock. Earlier in her life, she also had a strong attachment to Emerson, and her relationship to him, like Woolson's to James has been misinterpreted as one of unrequited love. Recent reassessments of that relationship see Emerson as Fuller's distant but intellectually compatible friend in much the same way that James was Woolson's. Fuller's sense of herself as homeless in a society that expected women to be what she could not be would have attracted Woolson. She may have discussed Fuller and her death by drowning in 1850 with James, who thought Fuller a disturbing force working on his psyche.[20]

"A Florentine Experiment" is one of Woolson's most Jamesian stories, heavily ironic with multiple levels of interpretive possibilities, as it leads its Margaret to home and a happy ending Woolson knew her audiences wanted. But, as is so often the case in Woolson's fiction, there is a distinct qualification to this happy ending. The story opens with Margaret Stowe talking to her friend Beatrice Lovell, a woman with money. Beatrice is quick to let Margaret know how much higher her status is as a widow rather than, like Margaret, as a spinster: "'You have beautiful theories, I know; but in my *experience*' (Mrs. Lovell slightly underlined this word as if in opposition to the 'theories' of her friend) 'the people who have those deeper sort of feelings you describe are almost always unhappy'" (502). Margaret's theory involves loving someone "deeply and jealously, and to the exclusion of all the rest" (502). Beatrice, with the status of a widow and the freedom and money to travel, is uninterested in love, so much so that she gives Margaret a letter from a suitor, Trafford Morgan. Later, Margaret meets Morgan and, we surmise, falls in love with him. He assumes she loves him and tells her that he, however, loves someone else. Margaret recoils at Morgan's arrogance and denies her love, claiming that she was cultivating an interest in him in order to forget someone else she loved. They part and in the interim before they meet again Beatrice marries. When Margaret and Morgan do meet again, he asks her to be the subject of his Florentine Experiment and allow him to forget another woman by trying to fall in love with her. Eventually, he proposes to her, saying he hasn't exactly fallen in love with her but that he does care for her and, once again showing his arrogance, saying he wants to marry her because she loves him. Again they part, and when they meet for the third time Margaret's aunt tries her own experiment, telling Morgan that Margaret is engaged. This time when Morgan proposes, he admits that he has finally figured out that he loved Margaret all along.

"A Florentine Experiment" is so heavily ironic that it is difficult to know if and when either of these characters loves the other, though Woolson does seem, finally, to agree with Morgan who comes to realize that to "marry without love" is a "wretched thing" (529) and to suggest that Margaret will simply hold out against Morgan until she is sure he really loves her. What is interesting, though, is that Woolson is also aware that marriage protects women from unwanted advances and, at least in Europe, that marriages of convenience allow women greater avenues toward freedom. We have no evidence that she ever seriously considered marriage while in Europe, though we do know that John Hay tried to arrange a marriage with Clarence King, and we surmise that there must have been speculation about her and James. Although he thought Woolson in love with King, Hay also calls her a "very clever person, to whom men are a vain show."[21] King had the reputation of a libertine and, had a marriage been arranged, Woolson might have found in him a husband willing to give her her liberty. But King was secretly married and Woolson probably had not met him when she wrote "A Florentine Experiment." Nor did she need King as a model, for almost immediately upon her arrival in Europe, she recognized the easy attitude toward marriages of convenience. As Morgan says in his first marriage proposal: "If [marriage] fails—if you are not happy—I promise not to hold you in the slightest degree. You shall have your liberty untrammeled, and, at the same time, all shall be arranged so as to escape comment. I will be with you enough to save appearances; that is all. In reality you shall be entirely free" (524).

One of the tensions in "A Florentine Experiment" involves the issue of sexual freedom. Although Woolson addressed the issues of marriage and sexuality only obliquely in her fiction, she does not ignore sexuality. Morgan's willingness to allow Margaret freedom if the marriage fails implies that, at least initially, the marriage will be sexual. John Kern believed that the "lovers in Miss Woolson's stories are so completely untroubled by amorous desires that the reader may be forgiven for suspecting their virility" (129), but Carolyn VanBergen has recently shown that this is not the case. In her discussion of the sexual and economic metaphors in *Horace Chase,* VanBergen finds ample metaphors through which Woolson could locate her characters' sexuality.[22] Early in her career, Woolson had written a provocative story, "On the Iron Mountain," that examines the role of sexuality within marriage. The protagonist, Helen Fay, is magnetic, restless, metaphorically sexual. At one point, she "seemed to be all pulse; pulses throbbed in her throat and the blood leaped through her veins" (228). In the story, Woolson develops the character of a mesmerist, who quiets Helen's sexuality and brings her so much under his control that she is willing to run away with him. His motive, however, is to force her other lover to acknowledge sexuality. The problem, though, is that for a woman sexuality becomes a loss of control over the self; it puts Helen first into the power of the mesmerist, then into the protection of a husband with whom she will be able to express sexuality only because he has been coerced by the mesmerist into giving his wife permission for sexuality. Throughout the story, Woolson associates Helen, the namesake of the woman whose beauty wields power over men, with the goddess Diana, who exacts revenge upon Actaeon when he sees her naked. The associations are ironic, for Helen gains autonomy neither through passion nor through chastity. Only if women can control their own sexuality can they find their own power.

Woolson's fullest and most sophisticated working out of the relationship of home to issues of sexuality, marriages of convenience, and the problem of divorce occurs in *East Angels,* not just through her treatment of that novel's heroine, Margaret Harold, but also through another examination of the girl-woman. Here, Woolson's girl-woman, Garda Thorne, defies society's mores to pursue the man she loves. Garda's defiance makes her, like Tita and Helen in *Anne,* more interesting than the simply virtuous Sara Carroll. Through both Garda and Margaret, Woolson hints at the sexual dimension implied in a marital home and at how that home may fulfill or stifle a woman's sexuality. One of the reasons Garda pursues marriage is that she is pursuing her sexuality, a trait most of Woolson's predecessors denied their fictional girl figures. In fact, Nina Baym's research on reviewers of pre–Civil War novels finds hostility among reviews to any treatment of sexuality.[23] Woolson subverts nineteenth-century literary models and expectations by suggesting that sexuality fulfills these limited women precisely because they do not need wider avenues for fulfillment. Furthermore, Woolson suggests that beautiful women have greater choices in finding their ideal marriage/sex partners. The beginning of *East Angels* contains a passage that articulates this view, one Woolson was especially sensitive to because, portrait evidence to the contrary, she thought herself lacking in beauty:[24] "For in their hearts women always know that of all the gifts bestowed upon their sex that of beauty has so immeasurably the greatest power that nothing else can for one moment be compared with it, that all other gifts of whatsoever nature and extent, sink into insignificance and powerlessness beside it" (19).

The question *East Angels* poses at first is what will become of the beautiful, sheltered, natural, restless Garda Thorne. Encouraged by her mother to become interested in a rich northerner, thirty-five-year-old Evert Winthrop, Garda complies. But enter Lucian Spenser, who engages in a brief flirtation with Garda. Spenser soon leaves Florida, the setting for the novel, and is enticed into marriage by a woman who has told him she is dying, but gets well after their marriage. This relationship is not central to the novel; however, it again reflects Woolson's sense of the sexual or emotional blackmail used to achieve marriage as well as her insight into how dull a life a woman can lead if she allows her family to dictate that she be reserved and wait for a suitably rich mate. When Garda can no longer pretend to love Winthrop, she breaks her engagement, taking what would seem a noble stance: "Everybody in the world seems to tell lies but me. . . . And everybody else seems to prefer it" (392). But nobility requires deeper feelings than Woolson develops in Garda. Because she does not have these deeper feelings, Woolson can reward her truthfulness simply by having Spenser's wife die and Garda marry him. In an unexpected plot twist, Spenser himself dies, but Garda finds a suitable second marriage to a handsome former admirer. By highlighting the dashing manners and physical handsomeness of both Garda's husbands, Woolson implies that being an honest and virtuous girl-wife is compatible with sexuality. In fact, sexuality becomes all the more crucial for wives whose intellectual dimension remains undeveloped. If one must marry to find a home, the sexual dimension to marriage should be fulfilling rather than endured for the sake of that home.

Unlike Garda, Margaret Harold does not find a fulfilling sexuality within her marital home but, instead, discovers how sexuality threatens to destroy a home. Margaret's husband, Lanse,[25] has had a long-standing affair in Europe, one she is expected to allow him, striving only to keep it secret so that his good name—and their facade of a good marriage—will be protected. But Margaret, who discovers soon after marriage that she does not love her husband, will have none of this double standard. Lanse leaves her for Europe and forbids her to follow him. When he eventually returns to America and Margaret, he remains oblivious to Margaret's growth and her needs. He cannot understand that his presence is painful to her, for he is willing to allow her to lead the life she is used to while he leads the life he wants. Thus, he believes, they can have a model marriage. Yet Lanse immediately contradicts this notion by insisting that Margaret conform to his notions of how she should dress, turning her into an ornament much as Henry James's Gilbert Osmond tried to turn Isabel Archer into an object for his collection. After all, Lanse has married Margaret for "her profile" (438) rather than for love. He dresses her according to his wishes and is pleased that she is such a "beautiful object" (440). Unlike Madame Carroll in *For the Major,* who finds this kind of role a satisfying one, Margaret finds it stifling, especially because she has fallen in love with Evert Winthrop during Lanse's absence. A scene between Margaret and Winthrop exudes the kind of passion Margaret is capable of feeling and that Garda's more fulfilling marriages contain. Lost in the sexually charged atmosphere of a swamp, Margaret and Winthrop acknowledge their mutual passion, but this is never consummated because Margaret chooses to remain faithful to Lanse. The scene in the swamp clarifies how much this loyalty betrays Margaret's natural instincts, but because she has refused to acknowledge Lanse's instincts to love another woman, she cannot act on similar feelings in herself. Lanse's parallel devotion to this other woman is long-standing, thus he leaves Margaret a second time. When he returns as an invalid, his illness suggests that the marriage will remain nonsexual.

Woolson uses Margaret's decision not to divorce Lanse, despite her unhappiness within the marriage, to illustrate how complex women's tendency to self-sacrifice can be. In an otherwise favorable review of *East Angels,* William Dean Howells criticizes Woolson's portrayal of Margaret as a sacrificial woman: "Neither Margaret nor Winthrop her lover appeals to our sympathy, perhaps because we cannot believe in them; they form for us the one false note of the book."[26] Woolson objects in a letter to John Hay that she "could not expect Mr. Howells to like 'Margaret,' for he does not believe in 'Margarets,'—he has never perceived they exist" (Petry 87, 30 July 1886). Nor, it seems, does Rayburn Moore believe they exist. He admits his own impatience with Margaret even as he recognizes the problem of dismissing her and thus denying the "generous impulses of feminine nature."[27] To accept Howells's or Moore's view is to dismiss Woolson's subtle portrayal of self-sacrifice, especially when the stakes of finding a satisfactory home are so high for women. Henry James serves as a better guide for understanding Woolson's position. He believes that she spends too much time in *East Angels* on feminine matters of love, but he also sees that if we "repudiate" Margaret, we deny "that a woman *may* look at life from a high point of view," deny "that there *are* distinguished natures."[28] Sybil Weir explains the matter from a more contemporary perspective, saying that we have lost the "religious referent available to Woolson" and that Woolson "saw clearly that it was almost always the woman, either motivated by a principle higher than self-love or forced by necessity, who was called upon to make the sacrifice" (565).

Unlike most interpreters of Margaret's refusal to divorce and re-marry, Joan Weimer argues that Margaret is attempting to choose autonomy within her bleak marriage over enslavement in a loving marriage to Winthrop.[29] This is a welcome interpretation because, typical of Woolson's fiction, the issue of self-sacrifice in *East Angels* is never clear-cut, and when James recognizes that there is a temptation to repudiate Margaret's choice to remain in her marital home, he realizes that Woolson is ambivalent about the value of women's sacrificial nature. A narrative passage from *East Angels* about Margaret's sacrifice and her friend Dr. Kirby's response to it illustrates one side of the issue:

> There are women who are capable of sacrificing themselves, with the noblest unselfishness in great causes, who yet, as regards the small matters of every-day life, are rather uncomfortable to live with; so much so, indeed, that those who are under the same roof with them are driven to reflect now and then upon the merits of the ancient hermitages and caves to which in former ages such characters were accustomed to retire. . . .
>
> The Doctor had had these saints as his patients more than once, he knew them perfectly. But here was a woman who had sacrificed her whole life to duty, who felt constantly the dreary ache of deprivation; but who yet did not think in the least, apparently, that these things freed her from the kindly efforts, the patience, the small sweet friendly attempts which made home comfortable. (565–66)

As admiring as Dr. Kirby's view is, Woolson knew that it is only one part of the issue. Garda takes an opposite view, believing that sacrifice is silly, that "two whole lives [have been] wasted—and all for the sake of an idea" (579). Winthrop takes yet another angle: "Women are better than men; in some things they are stronger. But that's because they are sustained . . . by their terrible love of self-sacrifice; I absolutely believe there are women who *like* to be tortured" (588).

Had Woolson simply admired sacrifice and seen it played out in martyrdom, she might have chosen to end her novel with either reward or doom. Instead, the ambiguous last line of *East Angels* shows Margaret still married to Lanse, never again meeting Winthrop, engaged in this cutting dialogue:

> "Do you know that you've grown old, Madge, before your time?"
> "Yes, I know it."
> "Well—you're a good woman," said Lanse. (591)

Margaret has sacrificed and lost love, has been tempted into the "terrible love of self-sacrifice" that is the mark of the "good" martyr. But something stronger than martyrdom also works in Margaret, much as it works in James's Isabel Archer, whose apparent choice to return to her marriage Woolson echoes. Like Isabel, Margaret had married naïvely, believing in fidelity only to discover opposing values in her husband and, again like Isabel, when she chooses with full knowledge to remain married, she upholds the value she believes reflected in the marriage vow, no matter her husband's cynicism about such vows. She wishes she could be like Garda, who "puts the rest of us (women, I mean) to shame—the rest of us with our complicated motives, and involved consciences" (244). But Margaret knows society too well to be like Garda and can analyze what lies beneath society's codes. She understands that part of the necessity to remain married comes from the stigma that would have been attached to her divorcing a man who, in her words, has not been physically abusive, who has not been an alcoholic, and who has not exerted a negative influence on any children (531).

An interesting commentary on society's attitudes occurs in *East Angels* when Winthrop overhears an older woman speaking to a younger one on a train: "*We* [women] do not exhibit our charms—which should be sacred to the privacy of the boudoir [i.e., the home]—in the glare of lecture-rooms; *we* prefer to be, and to *remain,* the low-voiced retiring mothers of a race of giant sons whom the Muse of History will immortalize in the character of soldier, statesman, and divine" (536). Aware of the frequency of this attitude, Margaret must struggle to find a place for herself in a society that allows her neither independence through divorce nor the fulfillment she might find in a public sphere "in the glow of lecture-rooms" or in a career analogous to the male occupations of "soldier, statesman, and divine." Woolson clearly does not endorse the attitude of the women on the train, and she may be suggesting that change can come only from a younger generation of women. Through Margaret's "complicated motives, and involved conscience" and Garda's naïveté, she may also be suggesting that as the younger generation carves a public sphere for women it consider the implications of this on the private sphere of the home. To widen society's acceptance of divorce for reasons of incompatibility would be to undermine the value of marriage in maintaining the private sphere. As a more public sphere has opened for women in the twentieth century, Woolson might well have predicted the difficulties women would face when they have to balance home and work, particularly if they have to do so as single mothers.

In *East Angels,* Woolson shows the price Margaret pays for upholding the sanctity of marriage her readers expected her to uphold. One of these readers wrote Woolson that she wanted the author to allow Lanse to be "taken" in order to provide a happy ending and still endorse the sanctity of marriage. Woolson answered this reader, saying that it is more realistic not to have Lanse die (Kern 88). She does not uphold the sanctity of marriage herself as much as she shows the degree to which women like Margaret have internalized society's norms. She does not make Margaret a "good" woman who finds sacrifice easy because she did not value easy sacrifice, believing, instead, that people are not especially good if what they do comes easily. Margaret is the genuine article—a person whose impulse to goodness involves great pain. Her marriage of convenience brings her no happiness, but it does bring some reward. Although the marriage and, along with it, her relationship to Lanse's hostile aunt are painful, Margaret also has gained something for herself. Three months before Lanse's return to the marriage, Margaret decides not to return to the isolated New England home of the deceased grandmother who raised her and has instead purchased East Angels in her own name. Knowing that a sense of place may help her replace her lack of a satisfying marital home, she tells Winthrop, "I shall do very well here if I have the place to think about . . . I shall have the land cultivated; perhaps I shall start a new orange grove" (524). At the same time, she also accuses Winthrop of wanting "no woman to lead a really independent life" (524).

Lanse's return undercuts Margaret's independence, but because he is now an invalid, she can still maintain control over her property. In fact, the narrative mentions a new orange grove just before Margaret tells Winthrop that she will remain married to Lanse (538). As much as Margaret sacrifices, her choice has had its compensations. We know that she has learned to live with the pain of Winthrop's loss because she counsels Garda that she, too, will learn to live with the loss of her first husband. She is even willing to have Winthrop marry Garda, and Winthrop reads this as a reflection of how much "you women think . . . of a home" (587). By the end of *East Angels,* Margaret has gained a richer home than she had in the past because both Lanse and his aunt have learned to treat her more kindly and because Garda, whom she cares about, is also likely to return to Florida and add the rootedness of place to the home she has in her new marriage. More important, Margaret has gained the integrity of the self-knowledge that, eight years after her refusal of Winthrop, though she is old before her time, she has become so for reasons that go beyond her personal happiness.

Early nineteenth-century novels, if they treated women's sexuality at all, tended to ghettoize it into nonmarital relationships that necessitated retribution. Woolson's subtle, but still clear, acknowledgement of a legitimate sexual dimension in a character like Garda Thorne moves toward the openness at the end of the century of novelists such as Edith Wharton and Kate Chopin. Like her depiction of sexuality, her depiction of marital abuse moves beyond the polemics of early novels that suggest that wives must somehow endure abuse or work toward the reformation of alcoholic husbands. Issues of alcohol abuse and its impact on domestic violence were widely discussed throughout the nineteenth century. Early in the century, crusades against alcohol often sensationalized the problem in ways that titillated rather than reformed. David Reynolds has called this tendency to sensationalize under the guise of reform "immoral didacticism" aimed at a "public accustomed to having its reform well spiced with violence and sex." Temperance works in this genre include "*Horrid Case of Intemperance,*" published in the *Salem Gazette,* showing a "drunkard burned to a crisp by a blacksmith's fire"; Mary L. Fox's *Ruined Deacon* (1834), showing the downfall of an alcoholic deacon, and novels with titles like *Letters from the Alms House* (1841), *Confessions of a Reformed Inebriate* (1844), *Confessions of a Rum-Seller* (1845), and *The Glass* (1849) that include wife beating and murder, psychopathological visions and insanity, child murder, and a case of self-cannibalism brought about by an abuse victim's being locked in a closet. Even Walt Whitman wrote a temperance novel called *Franklin Evans,* and Poe's "The Cask of Amontillado" and "The Black Cat" are derivative of the genre (Reynolds 65–73). Cathy Davidson has studied less-sensationalized novels and found that wives were expected to endure abuse rather than seek divorce.[30]

E. D. E. N. Southworth provides a living example of a woman who gained independence as a writer but chose not to seek divorce from a husband who had abandoned her and her small children.³¹ So, too, does the notorious case involving Mansfield and Ellen Walworth, an elite couple from Saratoga Springs, New York. Mansfield's father, Reuban Hyde Walworth, had been Chancellor of New York State and a friend of Cooper, Emerson, and Lincoln. When Reuban remarried, the young Mansfield met and soon married the daughter of his new stepmother. A novelist whose book *Mission of Death* (1853) went through twelve editions, Mansfield became an alcoholic and an abuser. The situation not only prompted Ellen to leave the marriage and open a school to support herself, in 1873 it also prompted the couple's nineteen-year-old son Frank to shoot his father. The case was highly publicized, including a lengthy piece in *Frank Leslie's Illustrated Newspaper* (June 21, 1873). Given the Walworth family's connection to Cooper and Mansfield's position as a novelist, Woolson would surely have been familiar with this situation. Cases like this triggered crusades against alcohol, which gained huge support among women, especially in the 1870s, when Ohio became one of the centers of activism and the birthplace of the WCTU. Women were tending to become politically involved and, by law, could ask that an alcoholic husband not be served at local saloons.³²

Woolson first addressed the idea of wife abuse obliquely in a story called "King Log." She does not name the source of the abuse, but her readers would have inferred alcoholism. The story deals with the reaction of a man whose sister has been trapped in an abusive marriage and who hears that the woman who broke her engagement to him has nearly succumbed to the same kind of marriage. More interesting is Woolson's portrayal of wife and child abuse in *Jupiter Lights,* in which the source of the abuse is alcohol. The novel is Woolson's most problematic, for it seems to endorse stereotypical attitudes about women as martyrs even if martyrdom requires enduring abuse. Yet beneath the surface of *Jupiter Lights,* we see Woolson struggling to come to grips with the issues of how women damage themselves when they remain in abusive relationships. Although the plot is melodramatic, *Jupiter Lights* neither titillates nor advocates wifely endurance. The novel examines how its girl-figure, Cicely Bruce Morrison, chooses not between sexuality and home or sexuality or home, but between sexuality/violence/home and loneliness.

Throughout *Jupiter Lights,* Woolson questions the conventional attitudes her characters too often display. In the novel, the widowed

Cicely has broken protocol by marrying Ferdinand Morrison before she has gone through the appropriate mourning period for her first husband, Eve's brother. She lives for only a few months with Ferdie before returning to her home at Jupiter Lights, Georgia. Eventually, she tells Eve that Ferdie, when drunk, has abused both herself and her son by Bruce, Jack. That Woolson was concerned about how marriage could be a physical threat as well as a refuge for women is evidenced in *East Angels* when she has Margaret declare that she has no grounds such as abusiveness or alcoholism for divorce. Woolson voices her dissent from this attitude when she has Eve indicate her disgust in a sarcastic comment: "And marriage makes everything perfectly safe . . . ?" (73). Just how abusive husbands and fathers can be is evidenced in the extent of Cicely's and Jack's injuries. Woolson does not sensationalize them but makes them realistic and serious: scars on Cicely's breast and shoulder and a broken arm for Jack that Cicely says "was easily set. Nobody ever knew about it, I never told" (79). And here, of course, is the problem. Although everyone who knows him loves and defends Ferdie, he misuses other people's money, misuses alcohol, misuses women, misuses children, misuses himself. The qualities Cicely and others love in Ferdie—his vitality, his handsome devil-may-care passion—are the very qualities that lead him to violence.

Although Woolson does not endorse Cicely's loyalty to Ferdie, she does accept the misconception that to break the violence may well be to break the man. Ferdie's half-brother, for example, says that "[d]runkards are death to the women—to the wives and mothers and sisters; but some of 'em are more lovable than lots of the moral skinflints that go nagging about, saving a penny, and grinding everybody but themselves. The trouble with Ferdie was that he was born without any conscience, just as some people have no ear for music; it was a case of heredity . . . " (339).[33] But Woolson's novel is not just another addition to temperance arguments that expect women to shoulder the burden of keeping men away from alcohol. It portrays alcoholism as hereditary and debilitating at the same time that it sees the danger of understanding the alcoholic, loveable or not. Thus Cicely's attitude of pretending that violence within the home does not exist by never speaking of the violence results only in a perpetuation of the cycle of violence.

Centering on the issues of home as kindred and home as violence, Woolson deepens her insights into how women pursue homes in her portrait of Cicely's more complex counterpart, Eve Bruce, her sister-in-law by her first marriage. Eve comes to meet Cicely for the first time after her brother's death, already disliking her for having married her brother and causing her, she believes, to lose the only family and connection to the feeling of home she has had. In fact, Eve's motive is to take her nephew Jack from his mother and build a home for herself with the child. Joan Weimer reads this as the result of Eve's incestuous fixation on her father, her brother, and her brother's child (*MG* xli). Though I do not like the term incestuous—Jack after all is only a toddler—Eve does seem to me a victim of social attitudes that expect female children to reify male family members and to appoint themselves as family caretakers. In that role, Eve breaks all taboos against violence when she discovers Ferdie chasing Cicely and Jack with a knife during one of his drunken rampages and shoots him. That Woolson has Eve rather than Cicely attack Ferdie enables her to focus on issues of passion and violence. Violence begets violence so that Eve finds she can shoot Ferdie, and Cicely, believing Eve wants Ferdie dead, strikes Eve. Cicely's passion is itself destructive and irrational. Not only does she excuse Ferdie on the basis that his violence "seldom happens" (80), she also believes herself "free; no one has any authority over me except Ferdie" (130). What she does not see is the extent to which this authority makes her not free.

Woolson uses Eve's gradual awakening to a passionate love for Ferdie's brother Paul Tennant to counterpoint Cicely's love for Ferdie. John Kern sees this working out of the plot as melodramatic, but it is so only if one fails to connect it to the issue of violence toward women, a subject he does not even identify as part of the plot of *Jupiter Lights* (90–92). Early on, Eve thinks of Cicely's wish that she drop her cold demeanor and learn the power of love: "To wish her [Eve] a love like her [Cicely's] own, this seemed almost a curse, a malediction . . . ; to love any man so submissively was weakness, but to love as Cicely loved, that was degradation" (90). Eve's anger here at Cicely is a revolt "against the injustice of all the ages, past, present, and to come, towards women" (90). But Eve's love for Paul is just as powerful as Cicely's for Ferdie. Like Cicely's, Eve's love tempts her to ignore social controls—at one point she meets Paul in the woods, the implication being that she is ready to have a sexual affair, and for a time she is willing to lie to him to ensure her happiness. Eve likes Paul's despotism, but only to a point. She claims that she wants someone stronger than herself, a protector. But if one has a despotic protector and no power, then the protector becomes the destroyer. What Woolson uses

Eve to achieve is a relationship that will bring support at the same time that it brings independence and personal power.

Paul does not have Ferdie's outward abusiveness, but he has similar faults that Eve knows about, condemns, and loves him in spite of. He trifles with other women, assuming that a sexual double standard is okay if the other woman is a peasant girl. The double-standard theme is strong enough that Woolson has Ferdie involved in a liaison; Paul's friend Hollis Clay, who also loves Eve, nearly seduces a barmaid; and Cicely's friend Judge Abercrombie condemns Ferdie's infidelity only because it, unlike his own, has touched a wife. Paul also trifles with Eve, treating her "like a child" he "long[s] to take care of" (325) and like a person who will, of course, bend to his will.

Only by having Eve love Paul can Woolson provide a way for her to understand how Cicely can continue to desire a home with Ferdie. But because she possesses a deeper nature than Cicely, Eve refuses to be bound to Paul in contrast to Cicely's bondage in love. She fears she will become a woman whose love will destroy her integrity and make her yet another victim of love, another woman who will accept a marital home, whatever the cost to her personal safety and integrity. "Once your wife," she says to Paul, "I know that I should stay on, even if it were only to fold your clothes,—to touch them; to pick up the burnt match-ends you had dropped, and your newspapers; to arrange the chairs as you like to have them. I should be weak, weak— I should follow you about" (324).

Woolson makes Eve's decision to leave Paul, because she believes she has killed his half-brother, strong enough that we have no question about its seriousness. Eve cannot marry Paul until Woolson provides a deus ex machina revealing that Eve did not murder Ferdie. The question we must ask is why provide this and save her from becoming, like Margaret Harold, a genuine martyr, one whose sacrifice is not easy, but hard, causing a great deal of personal pain. On a simple level, the answer may be that Woolson knew her readers would expect it. But as concerned as she was with the question of home, it is consistent that Woolson find a way to provide Eve a home that will not be one of bondage. She cannot give her Jack, for she needs Jack to provide Cicely with a home and for Eve to make her own home with them would be to enter into a different kind of bondage with a woman who hates her. Nor does Woolson want Eve to marry Paul's friend Hollis, a man who loves her but who is too much an older father figure and whom she does not love. The only home Eve can have consistent with her character is with Paul, but on her terms, not his. These terms include economic independence—Eve has an inheritance; social independence—she has broken society's code by shooting Ferdie; and physical power—she has rescued Jack from a near drowning without the help of a man.

Woolson reunites Paul and Eve at the end of *Jupiter Lights* in a scene that allows her to speak out against violence, suggesting that women like Cicely who have been tempted to tolerate violence for the sake of love and home have traded too much. Paul knocks down a priest at a charitable institution to get to Eve to tell her the truth about the real cause of Ferdie's death. This institution is an inappropriate refuge for someone of Eve's passionate nature and is, in fact, itself exploitative, largely, Woolson hints, interested in Eve's money. The woman in charge of the institution stops Paul just as he is about to force open the door that is blocking him from Eve: "Your violence has been unnecessary—the violence of a boor!" (347). Paul "laugh[s] in her face," opens the door, and takes "Eve in his arms" (347). Like the woman who blocks the door, we want to say, yes, his violence is, like Ferdie's, "the violence of a boor." But we also must surmise that despite, or maybe even because of, this display of violence, Paul wins Eve in a way that Woolson's readers might find satisfyingly dramatic. Woolson does not naïvely dismiss Paul's violence but, instead, shows the extent to which women commit themselves to relationships and the extent to which readers romanticize this kind of violence as evidence of love. But because Woolson has linked violence to Ferdie in a more instructive way, she forces us to remember that to be bound to home can constitute the kind of bondage that love has been for Cicely. Because she has earlier made Eve strong enough to resist the bondage of love, we hope that she will marry Paul, and escape the bondage of an institution that is also not a viable home for her, in a union that will allow him to see that violence should not be equated with loving passion.

In her portrait of the girl-woman in *Horace Chase,* Woolson does not expand beyond issues she has previously addressed, and though the novel reads well—it is her funniest, filled with the sarcastic and cynical wit that marks the majority of her fiction—it is also her least textured, as if she has reconciled herself to the inevitability of social codes that deny women autonomy and dignity. In this novel, Woolson explicitly links sexuality with shallowness. Ruth Franklin is spoiled, indulged, entirely natural; she is unconcerned about the implications

of sexuality and acts however she wants without thinking about social forms. Like an indulged child, she has her way in marrying Horace
Chase, who is much her senior, not in any search for home, but because she finds him fun to be with. Woolson exposes the attitude that
it is appropriate for older men to marry younger women by having a
minor character constantly remark on how women age in ways that
men do not. This is similar to the comment that Lanse Harold makes
in *East Angels* about marrying a girl fourteen years his junior because
he "always had a fancy for young girls" though he despairs because
they all seem to grow up (413). The irony, of course, is that, contrary
to the male viewpoint, Woolson shows that women are far better off
when they do grow up, whether this means losing their beauty or not.

In *Horace Chase,* Ruth can easily accept the older Horace because
he has money and can indulge her frivolous nature. Predictably, Ruth
discovers that she has a sexual nature that Horace is not fulfilling and
falls in love with his partner, the younger Walter Willoughby, a man
who flirts with her but ultimately marries the woman he really loves.
Ruth's awakening to her sexuality, late and outside her "happy" marriage, anticipates by five years Kate Chopin's theme in *The Awakening*. But, because she remains a childlike character, Ruth never gains
Edna Pontellier's awareness of the implications of sexuality outside of
marriage. Horace, the father figure, is really the right man for this
nonspeculative woman whose limited view of happiness is so different from Chopin's and from Woolson's own. Still, Woolson refuses to
condescend: given her upbringing and personality, Ruth is suited only
for play love. If Ruth is not cut out for a higher view of life or for
enduring and growing through suffering, she at least has the integrity
of her feelings and whims. She suffers and nearly dies because of her
love for Walter, but because Horace proves to be such a tolerant husband, she is protected from exposure to society and whisked off to
Europe, where we assume she begins to rebuild herself. Importantly,
she tells Horace that she cannot promise she will not do something
similar again and, given her character, we expect that she would follow her sexual instinct. Still, she is honest and fresh, and she may at-
tain the kind of happiness denied the person who possesses the deeper
intelligence Woolson was cursed by herself.

The marriage of Ruth's brother Jared to Genevieve Franklin represents an inversion of the marriage between Horace and Ruth, one in
which the male feels that the freedom he has longed for as a sailor
has been curbed by a serious-minded wife who pursues her passion

not for business but for philanthropy. In the process of gaining the kind of home she wants in marriage, she forces her husband, Jared Franklin, into a life-style he is unsuited for and thinks so little of his well-being that she is indirectly responsible for his death. Genevieve is the kind of wife Henry James Sr. seemed to extol, someone who has "her principles and plans . . . and her rules" (121), a dull do-gooder who would like to stay put and run charitable institutions, solicit donations for worthy causes, and keep an eye on the clergy, all kinds of reform she can pursue from within the socially accepted realm of the home. And yet, in her limited way, Genevieve loves Jared, and even as Woolson blames her, she does show that Genevieve has used her power to find freedom within her marriage to pursue an independent life. Still, Woolson is not so sympathetic to this philanthropist type as Henry James Sr. In fact, she suspected philanthropy as just another form of self-indulgence, writing in her notebook that people are philanthropic because this is what they enjoy being and that they are, therefore, not less self-indulgent than anyone who pursues a personal interest (Benedict 2:112). Woolson sees both Genevieve and Jared as victims of society's expectations. Society has taught them to value men according to how successfully they support a family, whether or not this material dimension provides a satisfying marital relationship, a sense of kinship, or even a permanent place to live. Jared's mother has valued the male within the home so much that she dotes on her son as the only male left in the family and even dies when he dies, as if to say that without a male there can be no home. Significantly the name of her home is *L'Hommedieu,* for home equates with the men she thinks necessary to support it.

Woolson's own character is apparent in all her complex heroines, but the personal connection is the strongest in her portrait of Ruth's sister, Dolly Franklin. She is the only major character in the novels who remains unmarried, and through her Woolson looks again at how the idea of home includes the importance of kindred and the importance of place. She had touched on both these issues before—in *Jupiter Lights,* for example, through Eve's longing for her dead brother in the guise of his child and in *East Angels* in Margaret's purchase of a house—but never without involving as well the idea of a marital home.

As the only unmarried woman in the novel not treated comically, Dolly Franklin represents Woolson's answer for how to reconcile home and independence, a reconciliation closest to the one Woolson sought for herself. She represents the same kind of strong woman that Woolson provides in her other novels in the portraits of Anne, Madame Carroll, Margaret Harold, and Eve Bruce. However, Dolly hasn't the sexual passion of any of these women. Speculation about Henry James to the contrary, at this point in her life Woolson seems less interested in seeing what passion calls forth in a woman than in what steadfast intelligence calls forth. Dolly's intelligence is especially nurtured because her arthritis-like condition, perhaps a metaphor for Woolson's tendency to depression and her habit of loneliness, has limited her options even more than society has limited them. Woolson surely intended Dolly's name to be ironic, for she is no pale, doll-like invalid, but with her acute and lively observations sounds much like Alice James. Even though Horace Chase dismisses her as a meddling spinster, she has superior insight about others and sees why Ruth and many like her need to marry men who will indulge them. At the end of the novel, Dolly reveals not just intelligence but also physical and moral strength when during a storm she saves Ruth, who has tried to run to Walter Willoughby. Dolly returns her to Horace, cautioning her not to tell him the truth because she underestimates his integrity and believes he, like most of society, will reject Ruth. Instead, Horace forgives Ruth and continues to love and value her as his wife. Because Ruth and Horace will now leave *L'Hommedieu* for Europe, Dolly has saved Ruth's marital home at the price of her own last ties to kindred.

Early in *Horace Chase,* Dolly articulates her understanding of how women tend to find homes and, therefore, of why Ruth's marital home is so important. In her comments, she locates the theme that permeates all of Woolson's novels: "Have you ever noticed . . . that the women who sacrifice their lives so nobly to help humanity seldom sacrifice one small thing, and that is a happy home? Either they do not possess such an article, or else they have spoiled it by quarrelling with every individual member of their families" (19). Through all her novels, Woolson presents a consistent vision of women who are homeward bound in the sense that they fight to find or to keep a home. When they sacrifice at all, as in the cases of Anne for Helen's marriage and Eve Bruce for her own integrity, they do so before they have found a home or, as with Madame Carroll's sacrifice of conventional honesty and Margaret Harold's sacrifice of love, they do so for a home.

Read in the light of Dolly's need to reconcile home and independence, the last paragraph of *Horace Chase* becomes more than just melodrama: "Horace Chase put Dolly aside—put her aside forever. He lifted his wife in his arms, and silently bent his head over hers as it lay on his breast" (419). The image of the wife, protected in the arms of her husband, represents the standard role for women in the nineteenth century, the one Woolson's readers would most value. But the image of a cast-aside woman is a fitting one in a society in which women have been so bound to the need for home that many feared that to remain unmarried was to bind them to homelessness and loneliness. Marriage represented to most of Woolson's contemporaries less the danger of limitedness and compromise than the promise of legitimized sexuality, social status, or security. But Woolson's portrait of Dolly Franklin, the woman who by the death of her parents and her brother and the marriage of her younger sister becomes the owner of *L'Hommedieu,* represents a different way to find a home, one that Woolson had touched on most explicitly in *East Angels.* In that novel, not only does Margaret Harold become rooted to East Angels, but Garda Thorne returns to it, and, before her death, Garda's widowed mother found satisfaction in performing household maintenance normally associated with men. That Dolly is cast aside by Horace, that she has no husband and now will lose her tie to kindred, just as Woolson had lost so many of her own ties to kindred, does not mean that she must be homeless. Woolson did not live to write a novel in which she examined closely the struggles a woman like Dolly Franklin might confront as she becomes bound to a home defined as the rootedness of place. But she clearly looked forward to this kind of home for herself, hoping to buy her own little cottage in Florida or to rent a permanent villa in Venice. Had illness, and possibly suicide brought on by her sense of homelessness, not cut short her life, she may have found herself bound to a home that did not limit her as it did so many of her characters.

7

Parents, Children, and the Ties of Family
♣

Jarvis and Hannah Woolson's experience as parents was marked by the sorrow of watching four young daughters die. But they never gave up their obligation to parent the children who lived, an obligation they seem to have approached in a manner consistent with mid-nineteenth-century trends that de-emphasized authoritarianism and emphasized family affection and unity. When their daughter Constance chose not to marry, she chose not to become a parent, but she had internalized parenting values enough that she maintained a strong maternal attitude toward children. She was especially close to her niece Clare Benedict, and she frequently asked about children in letters to friends and relatives. One of her most regular correspondents was her nephew Sam Mather, and in a letter to him she spends several pages asking about the new Mather child whose picture she has been showing off to friends. Her letters to John and Clara Hay often ask that they kiss the children for her and in one she speaks admiringly of Henry James, who "cares more for a child than for a grown person, any day! When there is a child (a nice one) in the room, he can't keep up a conversation" (Petry 42, 24 Apr. 1883).

But if the model of her parents taught her to love children, it also may have fostered in her and in those similarly situated a sense of obligation to relinquish the personal life in order to care for parents. Woolson was nearly thirty when her father died, at which time she chose, as the only unmarried daughter, to become her mother's companion. She replicated this pattern after her mother's death by becoming a traveling companion for her widowed sister Clara and Clara's daughter. Finally, it was Clare Benedict who continued the pattern, remaining a companion to her mother through eighteen journeys to Europe, eleven of them after Constance's death. The obligation to care for a parent fell to females because, though child-rearing models allowed similar freedom for both young boys and young girls, these models still mandated that girls give up tomboyish ways when they reached puberty and assumed that they would enter domestic and care-giving female roles.[1]

The different pattern of expectations for boys and girls was apparent in the Woolson family from the moment of the one son's birth. As Woolson put it in a letter to Sam Mather, her mother's "whole happiness, even her life I might almost say, depends, and has always depended upon how Charly is and how he feels" (WRHS, 24 Feb. 1877). The letter was written in 1877, when Charlie's adult behavioral patterns warranted concern, but the tone of the phrase "has always depended" indicates that Hannah Woolson's pattern of concern was long-standing. Indeed, Hannah's journal reflects just how keenly she saw Charlie as different: "after eight little girls comes the one boy. . . . I could not but notice the difference—throughout his infancy and childhood—between the sisters and this their only brother. He would not be petted, and made a baby of . . . " (Benedict 1:166). Because Hannah Woolson had borne eight children before Charlie and because the family had a predisposition to depression, it is impossible with the few records available to see how much Charlie's behavior was a result of family and societal dynamics and how much a result of heredity. Whatever his life was like, it was troubling enough that Clare Benedict went as far as leaving him off the family tree, and it added to the factors that helped shape Woolson's fictional themes.

All of these personal factors—the deaths of her sisters, her father's involvement in her childhood, her care giving to her mother, and her more highly valued but dissipated brother—combine with the context of the women's fiction published during Woolson's childhood and young adulthood to inform her vision of how parent-child relationships bind one to home. Nina Baym has located a substructure in nineteenth-century fiction that reveals women trying to overcome "recurrent injustices occasioned by [their] status as female and child." Within this structure, "there are very few intact families . . . , and those that are intact are unstable or locked into routines of misery." Nineteenth-century writers of popular fiction, says Baym, seek an end to injustice not through female isolation but by a redefinition of family: "men as well as women find greatest happiness and fulfillment in domestic relations, by which are meant not simply spouse and parent, but the whole network of human attachments based on love, support, and mutual responsibility."[2] Mary Kelley has argued that this attention to domestic relations enabled women to choose writing as a career without really entering the public sphere, a place open to them only at the expense of their more highly valued domestic roles.[3] Neither Baym nor Kelley discusses Woolson, because she wrote after the peak of the popular domestic genre and because her fiction is more consciously literary than that genre, but Woolson's own traditional but deeply scarred family background, her domestic habits, and her position as a woman who grew up during the heyday of the domestic novel and the primacy of debates over marriage and divorce shaped her into a writer keenly aware of the implications of valuing domestic roles, not only in terms of marriage but also in terms of how one behaved as a parent or a child.

Given the late appearance of Charlie into the Woolson household, it is not surprising that the impact of gender on parent-child relationships is especially apparent in Woolson's fiction. Recent studies about gender, particularly by Nancy Chodorow and Carol Gilligan, are remarkably consistent with Woolson's observations and measure how extraordinarily perceptive Woolson was. When Hannah Woolson wrote that Charlie "would not be petted, and made a baby of," she anticipates the findings of Chodorow, who explains the tendency for males to detach themselves from relationships in terms of their sense of difference from the mother. Because they identify themselves as not like the mother—in most cases their primary care giver—they emphasize their separateness rather than their connectedness to others. From a social science perspective, the validity of Chodorow's findings are suspect, and they have not been embraced by the social sciences as much as they have by the humanities. But the point for a study of a writer like Woolson rests in the perception of observable differences in gender relationships rather than in the cause of these differences or in their universality. The literary motif of the isolated male seeking his fulfillment in the West and the real-life case of Charlie, who left home and family for California, are simply extreme paradigms of normal male behavior in a society in which males are taught to value independence over connectedness. Females, on the other hand, relate to their care giver as the same. Gilligan's work emphasizes the increasing connectedness women find to others as they mature into responsible adults. Where the maturation of males works toward autonomy, the maturation of females works toward autonomy within connectedness; where males subordinate relationships to independent achievement, women subordinate achievement in order to preserve relationships. Again, the literary models of women as domestic nurturer and Woolson's commitment to her family despite its encroachment on her independence reflect current theories of female development.

Woolson did not have, or need, the benefit of Chodorow's and Gilligan's research, but, in addition to her observations of the social patterns of the nineteenth century, she had another model for seeing women as integrating with the mother, that of the goddess myths that were being uncovered and reinterpreted in the mid- and late nineteenth century. Cheryl Torsney's study of Woolson has discussed her emphasis on various myths as a subtext in her fiction. Of particular interest is her use of the Demeter-Persephone myth, in which Persephone has been kidnapped and raped by Pluto, the god of the underworld. Zeus intervenes and forces Pluto to free Persephone, who returns to her mother, Demeter, the goddess of agriculture and fertility. Demeter has been withholding her bounty from the earth as she mourns for Persephone, and when mother and daughter are reunited, Demeter renews the earth. But this ritual of renewal is cyclical because Persephone has eaten some pomegranate seeds and, as punishment, must return to Pluto for a few months each year.

Torsney reads this myth in terms of Woolson's treatment of the conflict between nature and art, with the female's creative spirit being threatened by male power—Persephone in some versions has been chosen by Zeus to be kidnapped by Pluto because she has intruded on the power of the gods.[4] Many in the nineteenth century saw similar gender implications in myths. Thomas Wentworth Higginson, Margaret Fuller, and Charlotte Perkins Gilman all were interested in uncovering goddess myths, and Annie Fields wrote a poem to Persephone. In her discussion of this primacy of the goddess myth, Sarah Sherman shows how the Persephone myth in particular reflects the same kind of findings that Chodorow and Gilligan discuss. Having been kidnapped by Pluto, Persephone is reintegrated with the mother in a way that is both independent and connective—she still returns to Pluto, but the result of her cycle of separation from and attachment to the mother is the fertility that results in the spring (Sherman 166–67). Consciously or unconsciously, Woolson had a model for independence that associated Pluto with her father and the freedom to join him in his travels. This independence enabled her to use her later transient life to develop friendships largely in terms of mutual professional interests, with people like John Hay, E. C. Stedman, and Henry James. At the same time, however, she maintained her connectedness to the Persephone figure through the companionship she gave to her mother, her sister, and her niece.

Woolson's treatment of parent-child relationships in her fiction is informed by this sense of herself as a daughter as well as by the societal and mythological paradigms of male-female roles. Her fictional themes develop in a way that is remarkably consistent with her own life experiences. She moves from exploring how the female child defines herself in relationship to the father, able to break from him only when he dies, to exploring how male children abandon mothers and how female children remain connected to them. Her parent-child relationships fall into three categories: the relationship between father and daughter, between mother and son, and between mother and daughter. Lyon Richardson believes that Woolson's father-daughter relationships are more fully realized than mother-daughter relationships, but if one takes all of the fiction into account it becomes apparent that Woolson focuses on fathers and daughters more often in her early fiction written shortly after the death of her father and that the notion of mothering becomes predominant in the fiction written in Europe after her mother's death. Furthermore, Woolson examines mother-child relationships with both younger and grown children, distinguishing here between male independence and female connectedness. Any father–younger child relationships are usually between fathers and sons and exist more as asides in the fiction than as developed relationships. In *Anne,* for example, the twice-widowed father has three young sons and a thirteen-year-old daughter by his second marriage, but the central relationship is between him and the sixteen-year-old daughter from his first marriage. In *For the Major,* the major, who is approaching senility, educates his son Scar into a gamelike code of honor that suggests a childhood friendship more than a father-son relationship.

In Woolson's fiction concerning fathers and grown daughters, the connectedness the daughter brings to the relationship is so strong that at least two commentators have read these relationships in terms of incest themes,[5] but they suggest less the sexual or incestuous than Chodorow's and Gilligan's theories about female development. Most often, the relationships depend on the daughter's caring for an ailing or inept father. As if she realized that too much care giving could inhibit women's growth, Woolson typically has the father die, freeing the daughter to abandon her role as nurse-wife and to marry more independently, according to her own wishes. Yet Woolson did not feel that her own father hindered her possibility for marriage, beginning to think of herself as a "desolate spinster" when her father was alive and healthy.[6] Rather than feeling freed by his death, she was haunted by the fact that she had been on a pleasure trip when he died. In a letter she wrote to John Hay after her father's death she indicates that the relationship had been extremely close: "I have never recovered from the sense of desolation I felt when I lost my father; the world has never been the same to me since, for he made a pet of me" (Petry, 26 Dec. 1885). In making a pet of her, he also hindered her ability to find her own identity, for it is only after his death that she began to write.

As Woolson sought her identity through writing the early fiction, she also confronted the loss of her father. The theme of the death of the father first appears in "Castle Nowhere," in which the girl Silver is not freed to marry until the death of Old Fog, the father figure. The death of the father motif occurs again in several stories in *Rodman the Keeper,* most fully in "Old Gardiston," in which the father figure is an old uncle who tries to keep the southern tradition alive by writing a meticulous genealogy and in which the female protagonist would rather starve than marry a northerner. With the death of her uncle and the burning of the genealogy and their dilapidated home, the young woman is freed from her southern pride and does marry the northerner. And again the motif occurs in *For the Major:* the subplot necessitates that the father figuratively die—by becoming senile—before the daughter plans marriage. In an interesting reversal of this theme, Rodman in the story "Rodman the Keeper," we learn, cared for his mother before coming south. Rodman's desire had been not to marry but to go west. Once his mother dies and he has fought in the Civil War, he gives up this dream and returns south, at this point fleeing from the rejection of a northern woman and choosing the solitary life of tending a cemetery in the South for northern soldiers. This is one of the few stories of Woolson's in which a significant male is a care giver and one cannot help but notice that the care giving is to the dead, where the connectedness does not allow for intimacy.

We see Woolson confronting her ambivalence about the love and confinement generated in father-daughter relationships most clearly in her first novel *Anne.* Anne's father, William Douglas, shares Woolson's father's tendency to be clinically depressed. This, the loss of two wives, and an artistic temperament combine to make Douglas a loving but dependent father who uses Anne to care for the younger children and to tend to the domestic chores. Woolson captures Anne's dilemma when the father is in the last stages of a depression that ends with his death: "For strange patience have loving women ever had with dreamers like William Douglas—men who, viewed by the eyes of the world, are useless and incompetent. . . . For personally there is a sweetness and gentleness in their natures which make them very dear to the women who love them. The successful man, perhaps, would not care for such love, which is half devotion, half protection; the successful man wishes to domineer" (91). The problem with this, as Woolson sees, is that the nondomineering, dependent father has the same impact on the daughter who cares for him as a more domineering man would have. For as long as she must care for her father, Anne can "never [live] for herself or in herself" (91). Still, Anne's service to her father has its compensations. Although she lives in a shabby and financially insecure home, she can dream of the time when she will be able to decorate each of the rooms according to her taste. She has a sense of place, she is loved and loves, and she has an important role in caring for the younger children.

Douglas's death provides the plot device Woolson needs to allow Anne to go to New York, where she will begin her journey to adulthood and her reintegration into connectedness that finally occurs in her marriage to Ward Heathcote. Her long period of independence allows her to awaken to herself and her own potential, a potential she could never have achieved had she remained the daughter of a loving but needy father. In the novel, Woolson also works out a more typical pattern of male-female relationships in the elopement of Tita with Erastus Pronando, Anne's fiancé early in the novel. We can read her elopement as an act of rebellion directed not just toward a sister who never recognized her as more than a child, but also toward a father who preferred that sister. In fact, while he lived, Douglas looked at Tita as a personification of his error in marrying her mother: she represented for him "his own mistakes" (12) and was someone he cautioned Anne to "stand by" but not to "expect too much of" because of "her Indian blood" (20). By having Tita and Pronando elope, Woolson provides Tita with space away from a home that has discriminated against her heritage even though that space depends on her finding a substitute father figure in the husband who is considerably older than she.

In the later fiction written in Europe, Woolson's patterns change to emphasize mothers' relationships with their children rather than fathers' with their daughters. Where the early fiction suggests that Woolson was confronting the loss of her father, the sense that families are always doomed to suffer losses, and the question of independence from care-giving roles, the later fiction suggests that with the death of her mother, she was now confronting questions about mother-child relationships. Although Woolson had approached the nature of mothering to young children in her early fiction, she did so only peripherally, using children to intensify the sense of loss she associates with mothering. In the early fiction, the loss usually centers on young male children, the gender that separates more than relates. She uses the death of a young male child as background to "St. Clair Flats" in the *Castle Nowhere* volume and the death of a genderless child in "Sister St. Luke" in *Rodman the Keeper*. In the latter volume, even the strongest mother-child story, "In the Cotton Country," distances the process of mothering by using a narrative method that reports the loss of a young son to a northern guardian rather than shows the relationship between the child and the mother figure. Later in her novella *For the Major*, Woolson uses mothering as the impetus behind her protagonist's duplicitous marriage, again associating mothering with loss. In order to marry and provide her female child with a home, Madame Carroll cannot even acknowledge the existence of her son, whom she believes dead. After the marriage, the child dies, and *For the Major*, like many of the mother-young child stories in *Castle Nowhere* and *Rodman the Keeper*, associates mothering with the child's death, an event Woolson experienced so often in her own family.

In her later fiction, Woolson looks more closely at mother-young son relationships, which center on exclusion rather than connectedness, as if women's desire for affiliation goes awry when the relationship involves sons. The boy in her story "In Venice" from *The Front Yard* collection, for example, is being parented by an aunt and uncle. A rather obnoxious Randolph Miller figure, he is carted around Europe and uses the excuse of illness to pester and to whine. The aunt caters to him so much that she nearly loses her husband to an infatuation for a younger woman. In fact, the marriage remains intact only because the boy dies, once again underscoring Woolson's inability to find a model for dual parenting: to parent seems to negate marriage; marriage, to negate parenting.

Woolson's novel *Jupiter Lights* is her most interesting presentation of parenting issues. It explores not just the relationship between a mother and young son but also how this relationship excludes the child's aunt, Eve Bruce. Eve wants to make the child her ward so that she can find a sense of family through him. Perhaps because her own mother died in childbirth, she has had a possessive love for her father and brother, both now dead, and she wants to continue this kind of love through her brother's son. The male orientation is strong enough that it earns her the comment that "[a]ny one can see that she has been brought up by a man" because she is sheltered and spoiled (15). Her desire is unrealistic and selfish, and ultimately she loses the child to his natural mother. As in so much of Woolson's fiction, there are no intact family units and the idea of mothering is associated with loss. An interesting scene encapsulates the theme. The young boy is stranded in a storm in a canoe, and Eve saves him. The rescue allows the boy to live, but for Eve the boy really dies in this scene because despite her heroic efforts, the natural mother will not relinquish him. Just as Anne Douglas in Woolson's first novel cannot become the natural mother of her stepbrothers and her stepsister, Eve cannot take the place of her nephew's natural mother. Nor can the process of mothering be fully realized through the natural mother because, like Woolson's mother, she has been traumatized by death, in this case not of other children but of her second husband. At the same time that the novel examines how much a mother—or an aunt—may love a child, it dramatizes a weak relationship between mother and child. So fraught with pain or so biologically impossible is mothering that Woolson, despite the love for children expressed in her letters, finds it difficult to suspend the idea of pain or exclusion to look at the daily interaction between mother and child.

Besides the issue of mothering and loss, *Jupiter Lights* addresses the issue of child abuse. The abuse is severe enough that the child here has his arm broken by his stepfather. Larry Wolff's study of child abuse in Freud's Vienna in 1899 indicates just how unrecognized a problem it was in the Western world even at the end of the nineteenth century. Vienna, according to Wolff, had a unique opportunity in 1899 to begin to focus on child abuse because of two highly publicized trials, one involving a mother who shot her illegitimate daughter and one involving a mother and father who tortured their eight children, one of whom died. In conjunction with these cases, the Vienna courts heard a rash of abuse cases, most having to do with overstepping the bounds of discipline. At the same time that parenting was becoming less authoritarian, physical punishment was still acceptable practice.

The main transgressions that surfaced in the Vienna case of the eight children were masturbation and other kinds of sexual experimentation. Antimasturbation devices included leather straps, metal cages, handcuffs, and spikes. Wolff speculates that this kind of obsession about children's sexual depravity was the basis for the governess's behavior toward the children in "The Turn of the Screw." Ellen Moers also has speculated that much of the childhood roughhousing in the nineteenth-century nursery came to be associated, in the minds of sisters, with the erotic (160–61), and Jean Strouse applies this theory to Alice James's relationship to her brothers, particularly the youngest, Robertson (28). The strength of the connection between childhood sexuality and women is reflected in the fact that concerns about masturbation and sexuality appear not just in references to children but also in the American medical literature about hysterical women.[7]

Woolson did not share the conflict with four brothers that Alice James had, or write a story in which the overtones of sexual abuse are as strong as James's "The Turn of the Screw" and "The Pupil." Although like much of her fiction, *Jupiter Lights* develops the link between women and children, the issues of childhood sexuality and the limits of punishment are missing. The boy is only a toddler and is attacked simply because his father is drunk. Woolson follows the pattern of her contemporaries and misses the variety of causes of child abuse by seeing it only in the context of alcohol abuse. The relationship between alcohol and abuse became a prominent issue in nineteenth-century life and literature. Barbara Epstein has traced an increase in alcohol consumption in the mid-nineteenth century, triggered by the movement of work outside the home. She has shown how men's drinking habits altered: as their lives no longer allowed alcohol consumption during work at home, they frequented taverns, which were no longer serving as family gathering places. Epstein has also shown that as abuses became more apparent, women enlarged their evangelical involvement to include social reform, particularly as it involved the temperance movement. However, neither these reform movements nor novels like *Jupiter Lights* or, later, Stephen Crane's *Maggie: A Girl of the Streets* precipitated an enlightened discussion of physical abuse outside the context of alcoholism. In fact, according to Wolff, not until 1962 with the publication in the *Journal of the American Medical*

Association of "The Battered-Child Syndrome," did people begin to acknowledge that there were all too many cases like the one Woolson depicts and that these were not all connected with alcohol.

Although Woolson fails to pursue the causes, outside of alcoholism, of physical abuse, she is keenly tuned to issues of emotional abuse. "A Transplanted Boy" should be read in terms of child neglect that is severe enough to result in a child's probable death. In the story, Woolson asks, "How does one parent without a sense of place?" and answers, "Badly," especially if that lack of a sense of place is accompanied by a lack of one's sense of herself as a woman free from dependence on men for financial survival. The fact that the child in the story is male actually makes the parental neglect worse. To fail to educate a female child is to ensure that she remain dependent on others, her success marked by how she can manipulate her appearance to attract men; to fail to educate a male child, especially when that child is, like Maso, unattractive, is to provide him with no way of surviving. Maso cannot take care of himself, yet society's expectations are that he will eventually take care of his mother. Because he is a male child, Violet Roscoe can leave him with a tutor and because he is male he can wander the streets of Italy looking for work. Before he has even reached puberty, he has internalized society's expectations to be manly and has tried to become a protector rather than a dependent, but his ill-education has transplanted him from a role as supporter/male to dependent/female, without anyone available for him to depend on. By failing to mother adequately, Violet Roscoe in the long run dooms herself as well as her child.

The gender implications in "A Transplanted Boy" are subtle, subordinated to Woolson's interest in the need for rootedness. In an earlier story in the *Rodman* collection called "Felipa," the gender implications as they connect to parenting are central and provocative. The child Felipa's parents are dead and she is being cared for by her grandparents. Like Maso, she lacks companions and has centered most of her affection on her dog. Dressing always in a dead boy's clothing, Felipa is so isolated that she has seen only three women before the arrival of the female artist-narrator, Catherine, and her friend, Christine: her old grandmother, a Seminole Indian woman, and the "wife of Miguel," who has no name of her own (*Rodman* 205). The narrator's wording here is apt, for Felipa's behavior in the course of the story points up Woolson's sense of the invisibility of women. Felipa becomes fascinated with the two women, particularly with Christine after her fiancé Edward Bowne arrives, and together these three become the parent figures. Unable to differentiate between Christine and Edward, she tries to win their love by copying Christine and dressing in a white dress that she thinks will make her pretty. The narrator helps her to sew a more appropriate dress for herself, one that she believes complements rather than wars against her Minorcan blood. This Minorcan blood makes her a southern version of Tita in *Anne,* an equation that represents a stereotypical connection of passion and race. Edward readily calls her pretty, but Catherine is more puzzled by Felipa's appearance and Christine, whose beauty is more socially contrived, rejects her entirely. When Felipa learns that Edward and Christine will marry and leave her, she tries to commit suicide by poisoning herself and to stab Edward before she dies. Felipa survives her attempted suicide, and the story ends with her grandfather saying, "It was two loves, and the stronger thrust the knife" (*Rodman* 220), an ambiguous comment that may refer to Felipa's love being stronger than the love between Christine and Edward.

With the male-female Felipa and the Christine-Edward unity, it is appropriate to read the story as one about androgyny. Joan Weimer reads it as one where "women [Felipa and Catherine] who love women lose them to men," emphasizing Felipa as Catherine's alter ego and Catherine's repression of her love for Christine into art, which cannot be successful because it represses rather than expresses feelings (*MG* xxxiv). Cheryl Torsney also emphasizes the story in terms of its portrait of the artist and the conflict between androgynous art and male-defined art. For Torsney, Christine is the male version of the beautiful woman and Catherine and Felipa are both marginalized from male-oriented culture, their own gender identification in a transitional position between the male-principled land and the female-principled sea.[8] Both of these interpretations connect sexuality or passion and art and show how the female voice has been repressed by patriarchal cultures where femaleness gets lost without beauty and without male approval. What matters is not that Felipa seems male but that she does not know what it means to be female. This connects to issues of parenting when we see Felipa rejecting the possibilities of connectedness offered by the mother figure embodied in Catherine. Felipa looks for a model of parenting that makes mother-father-child an inextricable unit rather than one based on negotiated relationships. Because she has not been parented to learn autonomy as well as connectedness, she can only feel rejected when the male-female love excludes her. Had Felipa been socialized as female, she might have accepted a connected relationship to Catherine or a marginalized one with Christine-Edward. Had she been socialized as male, she would have sought her independence.

In "Felipa," neither the mother-child nor the dual parent-child relationship is successful in providing a familial home, the first because the child rejects the mother, the second because the parents reject the child. But though Felipa may have found autonomy had she been socialized as male, Woolson does not suggest that Felipa's socialization as a male would have been preferable to her androgyny. In fact, if we look at Woolson's fictional relationships between mothers and adult sons, we see how much she associated sons with betrayal. We see the pattern of the adult male disappointing the mother first in "Miss Elisabetha" in *Rodman the Keeper,* in which the mother figure, a northern spinster-aunt, has come south to care for her orphaned nephew, who ultimately disappoints his industrious aunt by marrying a Minorcan girl with whom he leads an indolent life. This pattern becomes a prodigal son motif in *For the Major* and *East Angels:* in *For the Major* the mother nurses her adult son, who had been raised by his father, a murderer, and who led a mysterious foreign life until, impoverished, he returns to his mother in his dying hours; in *East Angels* one mother figure, an aunt, makes her home with her nephew's wife, Margaret Harold, while the nephew, whom she always favors over Margaret, whose maiden name she insists on using, has an affair in Europe. Even in *Jupiter Lights,* an unrelated spinster loves the abusive Ferdie Morrison "as the prodigal is often so dearly loved by the woman whose heart is pierced the most deeply by his excesses—his mother. . . . For she was a woman who would have rejoiced in sons; daughters would never have been important to her" (222). Four of the Italian stories collected in *The Front Yard* also develop the prodigal flaw into the kind of serious defect Ferdie Morrison possesses, and all four emphasize the mother's love for the son. One is a character only mentioned, a "ne'er-do-well, a rolling stone," a son who is not "dutiful" but whom the mother loves more than the daughter ("The Street of the Hyacinth," *FY* 186); one is a stepson, again the most loved child even though he gambles away the stepmother's carefully saved money ("The Front Yard"); one is a murderer and a robber whom the mother protects by working and pretending to be young, though she is past seventy ("A Christmas Party"); and one suffers from a hereditary disposition toward uncontrollable anger that results in a near-murder and his own suicide ("Neptune's Shore").

Only the last of these stories focuses on the son closely, for Woolson is less interested in characterizing a defect than in documenting her belief that heredity can account for some kinds of behavior. Thus this son possesses a disposition that he had "ever sence [*sic*] he was born" (*FY* 86), one whose turbulence is compared to Neptune's or the sea's. Again, though, Woolson misses an opportunity to examine how this hereditary disposition can impact on violence in the home. The story reveals what a terrible burden the mother is under, but it does not show the son abusive toward any family member. The mother is so worried and vigilant about her son that she can focus on nothing else. The son is a prodigal son, but only because of heredity, thus he is absolved of responsibility. Feeling a personal connection to a prodigal brother but also feeling limited in her ability to write from the male perspective, Woolson develops the archetype from the mother's rather than the prodigal's point of view. At the same time that she exposes the injustice of mothers' preferences for sons, she focuses on the pain the son causes the mother and on the mother's inability to betray the child who does not deserve her love. As in the stories featuring mothers and young children, in her stories of mothers and grown sons, Woolson expresses her dis-ease with the idea that mothering can be fulfilling as well as painful.

Woolson's vision of mothers and grown daughters shows as much dis-ease as her portraits of mothers and grown sons. Perhaps because her connectedness to her own mother inhibited her freedom, she fails to confront the issues facing mothers and grown daughters in her early fiction. She does not address these issues at all in the stories written before her mother's death, and even in the novels she subordinates them to other kinds of relationships. *Anne,* published shortly after the death of Woolson's mother, centers on a motherless protagonist; *For the Major* is primarily a father-daughter, mother-son story and although the stepmother and daughter do have a strong relationship, the daughter has been living away from home and sees her stepmother more as a friend than a mother; *Jupiter Lights* has no mother-daughter units. In *East Angels* and *Horace Chase,* the mother-daughter relationships cease when the mothers in both novels die.

The pattern is particularly interesting in *East Angels* because the mother wants her daughter to marry someone the daughter sees as a surrogate father. The daughter escapes this fate, however, when Margaret Harold, the woman whom her dying mother appointed as guardian, does not force the issue. As a result, the guardian mother figure, unhampered by the need to control the daughter's, and therefore her own, future, becomes the ideal mother, able to let the daughter choose her future. This future, however, is rather limited because while the mother lived, she spoiled the daughter so much that she is fit only to become a child-wife. The same kind of spoiling occurs in *Horace Chase*. Here, the mother defines herself so much in terms of her male child that she accuses his wife, with some justification but with unreasonable cruelty, of causing the son's death. She has replicated her preference for males in one of her daughters, who sees her brother's death as the loss of her only support, though she has a husband for financial support and a sister for emotional support. Believing her daughters taken care of by her son-in-law, that is by the male they need, the mother dies immediately after the son dies. Daughters, in here and in so many of Woolson's later works, are either literally motherless or are mothered in a way that denies them the love and autonomy accorded to sons.

Woolson addresses the mother-grown daughter relationship again in "The Street of the Hyacinth" (*FY*), though this is more a story about gender and art than it is about mothers and daughters. It does, however, portray a daughter, Ethelinda (Ettie) Faith Macks, who at first refuses marriage to Raymond Noel, a man she believes willing to accept her mother with her, but unwilling to respect the mother. The mother has been divorced and remarried, an aside Woolson tells us about for no apparent reason except to emphasize how much a spur she is in her daughter's side, especially in light of the nineteenth-century attitudes toward divorce. But instead of spurring her daughter to achieve as an artist, she spurs her to sacrifice her life to fulfill her role as the good daughter. In fact, Ettie defines her relationships according to how people treat her mother. An admirer, a famous painter whose proposal she refuses because she does not love him, she judges as having an "unbounded" goodness because if "he had lived he would have remained always a faithful, kind, and respectful son to my dear mother. That, of course, would have been everything to me" (*FY* 173). This admirer stands in marked contrast to Ettie's brother, whom the narrative calls "the dearest child of the two, as the prodigal always is" (*FY* 187). When Ettie goes to America to bury her brother, Noel attends to her mother so much that, on her return, Ettie listens to her praise him "most as if he was my real son" (*FY* 188). Ettie's loyalty to her mother has kept her from suicide when she began to believe herself an artist of no talent: "I had my mother to think of," she tells Noel in explanation of how she has survived her belief in her lack of talent, "my—good sense might not have been so faithful otherwise" (*FY* 175). When the home she and her mother have inhabited in the Street of the Hyacinth is about to be torn down, Ettie, despite her resolve not to marry Noel, breaks down, thus making the final sacrifice of marrying someone whom we have come to see as lacking both depth and integrity.

If we read "The Street of the Hyacinth" alongside "A Transplanted Boy," in which the young son serves his mother at his own expense, we see Woolson at the end of her career questioning the value of devotion when the giver loses so much for an undeserving person. Mothers serve their adult sons no matter what their defect while more typically adult daughters serve their mothers no matter what the cost to themselves. The adult male breaks away from the mother either by disappointing her or by dying; the adult female supports her mother, ultimately having to define herself by connectedness rather than independence. The displacement of this motif onto the young male child in "A Transplanted Boy" suggests Woolson's belief that to define oneself as connected keeps the female a child. But even in "A Transplanted Boy," Maso's devotion to his mother gives him an independence that none of the adult daughters find, an independence that Woolson herself found only after the death of her mother when she began to learn that independence also meant loneliness.

Woolson's observations about connectedness and disconnectedness are consistent with her relationship to her mother. The biographical connection is most prominent in "The Street of the Hyacinth," but Sybil Weir also sees Woolson's devotion to her mother reflected in *East Angels,* in which the protagonist gives up love to remain married and, thus, to continue her allegiance to her husband's aunt, one of the mother figures in the novel. Weir believes that Woolson was willing "to sacrifice her own ambition to care for her invalid mother" (145). Rayburn Moore concurs when, as Weir points out, he sees Woolson at her mother's death as being at last "free to live her own life."[9] At the end of her career, Woolson began to ask what might have been for her had she not been such a devoted daughter. Her ambivalence over mother-daughter relationships may also have been intensified by her relationship to Clare Benedict, thus explaining why the mother figures in her fiction are so often aunts. Woolson saw in Clare an almost frightening version of herself, writing to a friend about how mentally alike they were, though she learned to cover her own reticence: "I repeat, it is extraordinary how much she is like me! I see myself right over again as I was at thirteen (I mean mentally)."[10] Like Woolson, Clare Benedict remained single all her life and traveled as a companion to her own mother, who depended on her daughter's legacy for her financial well-being. Clare and Clara Benedict spent little time apart from one another. In addition to Clare's attachment to her mother, her attachment to her aunt was extraordinary, and even a bit embarrassing. If, before her death, Woolson had begun to brood on what might have been for her had she not devoted herself to her mother, she might well have been prompted by a sense of her niece's devotion at a time when her niece could have been developing attachments apart from her mother and aunt.

While one may speculate that Woolson was ambivalent about her devotion to her mother, she never regretted these years or admitted a wish that she had chosen a different path. As grieved as she was by her father's death, she was even more devastated by her mother's. She expressed this grief in a letter to her friend Jane Averell Carter, saying she is haunted by the question of whether she could have done something more to prolong her mother's life but feeling comforted by Carter's assurance that her efforts actually did prolong that life (Benedict 2:24–25). In a letter to Paul Hayne, she wrote about her "effort . . . to break up the depression which took possession of [her] after the death of [her] dearest Mother in Florida, just one year ago" (Hubbell 734, 16 Feb. 1880).

The late story "A Pink Villa," collected in *The Front Yard,* illustrates well the ambivalence Woolson felt. The story's mother figure expects her daughter to marry someone who would enable both of them to live comfortably in Europe. Instead, the daughter chooses her freedom, in effect leaving the mother stranded. The story ends with a question: "And the mother?" (*FY* 136). Whether or not this is the kind of question Woolson might have asked herself, she does show only two patterns in her fiction for the relationship between mother and child: mothers who demand, however subtly, service from their children, thus causing the children to lose their freedom; or children who die or in some other way renege on their filial responsibilities, thus betraying their mothers. Both paths are unattractive, and Woolson examines them more closely as she ages. Often expressing loneliness in her European years, she may have wondered if she might have been less lonely had she become a mother. But, with the societal pressures on women to produce large numbers of children and with her family's loss of so many children, she may have found the cost of parenting too high. As she confronts the nature of mothering in her fiction, she suggests that mothering replaces loneliness only when there is a corresponding loss of freedom. While she knew that others criticized her free life of traveling for its lack of "*duties*," she also was quick to defend her choice, asking in her notebooks why people without families shouldn't be allowed the pleasures of travel: "They did not marry and have children; then let them have the pleasures of such a life, since they have not those of the family. Family people appear to think that unmarried people are very self-indulgent because they want to amuse themselves. It does not occur to them that they (the married) gave themselves the pleasures which *they* preferred" (Benedict 2:111–12).

In studying the patterns of parent-child relationships in fiction, it is wise to remember that writers tend to confront those parts of life that they brood on, that they try to come to grips with. Happy families have never been the subject of much literature or have been the subject of literature relegated to the category of juvenile. The part of life that Woolson broods on in her fiction centers over and over again on the painful choices women must make. For Woolson's female characters, unlike for her male characters, life consists of negative either/or propositions: one can choose family and loss, or solitude and exile. Woolson had exile chosen for her when her mother died. Once her relationship to a parent was no longer an issue, she chose what Chodorow and Gilligan, perhaps too insistently, define as a male model of behavior. Freed from obligation to her mother, her wandering became her strength, for it gave her the freedom she needed to write and, despite her worries about financial insecurity, the financial means she needed to live. But in her bouts of depression, she did lament her lack of connectedness. Having been close to a family that shaped her and left her, she never engendered a family so that she could reproduce herself as mother to young children.

In Woolson's day, women had few models that joined both freedom and family, making it inevitable that this model would not be central in their literature or their lives. The belief that writing and child rearing are incompatible, as if child rearing saps a woman's creative juices, has been so long ingrained in our culture that only in 1989 did Ursula Le Guin pose the obvious possibility that child rearing, as much as it may slow the quantity of writing, may be the catalyst to some women's creativity. In Woolson's day, it was difficult to maintain a writing career and a family, but many women did so: E. D. E. N. Southworth raised two children after her husband deserted her, Helen Hunt Jackson had two sons, Kate Chopin had five children, and Harriet Beecher Stowe raised six. Still, even today, we mythologize the separateness of the female creative and procreative spheres, remembering more than mother-writers, women like Emily Dickinson, Sarah Orne Jewett, Mary Wilkins Freeman, Louisa May Alcott, and Charlotte Perkins Gilman, who was ostracized by society for not raising her child the way society demanded,[11] and Edith Wharton, whose experience with children was so minimal she once asked for help in understanding how they talked.[12] Although Woolson fits this model, she also observed fully its implications. She saw that family relationships involve more than the way parents raise young children, but that whether the children are young or old and the parents mothers or fathers, the burden for the relationship falls on women. The depth of this vision allows us to see Woolson as an example of a woman who observed closely the impact of limited choices on women and who examined parent-child relationships in a way that anticipates current theories about women's commitment to attachment and responsibility. At the same time, her successful pursuit of a career that has been open to women longer than the canon suggests and her choice of a life-style that allowed independence and solitude illustrates that women are not bound to accept patterns of behavior that are gender-identified within familial homes.

8

The Social and Economic Position of Spinsters and Widows

♣

When Woolson began to think of herself as a spinster, she did so against a social background that was dealing with rapid demographic change. After the Civil War, not only was it more difficult for a woman to find a home by marrying because of the shortage of males, but there also was increasing pressure on middle- and upper-class women to bear children, partly because of the fear that immigrant populations were outproducing Anglo-Saxon populations and, in addition, to replenish the country after its war losses. As early as 1817, historical records show discussion of abortion, and in 1832 Charles Knowlton peddled a book on contraception called *Fruits of Philosophy; or, The Private Companion of Adult People*. For this he was arrested, yet prior to the Civil War there were numerous thinly disguised advertisements for abortions as well as advertisements for diaphragms and condoms. After the war, the unrest about contraception and abortion turned into a major legal battle. The first conviction for an abortion-related death was handed down in 1871. In the 1870s, at least forty physicians, some of them prominent, were prosecuted for performing abortions. The YMCA initiated an anti-abortion campaign, but eventually diverted its campaign to its original spokesperson, Anthony Comstock, because of the unpopularity of its position. Comstock managed to have a law passed in 1873 making both abortion and contraception illegal.[1] Even though statistics show that the birthrate continued to decline throughout the nineteenth century, had Woolson married, she would have done so in an atmosphere that pressured women to bear children at the same time that it composed novels that had moved from showing graphic deaths in childbirth to offering alternatives to childbirth through education.[2] With a mother who had borne nine children, four of whom died in childhood, Woolson might well have seen spinsterhood, despite its low status, as preferable to childbearing.

The word *spinster* derives from the occupation of spinning, but by the seventeenth century it was the legal designation of a woman who had not married. As they defined the legal status of women, the United States and Great Britain both used William Blackstone's *Commentaries on the Laws of England (1765–69)* to interpret British Common Law. This interpretation allowed spinsters to own property, enter into contracts, write wills, be legal guardians, and administer estates, all of which a woman gave up when she married.[3] Her status then changed from *feme sole* to *feme covert,* wherein her rights were subsumed by marriage, with her husband having legal power and only a moral obligation to see to the welfare of his wife. By the nineteenth century in the United States, there was debate over and reform of women's property laws. Most new laws, rather than being initiated because of unfairness to women, were enacted in order to prevent a woman's property, usually the result of a dowry, from being seized if her husband had incurred debts or bankruptcy. Even under the old system, wealthy women had their property protected by their fathers, who often drew up trust funds and prenuptial contracts for their daughters.

By Woolson's day, most states had revised property laws so that women had full rights of controlling the property they brought to a marriage. The debate had been carried on in a body of fiction as well as in the press and the legislatures. Woolson's great-uncle, James Fenimore Cooper, was vehemently opposed to women's property rights, addressing the issues most explicitly in *The Pioneers* (1823), *Home as Found* (1838), *The Redskins* (1846), and *The Ways of the Hour* (1850). Fanny Fern's *Ruth Hall* (1855) and E. D. E. N. Southworth's *The Discarded Daughter* (1852) both supported women's property rights, the latter in large part because Southworth had her own financial well-being threatened by her profligate husband.[4] One of the issues for Southworth was the fact that by midcentury property law reform in most states had not extended to women's wages. Thus while Southworth could earn money through her writing, she did not have legal control of that money and, separated but not divorced from her husband, she still could be coerced by him to contribute to his support through the sale of her books.

After the Civil War, most states had enacted women's property laws, including the right to one's earnings, but given her great-uncle's involvement in the issue, Woolson was aware of the tendency for spinsters to enjoy greater protection under the law than married women. However, she was also aware that this was only part of the issue. Though women increasingly could keep their own wages, there was still much social pressure for married women not to work. This was particularly true in the higher status professions. For example, women who wished to become physicians were being denied education in the higher prestige male medical institutions and often had to choose between medicine and marriage. After the Civil War, many writers began to address the question of women doctors in their fiction: negative portraits included William Dean Howells's *Dr. Breen's Practice* (1881) and Henry James's *The Bostonians* (1886); more positive ones included Harriet Beecher Stowe's *My Wife and I* (1871), Mark Twain's *The Gilded Age* (1873), Elizabeth Stuart Phelps's *Dr. Zay* (1882), and Sarah Orne Jewett's *A Country Doctor* (1884).[5]

Although Woolson never created a portrait of a woman physician, she did support the idea. She believed that women should be allowed access to male medical colleges, and she must have known that six female physicians had successfully completed their medical education at the Cleveland Medical College in the 1850s. In a letter to Katharine Loring, she writes:[6]

> It opens a new field for women, & one that belongs to them fairly; one for which they are fitted. But do insist that they shall be educated with students of the other sex, and not kept by themselves; it is the only way, in my opinion, to widen the feminine mind. Do not suppose from that that I think the feminine mind inferior to the masculine. For I do not. But it has been kept back, & enfeebled, & limited, by ages of ignorance, & almost servitude. (BHSM, 19 Sept. 1890)

When Woolson and others spoke about women physicians, they addressed issues that by-passed the lower classes and that applied only to those few women who chose a career over marriage. Even middle- and upper-class unmarried women more often occupied the position of unemployed spinster living with family than that of self-supporting professional. Thus the original meaning of *spinster* as one who spins ironically designates much of the role of the spinster in the nineteenth century. If a spinster were middle or upper class, she could remain within a domestic environment—in someone else's home—or if she were from a lower class, she could spin on the new machines in the mills that were opened by men. The lack of economic opportunities for spinsters, coupled with the rise of spinsterhood after the Civil War, caused women to speak out in increasingly public ways about their status. One of the biggest controversies involved the issue of appropriate education for women. Henry James Sr. expressed one extreme in an 1853 article in *Putnam's Magazine* where he talks about the "very virtue of woman" "disquali[fying] her for all didactic dignity. Learning and wisdom do not become her."[7] By the end of the next decade, the debate was refueled by John Stuart Mill's "The Subjection of Women" (1869), which argued that women were not fitted for intellectual endeavor because both law and society's attitudes had taught them to be dependent and subservient and to cultivate beauty as their sole way of pleasing men, whom they depended upon for economic survival. Both Henry James Sr. and William James reviewed Mill's work, and Henry James Jr. read it in Switzerland, none of them at that time willing to take as profeminist a view as Mill was professing.[8]

A survey of the increased opportunities for women at the end of the nineteenth century indicates that even these avenues did not change the ideal that women should be trained differently from men. Not only were the numbers of women who attended colleges small, but their course of studies tended to focus on home economics or other areas that would prepare them for their roles as wife and mother. Colleges, both single-sex and coeducational—especially in the West, which needed women's money—continued to argue about whether excess intellectual activity would harm women's reproductive systems. By the end of the century, even fewer women attended college than midcentury, partly because studies showed that college-educated women were less likely to marry and that they had fewer children at a time when middle- and upper-class women were expected to increase the elite population base.[9]

Woolson did not doubt women's adequacy for intellectual work and, in fact, her most formative education came from her high school experience at the Cleveland Female Seminary rather than at Madame Chegaray's, her fashionable eastern "college." To her nephew Sam Mather's wife, she is quite blunt about her belief in the intellectual capacity of women: "Girls do so need a more thorough education! I never hear, or, rather, I seldom hear, one of my own sex talk long without noticing the lack of broad, reasonable, solid views. . . . But I am sure that education is all that is required. I do not think the feminine mind inferior." And again: she could see that Brugsch Bey, an Egyptologist whom she had met, "did not believe that women could be very profound scholars in anything; though of course he did not actually say so to me. I think we can—only our education must begin a hundred years before we are born—as some wit has said. By this I mean that it will take several generations of study and training before our girls can equal our boys in scholarship; or rather before our women can equal our men" (Benedict 2:49, 362).

In her belief that women could and should be educated, Woolson was as strong a feminist as anyone in the nineteenth century, even though she never joined the public ranks of feminism and did not have a lesson about women's rights as her primary aim in writing. She worked from personal observation more than from a political feminist agenda, perhaps because most of her fiction was written while she traveled in the South, which had been so damaged by the Civil War that it attended to what it saw as more pressing needs than women's rights, and in Europe, which was removed from the debates about feminism being carried on in mostly the northeastern portion of the United States. But though she lacked a political agenda, Woolson still saw fully the implications of legal, educational, and social controls on women. She addressed these issues by creating characters from within her rather conservative and higher-class social milieu. Her fiction serves as a mirror of the various attitudes toward and avenues for work and education open to large numbers of spinsters on whom these attitudes and avenues most impacted in the latter half of the nineteenth century. She portrays spinsters in lifelike situations and, knowing the dynamics that work on them, she refuses to impose strong judgments even when she does not fully sympathize with their choices. Her tone is sometimes witty, sometimes sympathetic, and sometimes angry, but it is not hostile or bitter. The one spinster in her novels who displays hostility and bitterness is Katherine Vanhorn in *Anne,* who is so warped by her decision not to marry someone who was unfaithful even during their engagement that she shuts herself off from all members of her family. This insight into what bitterness over the wrongs done to women could do to a person, plus her comfort within her role as spinster, helped Woolson to control her anger, so that it is more melancholic than bitter. At a time when many women felt forced to adopt extreme positions, Woolson moderated her voice in a body of fiction that, nevertheless, clearly illustrates the need for social change.

The story "Bro" from *Rodman the Keeper* is an interesting place to begin discussion of educational paths open to women because the woman in this story ends up denying her aptitude for math and marrying instead of finding a satisfactory role as a working spinster. "Bro" concerns a love triangle between Marion Manning, whose mother is worried because she is not married, a faithful but silent admirer Bro, and Lawrence Vickery, the returned grandson of an established family. The story is conventional enough: Marion loves Vickery; Bro uses money from an invention to buy land anonymously from Vickery for ten thousand dollars so Vickery will stay in town and marry Marion; Vickery complies and, years later, learns of Bro's purchase when Bro wills the land to Marion. Bro, an inventor, knows that with the loss of Marion his inspiration for inventing is gone, and he dismantles his workroom. John Kern believes that Bro's nobility is sentimentalized and that such unselfishness strains the reader's credulity, while Rayburn Moore is willing to accept his unselfishness in the context of Woolson's other writing and its stress on the nobility of sacrifice, whether by men or women.[10]

Despite the story's title, however, Woolson's main interest is not in the sacrificial character of Bro. She rarely centered on male characters, feeling that as a woman she had little access to their point of view. Rather than a story of self-sacrifice, "Bro" can be read as a statement of how a woman has been shaped by attitudes that assume she will marry instead of pursuing a career as an inventor. Marion is not only Bro's inspiration, she is also his mathematician, the one person who can figure the math so that Bro can get an invention patented. Lawrence Vickery is duly impressed with Marion's ability, and Woolson delights in exposing the kind of mentality that spurs his comment, "What will you do next? . . . Build a stone wall—or vote? Imagine a girl taking light recreation in equations, and letting her mind run hilariously among groves of triangles on a rainy day!" (*Rodman* 240). The response is doubly annoying when we learn that the math Bro had been working on for twenty years is done by Marion in an hour, but that it is too late, the invention already having been patented by someone else. The pleasure of arithmetic learned from a female teacher at the Episcopal seminary in town is really no more than a southern lady's idle hobby. If Marion is to become liberated intellectually, she must have access to education and to the avenues that can support the results of this education. Without these, she shows her feminine weakness when, well-timed, she swoons at the false news that Vickery is dead. In part, Woolson is suggesting here that even nonfeminine, intellectual women fall in love. But how strong can this feminine part of a woman be if that woman "had never said 'don't' or 'can't' in [her life]" (*Rodman* 235)? The freedom to accept such language, rather than the freedom to be both feminine and intellectual, is all that the liberated Vickery delivers.

Attitudes about appropriate education for women create an obstacle blocking Marion's chance for success as a mathematician. Another obstacle is the kind of teaching she has received at the Episcopal seminary. Teaching was almost the only profession widely open to women in the nineteenth century because the country needed women to fill the rising demand generated by the increase in public education. Teachers were by convention unmarried, the philosophy being that marriage would force them to divide their loyalties between home/family and school.[11] One survey has shown that of eight thousand women who graduated from college in the 1880s, only three thousand of those entered the work force, and two-thirds of that three thousand became teachers (Simmons 123). What we know of Marion's teacher is only that she was "an excellent though melancholy-minded teacher," "adept at figures," but "equally given to tears and arithmetic" (*Rodman* 227). This teacher's aptitude seems to have landed her in the only profession open to a woman who liked math. She is caught in a double-bind here, for if she educates her female students to value their mathematical ability, she knows that society will offer them work only in a profession in which their status will remain low.

Woolson respected teachers. She kept up a correspondence with Linda Guilford, her teacher from the Cleveland Seminary, whom she credited with helping to shape her into a writer. And later in life, she met Katharine Loring, who had been a history teacher for the Society to Encourage Studies at Home, an organization founded in 1873 to promote women's education without overstepping the male prerogative of university teaching. How much Woolson knew about these women's satisfaction with teaching is unclear, but the few asides she has about teachers suggest that she saw the profession as unsatisfying, one that Anne and Mlle. Jeanne-Armand in *Anne* and Madame Carroll in *For the Major* enter because it is the only way they can support themselves. Further, Woolson reflects just how difficult the profession was as a means for self-support in "Raspberry Island," in which two public school teachers share rooms in a city and can leave that city during their unpaid summer vacation only by taking jobs as raspberry pickers.[12] A woman's status in the field of education was never high. For example, in 1872 Harvard rejected the idea for an annex for women, and in 1879, when it finally adopted the annex, which eventually became Radcliffe, it used its own male faculty as teachers (Strouse 170–75). In 1978, Adrienne Rich complained that, even as late as 1947–51 at Radcliffe, she had still been taught by the "great men" from Harvard.[13] Because women teachers were forced to remain single and taught large numbers of students at lower grade levels and because teaching was one of the few professions in which women could try to earn a living, Woolson could say in one of her stories, "God help the woman who must be that dreary thing, a teacher, from necessity!" ("Rodman the Keeper," *Rodman* 39).

Besides teaching, the only other profession Woolson gives her spinsters is art, which raises issues complex enough to deserve a separate chapter. Because they have so few avenues open to them, Woolson at times turns a spinster's support of feminism into an amateur profession, allowing these characters to voice extreme positions she never voiced herself. As women in the nineteenth century emerged from private ways of reform through family and church influence and novels written within and about domestic environments into more public and political forums, particularly concerning abolition, temperance, and suffrage, suspicions of them widened. The schism among moderate and more radical feminists culminated in 1869 with the split of the Equal Rights Association, which critics complained was too influenced by males, into the conservative and largely upper-class American Women's Suffrage Association, led by women like Julia Ward Howe and Lucy Stone, and the more populist National Women's Suffrage Association, led by Elizabeth Cady Stanton and Susan B. Anthony (Strouse 215–16). Feminism had become so public—and so associated with the fear of the de-sexing of women through education—that its more outspoken members, especially those of a literary bent, earned the name "bluestockings." The term was adopted from British feminists at the end of the eighteenth century who had received the name from a tendency to eschew style and wear worsted "blue stockings" instead of fashionable (and presumably less comfortable) silk stockings.[14] Satirizing the fear that education would de-sex women, Woolson says of Anne Douglas in her novel *Anne* that she can learn Latin but not Greek lest it would "make what is called a blue-stocking of her" (42). One fear at issue here is that no one would fall in love with an overly educated woman, Greek being associated with philosophy and thus with the intellectual rigor that was thought to be harmful to women's reproductive systems.

Anne, of course, is no militant feminist even though she gains her independence at first by teaching, then by marrying on her own terms, but much of Woolson's fiction contains asides such as those in *Anne* about unmarried, educated, and outspokenly feminist women. Her fullest portrait of this type of woman is Maud Murial Mackintosh in *Horace Chase*. Maud Murial personifies the nineteenth-century fear that education and political autonomy would defeminize women. She defies patriarchy by modeling male behavior: she believes in women's suffrage; pursues a profession as a sculptor, using only ugly subjects; avoids instead of nurtures the children of her brother, with whom she lives; refuses to be a slave to fashion, believing that "[w]oman will never be the equal of man until she has grasped the conception that the position of her pockets should be unchangeable" (68–69); and in a wonderfully comic stroke, tries to smoke cigars. On the one hand, Woolson is satirizing radical feminism, but her portrayal is so pointedly aimed at the notion that women's rights will mean a loss of femininity that she ends by satirizing that fear more than any feminist type. One of the most telling scenes about this fear occurs when another character, a minister named Malachi Hill, becomes so impatient with Maud Murial that he kisses her to silence her. Her retort: The kisses "arc *very far indeed* from what is being described. There is nothing in them whatever!" (363).

Woolson knew that most theories about women's ideal relationships and about women's place in society were at bottom a sham. As early as 1872, she exposed these shams in a story called "Weighed in the Balance." Two men in this story articulate the past and future ideals for women: one does not approve of suffrage, believing that woman's power is love not intellect, that her "shrine is home, there is her place," and there one may "find [a] goddess"; the other looks to a future where "souls will recognize their soul-companions, and, in the white heat of idealized intellect, . . . hearts will blossom with fervid spontaneity. Then will woman reach her apotheosis; then will human intellect, embodied in the clear crystals of woman's mind, rise to its true place, the polar star of infinity, the germ of ante-cosmic vivication" (590). The story proceeds to have the boat these characters are on nearly plunge over Niagara Falls. In the crisis, the first of these male theorists exhibits his alcoholism, and his wife confesses she does not care if she dies or not, so difficult has her marriage been; the second shows himself a coward and joins in the drinking; and one of the idealized women shows herself a hypocrite as she thinks only of her own safety. In the end, the ship is saved by the separate bravery of a man and a woman, and the implication is that they will marry. A stereotypical ending, yes, but also an exposure of the falseness of ideal theories about women.

Woolson did not champion any theory about how women should behave or what they should be. Nor did she share the fear of some of her contemporaries that feminism would de-sex women. Her admiration for women who can combine not just femininity but also sexuality with feminism and the refusal to marry is apparent in a letter she wrote about George Eliot:

> How can you say George Eliot was unhappy? I think that she had one of the easiest, most indulged and "petted" lives that I have ever known or heard of—considering she was a woman without a fortune (which always makes the personal life easy), and without the least beauty, in fact, very plain. From first to last, she did exactly as she pleased—law or no law, custom or no custom! Lewes adored her; I heard all the details in London. She was surrounded by the most devoted, personal, worshipping affection to his last hour. True, she earned the money for two, and she worked very hard. But how many, many women would be glad to do the same through all their lives if their reward was such a devoted love as that![15]

Woolson continues by saying that she believes Eliot's nature craved men; she envies a bit their attention to Eliot and is annoyed that, having everything she wants, Eliot can preach to others less fortunate.[16] But Woolson does not condemn Eliot's sexuality or belittle her achievement. Still, Woolson is conventional enough in her fiction to keep her spinsters, whether they are feminist or intellectual or stereotypically old-maidish, celibate.

Apart from her artist-figures, most of Woolson's spinsters are minor, comic characters. They live alone or with family, often, like Woolson herself, serving as companions to nieces or nephews, without great wealth but somehow managing not to have to enter a work force populated by lower social classes. They are stereotypically spinsterish: old-fashioned, prim, asexual. For example, Miss Elisabetha in the story of that title (*Rodman*) has outmoded notions of fashion and music and thinks that her foil, an equally comic, aging opera star, is trying to seduce her nephew, though he is fifteen years her junior. Miss Elisabetha has inflated notions of her ability to teach music; the opera singer, inflated notions about her fame and attractiveness. In the story "Neptune's Shore," a spinster aunt is mocked by her nieces for being a stiff New Englander who has no knowledge of foreign cultures. Miss Billy Breeze in *Horace Chase* is given a male's nickname because she spends her life trying to catch a man—a safe, nonsexual one. She devotes herself to the study of extinct animals, a prime example of which is her current prey, the ancient-named Achilles Larue whose tombstone, says one character, should read "He was a verb in the passive voice, conjugated negatively" (357). Miss Teller in the novel *Anne* misses the point of all the conversations she hears.

It is interesting that in all these portraits of spinsters, Woolson uses humor, but the spinsters do not. Walter Blair and Hamlin Hill have shown that the New England spinster was a frequent subject for humor prior to the Civil War, and Woolson may have continued with this tradition as a refuge to deflect the attitudes she feared would be eventually directed toward her as a hard-of-hearing spinster. By the end of the nineteenth century, humor had moved away from situation and black or backwoods dialect to local-color humor. Woolson, however, rarely used this humor, which her friend E. C. Stedman disliked because of its "slang and nonsense spiced with smut and profanity" (Blair and Hill 273). Instead she used the sophisticated word play that developed by the end of the nineteenth century. But only a few women felt free to employ this device. The attitude toward women writing humor that persists well into the twentieth century is captured in a column from *Graham's Magazine* in 1842: "Women have sprightliness, cleverness, smartness, though but little wit. There is a body and substance in true wit, with a reflectiveness rarely found apart from a masculine intellect. . . . We know of no one writer of the other sex, that has a high character for humor. . . . The female character does not admit it."[17] Woolson and those like her who flouted nineteenth-century notions like these use humor in ways that subvert the power structure. A generation before her, Fanny Fern had turned her satirical eye against the male establishment.[18] Woolson is as likely to turn her wit upon women as men, but she does so in ways that expose misogyny rather than laugh at its victims.[19]

One of the ways that Woolson merges her criticism of a society that denies females power with her humorous portrayal of spinsters and her belief in the intellectual power of women is through the plot device of detective work. Several of Woolson's spinsters are attracted to mystery or detective work, and through these they can play out their fantasies, adopting roles that allow them power and pleasure that others found within domestic spheres. Miss Senter in "A Christmas

Party" (*FY*) satisfies her need for a mystery by buying an antique desk with a secret compartment that all the servants know about. The secret compartment here might be read as a metaphor for all those aspects of life, sexual or otherwise, that remain hidden from a woman whom society has forced to remain sheltered. These secrets of life are revealed in the course of the story through the images of duplicitous servants, theft, and even murder.

In *Anne,* Woolson's portrait of Miss Lois, her fullest and most sympathetic version of the comic spinster, equates the spinster with detective work. Miss Lois and Anne set about the very real and very crucial task of finding out who has murdered Ward Heathcote's wife Helen in order that they can free the accused Heathcote from jail. As high as the stakes are, Miss Lois still manages to have a grand time playing detective. She makes up false identities for herself and Anne that give them an imagined place in a home, including manufacturing for herself a dead husband who had been "something of a trial to her" (501). She would even like to equate her intrigue with a "popish" plot, but is "restrained by her regard for Père Michaux" (493), her longtime friend. She and Anne conduct their investigations totally free of a man's interference: "No man being there to weigh [their plan] with a cooler masculine judgment, it seemed to them a richly promising one" (492). And such it proves to be as they eventually track down the murderer. At this point, however, social constraints intrude and Anne and Miss Lois have to enlist the aid of Père Michaux to wrest a confession from the murderer. These women, who have shown themselves powerful and intelligent, have power denied. They receive no credit for their accomplishment, all the credit being taken by the representative of what is, in Woolson's vision, the patriarchal institution of the church. Yet Père Michaux is also a replication of Miss Lois and Anne—without family, he has the independence needed to obtain a confession that saves the man's soul even as it condemns him to prosecution for murder.

Hiding behind a self-protective comedy, Woolson uses expanded scenes or careful wording, such as those involving Anne's and Miss Lois's detective work, to indicate that spinsterhood has compensations and that a misogynistic society can be resisted. Though Anne may be a woman who feels she cannot be "homesick" because she "has no home" (360), and though Miss Lois may at times feel "loneliness" and "misunderstood-ness" and a "general sense of a useless ocean within [her], its breaking waves dashed high on a stern and rock-bound coast"

(135), they do have the advantage of independent movement. At one point in *Anne,* the omniscient narrator says that women living alone or with other women could more easily regulate their own household than if they lived with a man:

> A man, however mild, demands in a home at least a pretence of fixed hours and regularity; only a household of women is capable of no regularity at all, of changing the serious dinner hour capriciously, and even giving up dinner altogether. Only a household of women has sudden inspirations as to journeys and departures within the hour; brings forth sudden ideas as to changes of route while actually on the way, and a going southward instead of westward, with a total indifference to supper. (162)

Through comments like these, Woolson directs most of her humor against men, who force women to think in terms of domestic regularity. She is less likely to use humor when she portrays how this misogyny impacts on women's friendships. She knew that even relationships between unmarried women created strains and obligations, speaking in her letters about the frustrations of having to stop writing to move about with her sister and niece.[20] Perhaps because she wanted and could handle independence, she never formed a "Boston marriage" like the ones we see between Annie Fields and Sarah Orne Jewett or Alice James and Katharine Loring. She also saw that, if women were not committed to remaining single, the obstacles to women's friendships became more difficult. She confessed, for example, to her friend Arabella Carter Washburn her fear that Washburn's marriage would destroy their friendship (Benedict 2:18). On occasion, her married characters actually taunt her spinsters, but as much as she shows how relationships to males mar women's friendships, she also shows how they can occasionally deepen them. Such is the case with Anne and Helen Lorrington in their love for the same man. Helen freely acknowledges that had she known Heathcote loved Anne she would have made his life intolerable, indicating how full an understanding she finally has of herself and of her friendship with Anne. When Gregory Dexter, one of Anne's suitors, says to her that "a woman never knows a woman as a man knows her" (460), he means the word *as* to stand for *as well as.* But Woolson would seem to prefer the word to mean *in the same way as.* Whatever women's marriage status, Woolson recognizes that women's friendships develop against a backdrop that places more importance on male-female relationships than on female-female ones.

Besides the use of humor directed at men rather than the spinster at whom it appears on the surface to be directed, Woolson saw two other ways of subverting the misogynistic tendency of the nineteenth century to deny unmarried women homes, one by having a woman become an invalid, the other by having her a widow. Although, as Frances Cogan has ably demonstrated, female invalidism was not the only model for women in the nineteenth century, it was a prominent one. We can correlate this model with women's leisure, with the stresses of the conflicting attitudes towards women's place outside of marriage, and with the excess ratio of women in the population. Invalidism was both a product of and a rebellion against misogyny. Diane Price Herndl has studied the impact of male domination in the nineteenth-century medical profession, showing how medical men gained access to the female-dominated household by defining the female as ill and labeling such natural functions as menstruation and pregnancy as pathological. If a female ate strong food, her energy would flow to her stomach; if she danced too much, it would flow to her legs; if she read too much, it would flow to her brain—all these parts of the body deflecting energy from the woman's more essential reproductive organs. The nineteenth-century invalid was usually diagnosed as a hysteric and her symptoms associated entirely with her reproductive organs, not surprisingly given that these organs could easily have been damaged by the ubiquitous corset. But a woman also had something to gain through invalidism. She could avoid marriage and/or intercourse and demand that instead of serving others, she be served. She could maintain her purity by refusing gynecological care or she could accept this care and, in some cases, indulge a pure/perverted sexuality. Much research suggests the connection between social pressures and hysteria, though the medical practices of the nineteenth century undoubtedly exacerbated some genuine physiological problems.[21] We know today, for example, that many women experience hormonal-based symptoms of lethargy, irritability, and headache and that the inactivity prescribed for the hysteric in the nineteenth century was more likely to increase than relieve these symptoms.

Woolson's characterization of Dolly Franklin in *Horace Chase* derives both from her sense of her own debilitating depressions and from her sense of Alice James's invalidism. Like Woolson, Dolly fights her symptoms and rather than depending on others is willing, by the end of the novel, to live alone. From all commentators, one sees Alice James as more neurotic than Woolson or Dolly; however, Alice, too, was observant, strong, witty, and caustic, all traits that explain the kinship

Woolson felt toward her. But unlike Alice, Woolson was not attracted to invalidism. It is an interesting historical footnote that a writer named Abba Gould Woolson, perhaps Constance's distant cousin, railed against literary portrayals of sickly women in a chapter in her book *Women in American Society* (1873) titled "Invalidism as Pursuit."²² Abba would surely have approved Woolson's fiction, for, Dolly Franklin excepted, she does not develop invalids as admirable characters, the widow Mrs. Rutherford in *East Angels,* for example, illustrating just how nasty invalidism could be.

Like her spinsters, Woolson's portraits of widows tend to show them in roles other than invalidism. Some of these are comic. Betty Carew in *East Angels,* for example, monopolizes conversations so much that in one five-page monologue she manages to free-associate from hunters to fishermen to codfish to New England and Puritans to persecution of witches to her disapproval of witchcraft to the witch of Endor to a defense of historical groups to the question of Pocohontas's respectability—all before she is one-quarter finished! This is a bit taxing for the twentieth-century reader, an example that validates the charge that Woolson is cluttered. But, read with leisure, the passage is hilarious. More than comedy, however, Woolson's overriding attitude toward widows is captured in this statement in *Anne:* "Helen [prior to her second marriage to Heathcote] held what may be called a woman's most untrammelled position in life, namely, that of a young widow, protected but not controlled, rich, beautiful, and without children" (158). A recurrent motif in much of Woolson's fiction is the image of a woman who married briefly and then was freed from this marriage by the death of her husband. Through this motif, she suggests that widows have greater freedom of movement than spinsters as well as higher status in a society that expects women to marry. Thus, she does not surround her widows with the defensiveness of comedy, a device that upstages those who would laugh at a woman by laughing first. However, she knows that even if they occupy the enviable position of being "protected but not controlled, rich, beautiful, and without children," they still are not free from social pressures based on their gender.

In her fiction, Woolson's widows do not always have enviable financial positions. Like her sister Clara, her fictional widows often have to worry about money: in *For the Major,* Madame Carroll, believing herself a widow marries to provide for her child; in "A Transplanted Boy," Violet Roscoe manages for herself by traveling with men and in the process neglects her child; and in *Horace Chase,* Mrs. Franklin lives on the edge of poverty until her youngest child marries the wealthy Horace. If children are not involved, widows have an easier time, yet this does not mean that they use their status wisely. In "At the Château of Corinne," Katharine Winthrop loses the money her husband left her, though we never learn how. In *Anne,* Rachel Bannert, who has inherited all her husband's money, flirts indiscriminately, and Helen in the same novel realizes that her status makes it impossible to have friendships, male or female, that are not marked by her status as marriage bait. But at least Helen recognizes what she loses by her eligibility status. In contrast, a woman like the comic Mrs. Kip in *Horace Chase* has internalized society's expectations all too well. Twice-married and possessing both a child and a satisfactory income, she is looking for a suitable third husband because she thrives on marriage. She likes the married state so much that she always refers to her child as Evangeline Taylor in order that the name of her first husband not be lost in her second marriage. By novel's end, it is apparent that she is about to hyphenate her own name to Kip-Hill to honor her second husband as she marries a third. Woolson does not champion remarriage, but she recognizes that the tendency of widows to remarry is so prevalent in her society that a Fourth of July parade in *Jupiter Lights* can only find one Civil War widow who has not remarried.

The problems represented by the status of widow are central to Woolson's story "Neptune's Shore," collected in *The Front Yard.* The story is interesting because it is filled with unmarried women: Isabella, the spinster-narrator, who is the brunt of her eligible nieces' humor; Mrs. Preston, who has the power and freedom of an older widow free to choose men as companions because "[t]oo much lady talk dries [her] brain" (*FY* 71); and the eligible widow Pauline Graham. Pauline has a face that seduces men even though she does not want to seduce them. She is past the age of needing a chaperon but because she is so eligible she is urged to have a female companion. What she wants, however, is simply freedom to come and go as she pleases with or without men and without being judged in terms of her relationships with men. Her "passion for [horseback] riding at breakneck speed" (*FY* 56) becomes the metaphor for Pauline's urge to freedom. The story's plot ends with one of her suitors, a riding companion to whom she has made it clear that she wants no romance, killing a rival suitor. Through it, Woolson conveys her point that even the enviable status of widowhood cannot always offer women freedom in their relationships with men. If we want, like Leon Edel, to read Woolson's fiction in terms of her relationship with Henry James, we could match him story for story to illustrate that Woolson was fleeing from James rather than the reverse. But since we can only speculate about such matters, it is preferable to read a story like "Neptune's Shore" as another example of the social constraints placed upon women and, especially, of the difficulty presented in developing male-female friendships in a society that sexualizes so much communication between men and women.

One of the last stories Woolson wrote and the last story Alice James heard read to her, "Dorothy" centers on the pressures on young widows to remarry. Edel calls it a "story of the slow death of a woman who does not want to live,"[23] and, indeed, it is that, even a documentation of the overpowering influence of depression. While there is ample material in "Dorothy" to support Edel's interpretation of the Woolson-James relationship, there is also a strong current that suggests that part of the reason Dorothy does not want to live is because she is subjected to precisely the kind of speculation Edel engages in about Woolson and James. The story is busy with characters, most eligible young women or widows, or mothers who want husbands with money for their daughters. Throughout the story, judgments are passed on how each woman looks, on who will appeal to whom, and on who will become known as a spinster. The pressure is so great that one of these women leaves to work in an orphan asylum. Two widows, safely in their fifties with the status of having married, feel free to discuss another they call "that old maid" (555), speculating about whether she is unhappy because she is not married and whether marriage to a rich man would be wasted on her. Dorothy, widowed and rich at age nineteen, is judged to be in an ideal situation just as she had been judged before her marriage as flighty, shallow, and unsuitable for the dull man who became her husband. Married, she continued to flirt with other men so that people assumed she did not love her husband, something he too may have believed. Widowed, she at first plunges into a fury of activity to fight off the depression that eventually takes hold of her. The problem—and the reason she eventually dies—is that she loved her husband, but could convince no one, even him, of this. Having been talked about when unmarried in terms of what marriage would be good for her, she is talked about in the same way as a widow because nobody believes she might have married for love.

So many are the pressures Woolson saw on women in the nineteenth century that whether their status is married or marriageable, spinster or widow or wife, they are always judged in terms of that status, not in terms of their interests and achievements. So, too, are they denied education that will develop anything except appropriately female interests, thus insuring that they will remain under the thumb of patriarchy and continue to view themselves as of little value outside of their gender. The story "Dorothy" is a fitting farewell to Alice James, the woman whose culture helped shape her into an invalid who rejoiced when something physical—cancer—finally brought death. With all its banter about widows and spinsters and the "marriage business," "Dorothy" must have spoken to Alice's satirical side at the same time that it showed her how a woman who faced conflicting messages about sexuality, marriage, and gender-defined interests could embrace death as an attractive home.

9

The Challenge of Art
🎵

Woolson's life journey moved her away from the physical boundaries of her ancestors' and her parents' home, and because her life became one of persistent travel, she recognized midway through it that she was unlikely to find a place to call home. Once she chose travel and writing over place and family, she began to realize that she was breaking the boundaries normally associated with her gender. The issue of gender became increasingly important for her as she began to see the implications of seeking a literary home as a woman writer, though she was conscious of the issues even early in her career. In 1877, Woolson wrote a letter to E. C. Stedman that addressed his "entire disbelief in the possibility of true fiery genius in woman." "Well," she wrote, "I do not quarrel with you about this; and the reason is—that I fully agree with you!"[1] For a writer who pushed herself to be the best literary artist she could be and who created fictional characters with similar goals, the statement appears problematic. We could dismiss the letter as the product of self-doubt brought about by one of her depressions, but in the context of other remarks on women's genius, we come to realize that Woolson believed that "true fiery genius in woman" was unavailable because the definition of genius was a male-biased construct.

Most women in Woolson's day had not been given access to the education or life experiences necessary to cultivate genius in themselves or to recognize genius in others. In an early story titled "Duets," Woolson acknowledges this by satirizing the foolishness of two women when it comes to artistic judgment. One, Olive Dean, a dark woman associated with the natural, earthy world, seeks a marriage partner who represents the outdoors, the practical, the present; the other, the blonde, spiritualized Helena Mayberry, looks for one who represents the canonized art of the past. Each woman is proposed to by the man who represents the opposite of what she seeks, and each accepts the proposal. Not only does marriage take precedence over each woman's preference, each preference is compartmentalized as only physically natural or only artistic. Both women are also drawn to a female poet they nickname "Aurora Leigh," after Elizabeth Barrett Browning's popular feminist poem about a woman who refuses marriage not based on equality and who earns her living as a poet. Woolson's poet represents the two qualities Olive and Helena have been seeking: she carries an aura of mystery, living an isolated and earthy life on Lamia Island, after Keats's poem *Lamia,* and she represents the artistically successful woman, publishing in a magazine difficult to be accepted in. But all three of Woolson's characters represent the difficulty she saw for women to find places in society suitable to their needs. Olive and Helena lack the ability to form judgments that integrate both the natural and the artistically successful worlds. Even though the recluse poet should have both available to her, she lacks independence. She lives with her father and is coerced into publishing where she does, not because the magazine suits her but because it is prestigious.

When she began to write in the 1870s, Woolson had to learn that her literary home would develop in realistic rather than romantic modes. But from the beginning of her career, she was conscious of the difficulties presented by seeking a home in her status as writer. In her early fiction, she sets the idea of access to education that would foster artistic genius against a backdrop of attractions of the isolated western communities or quasi-communities. Her lake country stories, especially, show that as attracted as she was to the less settled parts of the West, she believed that to settle there would be to inhibit herself as an artist. In "St. Clair Flats," the issue takes the form of a debate between two male characters over the role of critics in determining what constitutes great art. One has written a poem based on his mystical, romantic vision of the wilderness, believing that this vision is enough, that the process and soul of creation is to be valued over the lesser talents of many accepted artists. But we do not learn if his poem is any good, and his companion, the narrator of the story, may be his only appreciative listener. If the poem is good, whether it survives or not, its depth comes not just from the wilderness but also from the tension between the poet's experience of civilization and his experience of the wilderness. Nor can the wilderness cleanse someone of the distortions of the critical establishment. Woolson makes this case in the story "Misery Landing," in which John Jay is a successful painter, living as a Thoreauvian recluse on an island in Lake Superior. He should be a painter of the sublime, able to use his experience within nature and his observations of the natural to inspire the imaginative. But his art fails to reflect his own passion rather than the expectations of a public drawn to the sublime as cliché. From the beginning, he earns our disdain because he is a false Thoreauvian, building himself a cabin in the woods because it is picturesque. He is a painter of surfaces, who sees flowers as "inanimate things . . . the toys of vegetation" (*CN* 214) and a limited artist, who cannot paint any portraits except those of women he judges beautiful.

Where "St. Clair Flats" and "Misery Landing" look at the impact of the wilderness on would-be artists, implying that access to artistic education or public acclaim may be corruptive, "Solomon" emphasizes the need for both private genius and public access. With her artist cousin, Ermine Stuart, the narrator of this story, Theodora Wentworth, visits a Zoarite community in Ohio. On the outskirts of the community near some sulphur springs, they find the home of Solomon and Dorcas Bangs and learn their story. Like so many of Woolson's women, Dorcas has given up her home to marry her soul mate, Solomon, a painter who becomes a coal miner because he can make no money at painting. Solomon's whole life is consumed with a mind-picture of Dorcas's beauty, but he cannot get this on canvas because his training does not match his imagination. Through the two visiting women, Ermine and Dora, Woolson shows the conflict—do we value the artist, the art work, or the life that is the inspiration to the art? Ermine values Solomon because he is an artist, but her real recognition of him comes only after she, a person of technical skill only, has shown him some techniques that enable him to create a great sketch. Dora, by virtue of being a first-person narrator, seems closer to Woolson as she complains that male artists get all the attention and that women like Ermine gather around them and never think about the plight of their wives. But she opts for the sentiment and the tragedy of Dorcas's life even before Solomon has transformed it into an art work.

All of Solomon's ill-executed paintings of Dorcas carry women's names from the Bible: Ruth, who represents the "power of hope"; Judith, the "queen of revenge"; Rachel whom Jacob loved (*CN* 260). Solomon and Dora recognize the power of women and the value of inspiration over the technically perfect art work. But the conflict is not resolved by simply valuing the artistic soul. After all, it is only after

Ermine gives skill to Solomon that he can do justice to his conception. The point is driven home in the last line: "Even then [after Solomon is killed and Dorcas dies of grief] we could not give up our preferences" (*CN* 269). We may prefer the inspiration to art—the woman in this case—or the person who can execute the art work. Either way is a dead end. Without society and the training available in society, Solomon's art is unrealized. As inspiration, Dorcas follows Solomon but becomes immersed in a culture that smothers her artistic sense—she loses the beauty she felt in her home in Maine and hates the Dutch with their ugly clothes and their "wooden shapes and wooden shoes" (*CN* 245). Hers is an Oriental beauty, and it has been squashed in this foreign culture that she, unlike the two travelers, does not find picturesque. To live a life worthy of art may be preferable to leading an insulated life, but it is also something that comes only at great cost.

In her southern stories Woolson continues to explore the theme of what constitutes art. Her story "The South Devil" looks at how a musician isolates himself in the Florida swamps to cleanse himself of his none-too-clean social experiences and to gain access to his creative abilities. The swamp finally reveals its music to him. Unlike the poet in "St. Clair Flats," this musician seems to have composed great music, but unfortunately it remains within his head because the swamp also kills him. The story "Miss Elisabetha" is a counterpoint to "The South Devil." Here the female character, Miss Elisabetha, has plenty of access to the charms of nature, in this case a Southern tidewater river rather than the swamps. But her experience does not blend the tension of passionate life experiences within society and the passion and mystery of the swamp. Instead, she has rested on outmoded and superficial concepts of music and taught these to her nephew, Dora. Her foil, an English prima donna, has had access to an entire world of music, but as in the story "Misery Landing," Woolson suggests that this has been equally corruptive. Dora escapes the influence of the prima donna, falls in love with a local girl, and happily raises a family, pursuing his music all the while. Although he has escaped corruption, he has also missed the opportunity for education and the informed rebellion of a character like the musician in "The South Devil," and thus his music remains at the recreational level.

When Woolson turns from writing short stories about the American landscape to stories set in Europe, mostly in Italy, the question of access to society in order to inform—or corrupt—art gets reemphasized into an exploration of how society has reified Old World values in art. The Old World values are captured in a story appropriately titled "In Venice." In the story, Claudia Marcy likes to wear velvet and to wander through old galleries looking at Raphaels and Titians, unlike her aunt, who is willowy and likes to wear lavender scarfs and shawls, representing the New rather than the Old World. Claudia sits for an American painter, Stephen Lenox, a mill worker with a new inheritance that has allowed him access to trying out his talent. She falls in love with this painter, though he is married and has a sickly child whom his wife dotes upon. Valuing Claudia and her representation of the Old World, Lenox goes in pursuit of a Titian drawing for her and misses the death of his child. In the end, however, he returns, never realizing that Claudia loves him, and is reunited with a wife who chose to follow the dictates of her heart by caring for her child rather than succumb to the Old World veneration of a particular type of art that she does not really understand. Claudia, too, has learned her lesson and recognizes that she has been following beauty without intelligence. The fact that Woolson locates the difference between the Old World and the New in terms of a male's imitation of and search for the old artists and a female's love for her child suggests that she recognized how much the old ways were male-centered and how the new ways need to value home and the love of "simple country lilacs" (*FY* 255) rather than to be locked into the dark velvet fashion of stylized antique portraits.

Although she was not willing to lionize the old masters, when Woolson moved to Europe, she began to write more often about their visual art. Besides being surrounded by Italian art, she was becoming increasingly deaf and unable to pursue her early love for and knowledge of music. To continue to find her literary home in realism, she needed to gain knowledge about aspects of the society she wished to portray. She educated herself in the visual arts so that she would not accept other people's standards of judgment without applying her own judgments as well. Like Claudia in "In Venice," she recognized that it is dangerous to accept beauty without intelligence. She had two major sources to help her develop her artistic judgment: Henry James, who introduced her to so many of the Italian art galleries, lecturing all the while, and John Ruskin, whose writing on art she refused to endorse. The distinction between Woolson's attitude toward these two men is important because it shows her accepting that she had had little access to the visual arts and that she needed to educate herself about how others thought before she could make her own informed judgments.

The excerpts Leon Edel selects to make his case that James was letting down his guard and that Woolson was falling in love with him illustrate that Woolson was listening to someone who knew art as well as she knew Florida; that is, someone whose knowledge of art was superior to her own. What Edel fails to mention is that Woolson weighed that knowledge against her own instincts in order to come to a more informed judgment, but one that did not simply accept the status quo: Henry James admired Giotto and she might one day do the same, but did not feel obligated to this; Henry James admired the Duomo, but, though he tried to make her do the same, she did not; Henry James said, "Of course you admired those grand reclining figures" by Michelangelo of Day, Night, Evening and Dawn, and she replied quite candidly, "No, . . . I did not[.] They looked so distracted." Woolson's assessment of "the nude" is especially revealing, not because it shows her, as Edel suggests, to be a women who was "clearly discomposed by the nudity of statues" but because it shows her total honesty about the limitation of her experience and knowledge. "The statue of Lorenzo in the new Sacristy of San Lorenzo is the finest statue, a thousand times over, I have ever seen," she wrote, "But I confess frankly that it is going to take some time for me to appreciate 'the nude.' I have no objections to it, I look at it calmly, but I am not sufficiently acquainted with torsos, flanks, and the lines of anatomy, to know when they are 'supremely beautiful' and when not. Now 'Lorenzo' is clothed and therefore comes within my comprehension and Oh! he is superb."[2] Rather than being finicky, Woolson is being candid. She was uncomfortable with nudes just as most of us are uncomfortable with anything we fail to understand. She was neither prudish nor moralistic and judgmental, perfectly willing to try to understand the physical body, though her society hid real bodies, male and female, under layers of clothing.

Woolson's growing confidence in her own judgments are revealed in her attitude, both in her letters and in her fiction, toward John Ruskin, an art critic who was admired by most of her contemporaries. In several of her fictional works, Woolson has characters object to Ruskin. Rodney Blake, a friend of Claudia Marcy's in "In Venice" is quite irreverent, claiming to like Ruskin but saying, "Ah, but he makes us work! In some always inaccessible spot he discovers an inscrutably beautiful thing, and then he goes to work and writes about it fiercely, with all his nouns in capitals, and his adjectives after the nouns instead of before them—which naturally awes us. But what produces an even deeper thrill is his rich way of spreading his possessive cases over two words instead of one, as 'In the eager heart of him,' instead of 'In his eager heart.' This cows us completely" (*FY* 245). The satire is unmistakable and we might even be tempted to wonder if Woolson is poking a bit of fun at James, though this seems unlikely because James had not yet entered his late phase.

Woolson objected all her life to critics who made pronouncements about literature or art but had never tried anything creative themselves. For Woolson, Ruskin was an especial anathema because, unlike Matthew Arnold, she found him to be arrogant and moralistic, unwilling, even though he professed the need for economic and social reform, to support the masses. Oddly, Woolson's niece Clare Benedict writes that her aunt admired Ruskin's "splendid prose." Benedict then quotes passages from Ruskin with Woolson's marginal comments. What she considered admiring is strange, indeed, including such examples of Woolson's comments as: "Ruskin, being very near-sighted, can see nothing without a ladder, or a magnifying glass"; "The general effect of the whole, from a distance—this escapes him entirely"; and "poor little Ruskin! You should have been a priest in the days when the priest's word was law. How you would have knocked us about!" (Benedict 2:88–89). She even wrote to Katharine Loring about Ruskin, saying, "I hate him, and hate's very enlivening" (BHSM, 19 Sept. 1890). The fact that Benedict so mistook her may signal exactly the problem Woolson saw with Ruskin—that people took his word whether they understood it or not.

Woolson expanded on her objection to Ruskin in her novel *Horace Chase,* and her fictional comments here help us to see why she objected to a man who ostensibly supported reinvigorating art with a creativity that had been undermined by technology. That technology threatens to take over art is evidenced in Horace Chase's desire to have sculptures mass produced for his proposed resort. While Ruskin opposed mass-produced art for a populace who had little artistic judgment, Woolson did not trust his desire to connect to the masses. "If [his] theory is true," says Woolson's sculptress Maud Murial, "very good persons who visit the poor and go to church, are, if they dabble in water-colors, or pen-and-ink sketches, the greatest of artists, because their piety is sincere" (67). Maud Murial chastises her friend Miss Billy for trying to imitate Ruskin in her writing. She claims that Ruskin assessed sculpture "without any practical knowledge whatever of human anatomy; a man who subordinates correct drawing in a picture to the virtuous state of mind of the artist!" (67). Woolson pushes the point even further as she reiterates her own refusal to be shocked by nude statues: another of Maud Murial's friends, Mrs. Kip, questions her morality in sculpting a naked view of her own back, a subject that Mrs. Kip believes is inappropriate for "*lady* artists," who should be carving "angels" (354). Maud Murial may be a product of satire for her mannishness and her insistence on using only common or ugly subjects rather than beautiful ones for art, but she is also Woolson's spokesperson for freedom of expression. In her marginal notes on Ruskin, Woolson complains that he wants to keep people "ignorant and childish" (Benedict 3:89). Given the alternatives, Woolson prefers Maud Murial.

As both Cheryl Torsney and Joan Weimer have shown, women artists are the central character figure in Woolson's fiction. Torsney sees these figures in terms of the grief that artistry brings to women, Weimer emphasizes that Woolson's female artists prefer exile to the compromises that a home would bring, and both look at her work in terms of the expectations of a male-defined art and literary industry.[3] From the beginning of her career, Woolson looked at artist figures more than any character type, and after she began writing fiction centered in Europe the complexity of the issues surrounding those artist figures deepened. In Europe, she began to see the expectations of Americans who had come to tour the artistic capitals of the world clash with the qualities of that world; she deepened her understanding of European art and literature; she met in the person of Henry James the greatest writer she was ever to meet and undoubtedly deepened her own perceptions simply because of the level of their conversations; she began to see the full implications of choosing the solitary life of an artist, a life now largely free of family obligations; she became established with the publishing industry and learned that female writers had to deal with male publishers; and she reached the maturity of middle age. Four of Woolson's finest stories—"The Street of the Hyacinth," "Miss Grief," "At the Château of Corinne," and "In Sloane Street"—look closely and hard at what it means to find a home as a female artist.

"The Street of the Hyacinth" is the only one of these four stories that involves visual art. It is easy to see echoes in it of Woolson's relationship to Henry James, which as Cheryl Torsney has listed them, include her introductory letter to James, the guided tours James gave her of Italian art galleries, and his habit of referring to her via her middle name.[4] Joanne Vickers has also traced the James connection by reading the story as Woolson's version of *Daisy Miller,* a version that "vindicates the young American heroine as a strong, self-reliant, and intelligent woman" (288). Since the story centers on the dangers of lionizing an art critic, it may be that Woolson controlled this tendency in herself by looking squarely at it in her writing. It may also reflect her feelings toward the at least moderately talented Lizzie Boott, who married her art tutor, Frank Duveneck, who married this student whose money could support him. In the story, an American woman, Ethelinda Faith Macks, comes to Italy with a letter of introduction to the art critic Raymond Noel. She hopes that Noel will show her the galleries in Rome, look at her paintings, and recommend a teacher to her. Noel complies with the latter request in order to have Ettie, or Faith as he comes to call her, off his hands; however, when he stumbles on her in a gallery he acts as her guide and, later, lies about his assessment of the quality of her paintings.

There is a double-edged quality to this story, for Ettie is not only lionizing Noel but also actively pursuing him, yet when she wins his love, she refuses, at first, to marry him. Noel judges her as naïve when, in actuality, she seems to know exactly what she wants. Others call her clever or intelligent, and one of the reasons we do not doubt their judgment is that she remembers verbatim everything that Noel says about art. Two men eventually propose to Ettie—a count who has money but no culture, and the art teacher Noel recommended to her, who has culture but no money. Ettie wants neither of these men, but neither does she want to ensnare Noel if he does not love her. Eventually, Ettie has to take a trip to the United States because her brother has died, and at this time, Noel makes himself indispensable to her mother, whom he had before found nearly intolerable, particularly because of her tendency to wear ostentatious clothing. In mourning, the mother becomes more conventional and wears black, so that Noel can comfortably begin to pay attention to her and to prove himself to Ettie through this attention. If we read the mother's unconventional clothing as a metaphor for the female artist, as Torsney does, we begin to see that Ettie's return and acceptance of a pacified Noel represents a sacrifice of artistic integrity. It is quite possible, as well, that Ettie no longer loves Noel and marries him only because he replaces the son her mother has lost, not, as Vickers believes, because he has proven himself sincere. Ettie's feelings and motives aside, Woolson gets a final revenge on Noel by saying in a wonderfully ironic last sentence that the mother, who is beginning to abandon the role of a grieving invalid, is no longer "confined to her bed; she drives out with her daughter whenever the weather is favorable. She wears black, but is now beginning to vary it with lavender" (*FY* 193).

We may find poetic justice in "The Street of the Hyacinth" if we read the ending as a metaphor for the female artist ensnaring the resisting critic, but we still must deal with Ettie's decision to marry Noel as the central concluding action. If we read the marriage as a conventional happy ending, the story is unsatisfying because Noel never engages the sympathy of most readers. If we read it as Ettie's self-sacrifice for her mother, the story fits Woolson's tendency to portray sacrificial heroines, but since in no other story does a woman marry as a sacrifice, this is a tenuous interpretation. We could suggest that Ettie gains her own revenge on Noel through the marriage, but such an interpretation places Ettie in the position of revenge seeker, hardly an admirable role. The best way out of the problem is to admit that Ettie loses our admiration and that Woolson intended this and also gained her own authorial revenge by foreshadowing that the marriage will become a trial to Noel. Woolson undoubtedly intended the story to be problematic since the issues of women and marriage, women and art were highly problematic ones in her day.

Regardless of how we see Ettie's character, the story is quite pointed in its treatment of issues related to art. Noel believes that artificiality is an intrinsic and valuable part of art. Thus he can flirt with a French woman and find that "[s]he was not artificial, because she was art itself. Real art is as real as real nature is natural" (*FY* 163). Noel values the ornamental, the kind of artificial beauty in a woman that allows her to be an art object and that absolves him from seeing the woman beneath the ornament. He also values "execution," the established, definable, and, we might say, male techniques of art while Ettie sees "execution" as "secondary" to "the subject, the idea," which is "the important thing" (*FY* 165). This is why Noel discredits Ettie. Her technique, he believes, is abysmal, and her art teacher concurs. Both, though, at first lie to Ettie, Noel to be rid of her and the teacher because he loves her. Two other male artists, we learn, tell her that she has no real talent. Woolson never provides the grounds for these last two negative judgments, the problem being not the quality of Ettie's art but her faith in these judgments, so that she eventually comes to believe that her art is no good.

We cannot, however, assume that Woolson intends us to disagree with male judgments about art. In one scene, for example, Noel takes

Ettie walking through a Roman market because "he was very fond of the old streets, and was curious to see whether she would notice the colors and outlines that made their picturesqueness. She noticed nothing but the vegetable stalls, and talked of nothing but her pictures" (*FY* 152). This is Noel's judgment of what Ettie fails to notice, but she does sound a great deal like the American woman in "The Front Yard," who wants only a New England front yard for her house and never notices that she has an extraordinary view of the Italian landscape. As the criticism of Ruskin confirms, Woolson knows that artists can get lost in details and miss the broader picture, whether visual or literary. But she also knows that the avenues to great art are not all the same and that the female way of seeing tends to be disparaged. Ettie does not stop trying to be an artist until she realizes that four males judge her as lacking. She begins with an idealized view of the artist that causes her to seek Noel in Europe: "there comes a time when [artists] have to live on hope and their own pluck more than upon anything tangible that the present has to offer. They have to take a risk" (*FY* 143). She ends with a pragmatic view that without an audience she will trade art for teaching. But as she does so she has also formed her own judgments about art. Though Noel takes her to the nine "right" galleries, she wants to see twenty and, like Woolson with James, says she needs to understand Noel's judgments in order to make her own on solid, intelligent grounds.

Ettie's relinquishing of art cannot be attributed to one cause. She may have taken the pragmatist view because she decides it is not worth the effort to paint from a female perspective; she may have done this because she has bowed to male perspectives and judged her work as lacking; or she may have stopped painting because her independent judgment has shown her that whether from a male or a female perspective her painting is lacking. Whatever the case, it is significant that her marriage is less to Noel than to her mother's son-in-law and that Woolson does not intend us to admire Noel. Woolson constantly undercuts him with sentences like "when [Ettie] was his wife he would tell her the truth, and in the greatness of his love the revelation would be naught" (*FY* 173). Noel may, as Vickers believes, change by the end of the story, but this seems unlikely because Woolson exacts such a neat revenge on him in the guise of the mother. Again, we are left with the sense that Ettie, too, has been defeated. Both Cheryl Torsney and Joan Weimer support the notion of her defeat through the image of Hyacinth, who was accidentally killed by Apollo, his teacher.[5]

Hyacinth's death, in this interpretation, represents Ettie's death as an artist and her defeat in marrying Noel. We can give this another twist, however, especially if we take a cue form Torsney and translate Ettie's full name, Ethelinda as German for "noble serpent." With this twist, we can see Noel as slain by his teacher, Ettie, when she dooms him unintentionally, if we want to be true to the myth and to Ettie's defeat in marriage, to an alliance with a mother-in-law who flaunts all the "wrong" artistic tastes. In the end, the shabby Roman Street of the Hyacinth is torn down, but Hyacinth rises again in the purple and lavender shades of the mother's clothing, a reminder for Noel that the grief of losing Ettie might have been preferable to the grief of gaining her mother.

That Woolson associated art with grief is apparent even in the title of what is perhaps her most extraordinary story, "Miss Grief." The story concerns a female writer trying to get a manuscript published and it becomes especially meaningful if read against the backdrop of the publishing establishment as it existed in Woolson's day. Discussions of American literary history generally connect the development of fictional forms with the American writer's need to show autonomy from British traditions in the aftermath of the political freedom won by the Revolutionary War. Thus we hear in the famous Melvillian accolade of Hawthorne that "we want no American Goldsmiths, nay, we want no American Miltons. . . . no American writer should write like an Englishman or a Frenchman; let him write like a man, for then he will be sure to write like an American" (Melville 1470–71). To contend that American fiction developed outside the purview of British fiction would be incorrect—Washington Irving and Charles Brockden Brown, for example, sought American locations and atmospheres for the Gothic form they had seen develop in Britain, Cooper has been dubbed an American Sir Walter Scott, and many women aspired to emulate the Brontë sisters. But because the fictional form is new in comparison to the dramatic or poetic, American writers gravitated to this new form that was shaping itself as the new country shaped itself. At the same time, American women were beginning to see themselves as able to maintain their private sphere and still write for public audiences.[6] As they broadened their avenues for work, their educational base, and their ability to earn wages, they, too, gravitated to a new literary form in which they could sound their new voices. But as much as women were allowed to write and even were courted by publishers, they still had more strictures put on them than their male counterparts. Even at the end of the century, Woolson could write to Henry James, "Fancy any woman's attempting a portrait of a gentleman!" and could complain to him of woman's inability to be "a complete artist," a comment that seems to refer to the publishing pressures on women writers to provide happy endings.[7]

By Woolson's day, the publishing scene had changed in ways that Susan Coultrap-McQuin has argued undermined women's mode of working. In the middle of the nineteenth century, says McQuin, the author-publisher relationship centered on "personal regard, benevolent paternalism, loyalty, noncommercialism, and advocacy of Victorian morality," and was more hospitable to women than at any other time in the history of publishing (xii). This does not mean that publishers valued women over men; in fact, they routinely omitted women from celebratory occasions such as one the *Atlantic Monthly* sponsored in 1877 to honor John Greenleaf Whittier. Still, the publishing industry's vision of itself as the guardian of culture and morality allowed it to subordinate the profit motive and to abide by a gentleman's agreement not to steal other publisher's writers. Marketing strategies and competition began developing in the 1830s, but the ideal of the Gentleman Publisher did not become subordinate to the profit motive until after the Civil War. By the time Woolson was publishing, the Businessman Publisher was emphasizing efficiency, profit, objectivity, and audience appeal; it was, as Coultrap-McQuin says, becoming more centered on male values of aggressiveness and competition, even going so far as rejecting manuscripts from established writers. In England, as well, the position of the female novelist was changing. Gaye Tuchman and Nina Fortin have studied the Macmillan Archives to show that before 1840, more women than men submitted to Macmillan; from 1840 to 1879, when the novel had become a legitimate forum for the dissemination of ideas, men began to submit more often though not as frequently as women; and from 1880 to 1899, they submitted more than women, with equal acceptance rates (7–8).

Woolson was caught within the dynamics of this change. She settled in Europe and came into her own as a writer at exactly the time that men began to achieve primacy as writers of novels. Cheryl Torsney has shown that the changes directly affected Woolson and has traced her difficulties with the Osgoods, who failed to promote her work, and with the Appletons, who would not release the copyright for *Anne,* a book they claimed they could not pay her for because they had not paid their own expenses.[8] On the one hand, she was criticized early in her career for "infesting the magazines"[9] with her work rather than staying with one publisher; on the other, she was, later in her career, committed to Harper's, one of the most commercial of the publishers, to such an extent that she constantly worried about meeting their deadlines at the same time that she wrote more slowly the more pressure built on her. Her letters to Sam Mather, who handled most of her financial affairs, indicate that she felt dependent on the money she made from her writing, that she hoped diligence and thrift would enable her to save enough money to settle in her own home in a congenial climate like that in Venice or Florida, and that she felt an obligation to fulfill her commitments to Harper's. Woolson was a professional writer in a marketplace that was increasingly competitive and was unable to write hasty potboilers to please this marketplace.

Woolson's "Miss Grief" illustrates the tension for women trying to write in a marketplace that imposed strictures on them that it did not impose on males and that valued male writing over female even though for a large portion of the century nearly three-quarters of its writers were female. The story explores the relationship between the writer and society and between the writer and disciple.[10] Modeling himself on Balzac, the narrator of "Miss Grief" judges himself a "literary success" (*MG* 248). By this he means that he is successful in a Balzacian kind of social world, and he is convinced that hard work has made this success deserved. As a mark of his success, he is much sought after for dinner parties and is known as the author of "those delightful little studies of society" (*MG* 248). This society is represented by the narrator's fiancée, Isabel Abercrombie. Representative of art, on the other hand, is Miss Crief, a name the narrator has misunderstood and translated to "Miss Grief." Much as Woolson in 1880 approached James, and Ettie approached Noel in "The Street of the Hyacinth," "Miss Grief" approaches the narrator. Her visits have been fruitless until finally one evening this hard-working writer, because of difficulties with Isabel, remains at home. "Miss Grief" asks the well-known writer to read her work: a play, a prose piece, some poems. He is greatly impressed but he also sees the work as greatly flawed. Nevertheless, he tries unsuccessfully to have the work published. This failing, he tries to correct the flaws, but they will not be corrected. Having done as much as he is willing, he still keeps the work for months. He sees "Miss Grief" again only when he chances to meet her aunt-companion in the street. "Miss Grief" is now dying. At her deathbed, the narrator lies about having found a publisher for her drama. He promises to see the manuscript through and to bury her other work with her. The latter he does. The drama he keeps, stating in his will that it should be buried with him, unread.

The narrator of "Miss Grief" is culpable on many levels. He praises "Miss Grief" not for her genius but as an "antihysteric" (*MG* 258). The aid he gives her is at best half-hearted. When he invites her to dinner, he arranges for her early departure. When he sends two of her pieces to publishers, the publishers are both inappropriate ones. Finally, he accepts Isabel's worldly judgments of her poems and from then on never shows her manuscripts again. One of "Miss Grief['s]" manuscripts has a physician hovering behind a conventional, approved plot of a dying girl and the man who pretends to love her in order not to break her heart. Woolson's narrator-critic cannot understand the physician's role: to "Miss Grief," he is a messiah; to him, he is simply a murderer.[11] Males and females read differently, Woolson says, yet if the male could open himself to women's writing and their ways of reading, he might find liberation rather than death. Without this open-mindedness, he will continue to dismiss women writers as "authoress[es]! . . . worse than old lace" (*MG* 253) and women and their work will be buried unappreciated and unread. When the narrator denies "Miss Grief," he also denies the suffering of genius and accepts, instead, the shallow happiness represented by Isabel, a woman who has adopted male visions of what women should be. The possibility of another self that encompasses genius does exist for the narrator and did, in fact, surface once in a piece of writing that drew "Miss Grief" to him in the first place. But the narrator denies his alter ego, his genius, and remains only a writer of talent.

Through the narrator's culpability and "Miss Grief['s]" buried work, Woolson creates a feminist statement about the problems women writers face. The male writer has success, the publishing industry is represented by males, the male can keep the female's manuscript for months. The female, especially if she is not young or attractive, has only her writing to validate herself, yet if she speaks in a different voice, she is not heard and her work is tampered with by the male critic. Such, again, seems to have been Woolson's fate at the hands of Leon Edel, who reads "Miss Grief" in terms of Woolson's "deep literary ambition," her "exalted notion of her own literary powers," and her lionizing of James.[12] Joan Weimer offers a more plausible interpretation of Woolson's motives when she suggests that "Miss Grief" represents the fate of a woman who writes as she pleases rather than as the literary establishment dictates, and that Woolson suppressed some of her own writing in order to survive as a professional (*MG* xxxvii–xxxix). By putting "Miss Grief" into the context of Woolson's publishing history and asking why her publishers did not include the story in her two posthumous collections of Italian stories, Cheryl Torsney makes a case that the publishing industry acted much like the narrator of the story, suppressing a work they found intimidating. For her, "Miss Grief" is a "paradigmatic story of nineteenth-century woman's artistry, a narrative that, given late twentieth-century hindsight, offers an ironic comment on the canonization of literary texts by implying that many powerful works by women were, in effect, suppressed by those male readers, editors, and publishers in positions of power."[13] Whether we regard Woolson's publisher's decision as conscious or not, as late as 1967 this fine story was collected only in Rayburn Moore's *For the Major* edition. Thanks to Torsney and Weimer, it is now available in a *Legacy* reprint and in *Women Artists, Women Exiles*.

Torsney and Weimer have also helped to resurrect another of Woolson's artist tales, "At the Château of Corinne," a work collected in *Dorothy*, a collection that has never been reprinted. At first glance, the story, which Weimer includes in *Women Artists, Women Exiles*, is a feminist's nightmare, as illustrated in a brutally direct assessment the character John Ford makes of poems by the young widow Katharine Winthrop:

> We do not expect great poems from women any more than we expect great pictures; we do not expect strong logic any more than we expect brawny muscle. A woman's poetry is subjective. But what cannot be forgiven—at least in my opinion—is that which I have called the distinguishing feature of the volume, a certain sort of daring. This is its essential, unpardonable sin. Not because it is in itself dangerous; it has not force enough for that; but because it comes, and can be recognized at once as coming, from the lips of a woman. For a woman should not dare in that way. Thinking to soar, she invariably descends. Her mental realm is not the same as that of man; lower, on the same level, or far above, it is at least different. . . . Every honest man feels like going to her, poor mistaken sibyl that she is, closing her lips with gentle hand, and leading her away to some far spot among the quiet fields, where she can learn her error, and begin her life anew. (*MG* 233–34)

Ford, who sounds rather like Schopenhauer, a writer Woolson had read,[14] makes similar comments throughout the story. He talks about loving Katharine "in spite of" himself (*MG* 243), about wanting her to lose her money so that she will need him, about how childlike she is with her small foot, and about wanting her to be "dependant upon [her] husband" (*MG* 243). With a distinctly homophobic attitude, he dismisses Katharine's fiancé, Lorimer Percival, as effeminate and convinces her, finally, to marry him instead.

There is much we do not know in this story. We do not know if Katharine broke her engagement or was jilted, or if she chooses to let Ford think she was jilted in order that he will think she depends on him. We know that her engagement to Percival replicates her first marriage to an older man, but we do not know if her marriage to Ford is a better match. More important, we do not know if Katharine's poem is bad only from Ford's male standard, but we do know that Ford is blatantly honest and that through him Woolson opens up the issue of a woman trying to write like a man. Through him, she also raises the question that informs so much of her writing throughout her career, that of having a public life as a writer or a private life within a home. The centrality of this issue is apparent in a brief exchange about Corinne between Ford and Katharine:

> Katharine: "A woman of genius! And what is the very term but a stigma? No woman is so proclaimed by the great brazen tongue of the Public unless she has thrown away her birthright of womanly seclusion for the miserable woes of pottage called 'fame.'"
> Ford: "The seclusion of a convent? or a prison?"
> Katharine: "Neither. Of a home." (*MG* 229–30)

The dilemma between art and home plays itself out when Katharine chooses the home Ford offers. The centerpiece of that home is a picture of Coppet, the Château where Madame de Staël wrote *Corinne,* and a collection of Madame de Staël's books. The courtship between Ford and Katharine took place in four meetings at Coppet, a fitting environment given the reification of de Staël as a woman of genius by many nineteenth-century women writers.[15] Although Katharine, unlike de Staël, chooses home, she also venerates the woman who defied men and who suffered criticism and "dreary exile" (*MG* 229) because of her choice. This, plus a puzzling last line that Benjamin Franklin, the keeper of the Château of Corinne, understood English after all, suggests that Katharine is trying to forge a new, American way, one where a woman can be honest, independent, and cooperative. This new way also requires a change in men, so that Katharine accepts Ford as a husband only when he kneels at her feet with tears in his eyes, not fully changed but ready to try. Certainly, we may want to read Katharine's acceptance of Ford and her abandonment of her art as a defeat. Cheryl Torsney reads it as an action precipitated by Katharine's financial need and one where she is "[t]aken under her husband's control, put into his library, . . . ranged separately on a shelf, a collectable, a conversation piece, an objet d'art."[16] The blatantness of Ford's sexism indicates that, whatever the reader's assessment of Katharine, Woolson also wanted to expose the dilemma faced by female artists in the nineteenth century and to challenge her readers to think about the "woman question." As Joan Weimer so aptly puts it, the "torrent of misogyny" that "Woolson assigns Ford is a clear sign of her disapproval of his stereotypical masculinity, while the space she gives his violent opinions indicates her belief that such opinions were a very serious obstacle to women writers" (*MG* xxxvii).

Unlike "Miss Grief" and "At the Château of Corinne," Woolson's "In Sloane Street," another of her first-rate stories about writers, is not available in modern reprints. As the only story Woolson set in England, it found no place in any of her collections and so must be looked for in its original magazine version in *Harper's Bazar,* June 11, 1892. That publishing date places it at the end of Woolson's career, but the story harks back to the time she spent in Sloane Street in London in 1884, and internal evidence suggests the story may have been drafted at that time. It was during her stay in Sloane Street that Woolson learned of her brother Charlie's death, and perhaps because of this memory, she wrestles in this story more than in any of her other works about the conflicts between commitment to family and commitment to art.

Woolson was never one to stereotype her characters unless she undermines this with ironic narrative commentary or provides some kind of twist to the stereotype. The twist provided in "In Sloane Street" is that the writer in question, Philip Moore, is male and that the choice he makes for family comes because his wife wants to be supported in style, which can happen only if he gives up his serious writing and moves to Washington, where he can devote himself to writing popular novels. Woolson by no means insists that his is a lesser choice, but it is a choice between two roles she saw as incompatible—that of family person and that of writer—made because Philip is devoted to his children. The complexity of how to interpret Philip's decision is deepened by the character of Gertrude Remington, his friend and lionizer since childhood, who is an aficionado of art and literature though she claims not to write herself. The story allows Woolson to ask a number of questions about art, particularly writing, none of which, as typical in her fiction about art, has a clear answer. By the time the story has ended, we are asking about the relationship between gender and literature, about the pressures on women to write children's literature, and even about the relationship between artist, critic, and reader.

Woolson names three women writers in "In Sloane Street," and they all tell us something about attitudes toward women who write. Her reference to George Eliot comes from a visit to her grave by Gertrude and by Moore's wife, who implies a criticism of both Gertrude and George Eliot when she says that "a tall thin woman in a tailor-made gown, with hair dragged lightly back from her face, and all sorts of deep books—why, naturally all men are afraid of her" (474).[17] Woolson, however, admired George Eliot, particularly her ability to "do exactly as she pleased—law or no law, custom or no custom,"[18] so that she clearly does not intend us to accept the Moores' assessment, as much as this assessment may represent the prevailing attitude toward women writers. Nor does Mrs. Moore like Marie Bashkirtseff, the Russian whose posthumously published journal was in vogue, partly because of its morbid introspection. While Mrs. Moore finds the journal "unnatural," something to be dismissed as a weird French thing, Gertrude finds it entirely "natural." But this is not because she admires Bashkirtseff; in fact, she may see her as a reflection of the kind of woman Mrs. Moore appears to be—self-indulgent and inattentive to family. Gertrude lambastes Bashkirtseff for "her behavior to her mother and her aunt [which] showed indifference, and often scorn; her one thought was herself" (475). This kind of selfishness was particularly troubling to Woolson, who disliked Tolstoy because he ignored his family and, though professing commitment to the masses, never sacrificed his comfort for them.[19] In a journal entry about Bashkirtseff, Woolson says that "[a]ny journal written with absolute truth would be equally interesting," but the entry makes it impossible to discover if she thinks Bashkirtseff, like Tolstoy, is at heart untruthful (Benedict 2:104).

As someone who became a traveling companion to her mother and later to her sister and her niece, Woolson valued family, yet she also recognized the way family can place tremendous obligations on writers to publish what will support them. Thus the third woman writer named in "In Sloane Street" is Louisa May Alcott, who died four years before Woolson published this story and whose recently published biography, Ednah Cheney's *Louisa May Alcott: Her Life, Letters, and Journals,* Gertrude has been reading.[20] Gertrude values Alcott, marveling that she "worked all her life as hard as she possibly could, turning her hand to anything that offered, no matter what, and her sole motive was to assist her parents and her family, those dear to her; of herself she never thought at all" (475). Cheryl Torsney reads this story in terms of what Woolson values: "art, loyalty, self-sacrifice, hard work [which] were no longer validated by society" at the approaching turn of the century.[21] But as much as Woolson may be seeming to endorse Alcott's way through Gertrude's voice, she still portrays a Gertrude who holds a double standard: Gertrude admires Alcott because Alcott sacrificed for the sake of family, but she despairs when Philip chooses to sacrifice his serious career for the sake of family. Gertrude is Philip's "chief incense-burner" (474), but Woolson, typically, gives us no way of knowing how good a writer he is. Through his many comments about women being unfit to write seriously, Woolson compels us to doubt Philip's abilities but to see also that he has the option to write seriously, which women do not have. In some ways, he is also a victim of the segment of society that Gertrude represents: those who believe that a man must sacrifice family for the sake of art. Fortunately for Philip, he also has a wife who is happy to let him become the female-identified character, directing his attention to the needs of his family, especially his children.

The society Woolson depicts in "In Sloane Street" relegates women's creativity to the frightening and their intelligence to the overly emancipated represented by Philip's sisters, who advocate college for women. But of all the shackles put on women, Woolson seems most upset about the assumption that women can write "children's stories—yes; they can write for children, and for young girls, extremely well" (474). Woolson's own first book, *The Old Stone House,* was a children's book, published just five years after *Little Women.* The success of *Little Women* caused publishers to pressure women to write children's stories, but Woolson abandoned this genre early on and, in a letter to her former teacher Linda Guilford, recalls disliking the tendency in the United States to exalt "stories for children to a place which it did not seem to me belonged to them." She continues the letter complaining about having to hear another of her former teachers deliver "an hour's eulogy of [*sic*] Miss Alcott's 'Little Women'—which I, too, liked, but could not place above all else in the world." Still, she admires Alcott and the "heroic, brave struggles" she went through (Benedict 2:41–45).

This is not surprising, because Ednah Cheney's biography of Alcott portrays someone much like Woolson. Early on, Alcott chose spinsterhood in order to support her parents: a mother who had eight pregnancies and much household care, and a father who, helpless though he was in practical matters, did teach her to love both learning and exercise. Alcott frequently worried about the money she was making, but still she took pride in her ability to remain unmarried and independent even though this put her at odds with other more feminine women. Unlike Alcott, Woolson made a firm break with the notion of writing for children even before the time she lived in Sloane Street. In 1883, she refused an offer from the *Companion* to write a children's story, politely saying that many other authors have the talent to write for them that she does not possess and that these authors would accept the "generous terms" the *Companion* was offering.²²

Not only does Woolson use the Alcott reference to underscore the dilemma of needing to write for children against one's natural inclinations, she reinforces gender attitudes in her portrait of the Moore children's creativity. Their childhood play is with dolls and it involves having the dolls seek a water cure for sickness, specifically "the *mind-cure.*" Of course, the boy is the "head doctor" (275), both in terms of his importance and in terms of the notion that women need mind cures in a society that tends to deny them the power to write. Throughout her career, Woolson recognized that society denied women power by denying them access to serious art. The general population of women is like Mrs. Moore, whose words open the story: "Well, I've seen the National Gallery" (473). High art is a sense of duty; analytical novels, which Gertrude wants Mrs. Moore to read, are dismissed as "that analytical thing? I hate analytical novels, and can't imagine why any one writes them" (474). Preferable are popular novels that are "easy to read" and that make women like Mrs. Moore "laugh" (475).

Yet it is not just popular tastes that artists have to deal with. They also have to contend with how much critics shape taste. As early as her lake country stories, Woolson raised questions about the power of critics. Here, at the end of her career, she makes the same point through Gertrude, who complains of a friend who "thinks that painters, as a rule, are stupid—have no ideas; whereas the art critics—that is, the two or three she likes—really know what a picture means"; "it is the art critic . . . who discovers the soul in their productions" (473). In particular, Gertrude, like Woolson, singles out Ruskin, saying that "all his later books are the weakest twaddle in the world, violent, ignorant, childish" (473). Philip, it seems, is caught between a rock and a hard place. If he relies on popular audiences, he is ignored; if he relies on critics, he is also ignored. However, he does not really seem to care, complaining to Gertrude that his works are of no interest to him once they are printed: when readers "get hold of them—I'm taken up with something else, and miles away. Yet you always try to drag me back" (474). Gertrude, on the other hand, believes that there is some purpose to art represented in the analytical novels that Mrs. Moore hates so much. People write them and read them because they "are interested in the study of character generally," as Gertrude and Mrs. Moore "are interested in Philip's in particular" (474).

And here is the rub of the story. Woolson is interested in character: to a small extent in Mrs. Moore's as representative of the cultural norm; to a greater extent in Philip's for abandoning the role of the starving male author who forces his family to live on the bottom floor of a house in dark, dreary Sloane Street with its "battered" pavement (474). She is also interested in Gertrude, who seems like the "battered" women of Sloane Street—like the "vine [that] was attached to one of these dwellings, [whose] leaves, though dripping, had a dried appearance" (474). But unlike Gertrude, who has her love for art and her love for Philip's character, Woolson could transform a voyeuristic study of an individual into a creative understanding of the complexity and ambiguities of even the most stereotypical nineteenth-century character types.

Although she never sacrificed her duty to family, Woolson did choose to devote her life to art. That she plunged into depression after each of her books indicates that she could not, like Philip, so easily forget her work once the public got hold of it. Given the fact that she has been championed by neither the public nor the literary establishment in the twentieth century, it seems appropriate that she has Philip choose family life over art. In the light of the neglect of Woolson in the twentieth century, a journal entry she wrote about painting becomes especially poignant: If a picture, she asks, remains unfinished and then not looked at by anyone, "Was this work, this life, useless?" (Benedict 2:103). On the one hand, Woolson needed her work to be looked at in order to support herself, and she found this work continually exhausting. On the other, she knew that the art work could never be complete in the sense that it could render absolute truth divorced of its social and cultural milieu. So a dialogue in *East Angels* centers on the question of whether a painter is painting the "true" blue of the sky (165) and an uncollected story called "The Old Palace Keeper" asks if a fresco of an angel can be copied, if it, as ideal as it is, could approach the truth of angelness, and if, destroyed, it becomes less of an ideal portrait than it had been. Unread though she has been in the twentieth century, we still must answer that Woolson's life, her work, was not useless. Art provided an outlet for this extraordinary woman, who knew that she could not create an abstract "true" blue sky or an ideal angel. Instead, she maintained a connection to a society that she understood fully, that she often did not approve of, but whose members she refused to condemn because she knew the weight of societal pressures.

At Home in the Canon

♣

New methods of subjective literary criticism have taught us to become self-conscious about what draws us to particular literary figures and about how we interpret their texts. As I conclude this study of Constance Fenimore Woolson, I enter my fifties and realize that part of why I am drawn to her comes from my sense of being born into a lost pocket of time. Where Woolson, born in 1840, is counted neither pre–Civil War nor post–Civil War, those of us born in the early 1940s are neither pre-Vietnam children of the fifties nor post-Vietnam children of the sixties. Many of the males among us were drafted into a war that crept into our awareness before the first draft card had been burned. Now we hear commentaries about the first baby-boomer president and wonder what happened to the generations between our elder statesmen and the baby boom. As a woman born in 1943, I was not unusual in my decision to attend college. But I managed to finish both undergraduate and graduate school without having studied with a single female professor. I had the benefit neither of those women who came before me and were just beginning to teach in and shape the feminist agenda of the academy from which I was graduating, nor those who came after me and benefited from their mentoring. Recently a young professor struggling with how he and his wife, a professional outside academia, juggled child-care issues asked me how I had managed and seemed to admire that I was "a generation ahead of my time." But what this meant for me was nearly ten years of part-time employment in a glutted job market, so that my child-care issues were easily resolved. Still, I regret few of my life choices and accidents and feel no envy toward the young professor and his wife who must balance full-time careers and child rearing. Instead of feeling burned out by the

pressures of a publish or perish environment, I look forward to another two decades of research and writing, assuming I do not follow
Woolson to an early grave.

Just as my sense of being born into a lost pocket of time draws
me to Woolson, so, too, does my sense that much time is left for her
in our evolving canon. What might we find if we studied writers born
in the early 1840s? Surely there are more than Woolson and the Jameses
who deserve our attention. Or if there are not, might we discover why?
Were too many of the men of talent killed in the Civil War so that our
best-known Civil War novelist, Stephen Crane, was not even born until
1871? Did the women who might have chosen authorship redirect their
talents into the social causes that emerged after the war? What do the
records of publishing houses reveal about submissions in the war years
by men and women hovering around the age of twenty? In those like
James and Woolson who do choose writing as a career can we see
overlapping themes, such as the ones of homelessness and exile, that
are a by-product of the tumultuous change young people who came
of age during the war experienced and are there connections that we
can draw to our contemporary writers who came of age during the
Vietnam war? As we move out of our tendency to study literature in
terms of periods, we have much to gain by including in our studies
writers who do not fall easily into period groups.

The accidents of Woolson's life, not the trends of a rigidly defined
literary period, shaped her conception of home as physical sanctuary
and metaphorical belonging. Had she married, had her father lived
longer, had her mother's health and financial constraints not led her
south, Woolson might never have begun to write at all, or she might
have remained a journalist for the Cleveland newspaper that published
her first travel sketches. But at least to some extent writers are born,
not made. Had she stayed in Cleveland, Woolson would likely have
developed into a local-color writer associated with one region, and,
with that regional identification, might today be better known. Because
of her penchant for observing the present and the actual, I believe
that she would still have moved away from the domestic realists whose
social milieu changed too much with the influx of immigration and
industrialization and the disruption of the Civil War for Woolson to
imitate. She also would have moved away from Cooper's brand of
romance because it was too ideal and from Hawthorne's because it
was too grounded in the imagined past.

Woolson's talent always lay in her ability to create the nuances of the local and the present. Her movement out of the boundaries of her lake country home was fortuitous, for though these boundaries may have seemed limitless before the Civil War, by war's end they were fast becoming limited by the established morés of town and city dwellers. Equally problematic, if they remained untouched by evolving civilization, they would lack a cultural milieu out of which Woolson could shape her art. Woolson's move south during the turmoil of Reconstruction and then her move to Europe gave her access to other writers so that she could become more conscious of the kind of writer she wished to be. It also expanded her sense of place and of the contrasts between places.

For each of the places Woolson wrote about, she saw how region generates different issues, particularly for women seeking a place to call home. In her fiction, the West, with its untapped lands, represents the temporary possibility, usually unfulfilled, of finding a new way in connection to the land and outside the rigid social expectations of established society. The South has social expectations so embedded that its connection to the past inhibits its vision of the future and causes it to insist on enmities with other regions of the United States. Describing a character's preference for the South in *Jupiter Lights,* Woolson puts it this way: "It might have been said, perhaps, that between houses and a society uncomfortable from age, falling to pieces from want of repairs, and houses and a society uncomfortable from youth, unfurnished, and encumbered with scaffolding, there was not much to choose. But the judge did not think so; to his mind there was a great deal to choose" (140). In this novel, Woolson prefers the West with its freedom from enmity and its naturalness represented in the image of the jupiter light, a lighthouse where one might live close to nature and apart from all social ties. But there is also a jupiter light in the South, and Woolson recognized another dimension in the South that escaped the obsession with the past: as in the Florida swamps, it had some untapped and unexplored regions that could help to open men and women to their untapped and passionate selves. In contrast, in Europe she came to see that Americans have no way to transform themselves except as visitors living as Americans on the fringes of society.

The expanding range of Woolson's fiction makes it an invaluable source for understanding nineteenth-century issues. The fiction helps us to understand the impact of demographic change and the rise of industrialism. It provides a window into attitudes toward social class and the insulation of the elite and the struggle of those on the fringes of the elite. It provides insights into race relations and ethnicity, particularly as these are mirrored in the diverse regions of the United States and in the position of Americans in Europe. And it helps us to see how women's places—as wife, mother, daughter, widow, spinster, artist—are socially prescribed merely because of gender. My approach to Woolson's treatment of these issues as they show her feeling bonded to and bounded by home has been general and comprehensive rather than specific and exhaustive because I believe that at this juncture in Woolson studies we need an overview of her corpus of fiction to give us a full sense of its richness and variety and the appropriateness of its home in the literary canon.

That Woolson deserves this home is represented as much by what I have left unwritten as by what I have written. Besides studying Woolson in relation to other writers born into a lost generation, we will find a wealth of material to pursue as her work becomes better known. Much, for example, remains to be done on the connection between Woolson and James. The path of influence cuts in both directions and a profitable area for study here might attempt to describe how the two writers bring different gender perspectives to similar germ ideas. Other literary comparisons would also yield rewards, the most obvious being to Howells and Harte, but with possibilities also apparent in the women writers a generation older than Woolson—Elizabeth Barrett Browning and Margaret Fuller might prove fruitful because of the European connection—and in women a generation younger—one thinks especially of Edith Wharton—who may have been shaped by her well-respected work.

It would also be rewarding to study more fully Woolson's treatment of specific issues in the light of magazine and news accounts of the day; for example, reported cases of wife and child abuse and the extent to which these are connected to alcoholism, or debates about Social Darwinism and the extent to which they are connected to debates about education for American Indians and African Americans. A study of Woolson's treatment of specific regions might give us a fuller picture about women's relationships to nature. How did the landscapes and myths of Mackinac Island inscribe her fiction and what does this tell us about the island's growth as a resort community? How does her fiction about Florida differ from that of other regions of the South and can this help us to understand how landscape shaped different ways in which the South reconstructed itself after the Civil War? A more philosophical approach might enlarge the study of Woolson's artist figures to see them not only in terms of gender but also in terms of self-conscious theoretical questions about the nature of art that place her into the context of modernism. Her fiction reminds us that nineteenth-century artists explored attitudes toward the relationship not only between art and gender but between art and reality, between artist, critic, and reader, and between art and commercialism in ways that could be as sophisticated as those of today's literary theorist.

Besides fiction, Woolson wrote travel sketches and poetry and she kept a notebook and carried on a large correspondence, all of which represent untapped areas for those interested in Woolson studies. But it is her fiction that is especially valuable for us today because it situates itself in the decades after the height of romantic and domestic fiction and before the more outspoken and self-conscious fiction of the turn of the century and so reflects a society on the brink of change. If we begin to read it again, it can show us much about our own brink in order that we may learn from the society of a hundred years ago and construct a world that a hundred years hence will be less fraught with racism and sexism and less fractured into unequal social classes and biased regionalism. Constance Fenimore Woolson was bound to the past and to the future, a difficult place to call home, but one we need to remember by placing her again at home in the canon.

Notes

♣

Frequently referenced works are cited in the text using the abbreviations below. Other in-texts references are coded to the bibliography. References to Woolson's short fiction are to her collections or the most easily available source.

Benedict	Clare Benedict, *Five Generations (1785–1923)* 3 vols. (London: Ellis, 1929–30)
BHSM	Katharine Loring Papers, Beverly Historical Society and Museum, Massachusetts
CN	Woolson, *Castle Nowhere: Lake Country Sketches* (New York: Garrett, 1969)
FY	Woolson, *The Front Yard and Other Italian Stories* (New York: Books for Libraries Press, 1969)
Hubbell	Jay B. Hubbell, ed., "Some New Letters of Constance Fenimore Woolson," *New England Quarterly* 14 (Dec. 1941)
Major	Rayburn S. Moore, ed., *For the Major and Selected Short Stories* (New Haven, Conn.: College and University Press, 1967)
MG	Joan Myers Weimer, ed., *Women Artists, Women Exiles: "Miss Grief" and Other Stories* (New Brunswick, N.J.: Rutgers University Press, 1988)
Petry	Alice Hall Petry, "'Always, Your Attached Friend': The Unpublished Letters of Constance Fenimore Woolson to John and Clara Hay" (*Books at Brown,* 1982–83)
Rodman	Woolson, *Rodman the Keeper: Southern Sketches* (New York: Garrett, 1969)
WRHS	Samuel Mather Family Papers, Western Reserve Historical Society, Cleveland

Introduction

1. Cheryl B. Torsney, *Constance Fenimore Woolson: The Grief of Artistry* (Athens: Univ. of Georgia Press, 1989), 5–21.

2. Clare Benedict, *Five Generations (1785–1923)* (London: Ellis, 1929–30). The *Five Generations* volumes are titled *Voices Out of the Past, Constance Fenimore Woolson,* and *The Benedicts Abroad.* Benedict, who published a revised edition in 1932, gave away, but did not sell, these privately printed books.

3. Clare Benedict, *Appreciations* (Leatherhead, Surrey: F. B. Benger, 1941).

4. I am indebted to Colin Sanborn of the Claremont (New Hampshire) Historical Society and Marilyn Nagy of the Fiske Free Library, Claremont, for information on the Benedict connection to Claremont.

5. A variety of correspondence about the Mackinac Memorial is with the Mather Family Papers at the Western Reserve Historical Society, Cleveland.

6. The Woolson House is now a lounge for the English Department of Rollins College and its connection to Woolson studies tenuous at best. For a discussion of the neglect of Woolson House, see Cheryl B. Torsney, "In Anticipation of the Fiftieth Anniversary of Woolson House," *Legacy* 2 (Fall 1985): 72–73 and "The Strange Case of the Disappearing Woolson Memorabilia," *Legacy* 11, no. 2 (1994): 143–51.

7. Rollins's continued disinterest in the Woolson material is especially ironic given that Clare Benedict chose this college because she felt the material would be "more appreciated" there than at the University of St. Augustine, whose interest was more in Spanish material. See letter from Clare Benedict to Katherine Mather dated 23 Apr. 1914[?] and housed at Western Reserve Historical Society. See also Evelyn Thomas Helmick, "Constance Fenimore Woolson: First Novelist of Florida," in *Feminist Criticism: Essays on Theory, Poetry and Prose,* ed. Cheryl L. Brown and Karen Olson (Metuchen, N.J.: Scarecrow Press, 1978), 233–43.

8. Fred Lewis Pattee, *The Development of the American Short Story: An Historical Survey* (New York: Harper, 1923). A copy of the 1938 Dedicatory Address is available at the Western Reserve Historical Society as well as at Rollins College. Pattee used portions of it in "Constance Fenimore Woolson and the South," *South Atlantic Quarterly* 38 (Apr. 1939): 130–41.

9. WRHS. Cited from a letter Richardson wrote to Katherine Mather, Woolson's niece, on 26 Aug. 1938. See also Lyon N. Richardson, "Constance Fenimore Woolson, 'Novelist Laureate' of America," *South Atlantic Quarterly* 39 (Jan. 1940): 18–36.

10. See Arthur Hobson Quinn's discussion of Woolson in *American Fiction: An Historical Survey* (New York: D. Appleton-Century, 1936).

11. For discussions of the formation of the American literary canon, see Paul Lauter, "Race and Gender in the Shaping of the American Literary Canon: A Case Study for the Twenties," *Feminist Studies* 9 (Fall 1983): 435–63, and

Elizabeth Ammons, *Conflicting Stories: American Women Writers at the Turn into the Twentieth Century* (New York: Oxford, 1991), 15–17.

12. Rayburn S. Moore, *Constance F. Woolson* (New Haven, Conn.: Twayne, 1963) and Rayburn S. Moore, ed., *For the Major and Selected Short Stories,* by Constance Fenimore Woolson (New Haven, Conn.: College and Univ. Press, 1967).

13. Many of the editions I used have been taken over by other publishing companies. The following novels or collections are listed in 1994–95 *Books in Print: Anne* (1882; Salem, N.H.: Ayer, 1977); *Castle Nowhere: Lake Country Sketches* (1875, Reprint Services; New York: AMS Press, n.d.; Manchester, N.H.: Irvington, 1972); *For the Major* (1883, Reprint Services); *The Front Yard and Other Italian Stories* (1895; Salem, N.H.: Ayer, n.d.); *Horace Chase* (1894; Manchester, N.H.: Irvington, 1986); *Jupiter Lights* (1889, Reprint Services; New York: AMS, n.d.); *Rodman the Keeper: Southern Sketches* (1880, Reprint Services; New York: AMS Press, n.d.; Manchester, N.H.: Irvington, 1972, 1986).

14. Leon Edel, *The Life of Henry James,* 5 vols. (Philadelphia: Lippincott, 1953–72).

15. Joan Myers Weimer, ed., *Women Artists, Women Exiles: "Miss Grief" and Other Stories* (New Brunswick, N.J.: Rutgers University Press, 1988), hereafter abbreviated as *MG.*

16. Cheryl B. Torsney, ed., *Critical Essays on Constance Fenimore Woolson* (New York: G. K. Hall, Macmillan, 1992).

17. Some anthologizing of Woolson is beginning to happen. Volume 2 of the *Prentice-Hall Anthology of American Literature,* ed. Emory Elliott, Linda Kerber, A. Walton Litz, and Terence Martin (Englewood Cliffs, N.J.: Prentice-Hall, 1992) has included "King David," and *American Women Writers: Diverse Voices in Prose Since 1845,* ed. Eileen Barrett and Mary Cullinan (New York: St. Martin's, 1992), has included "Miss Grief."

18. Susan K. Harris, "'But is it any *good?*': Evaluating Nineteenth-Century American Women's Fiction," *American Literature* 63, no. 1 (Mar. 1991): 43–61. Harris uses Hans Robert Jauss, "Literary History as Challenge," in *Toward an Aesthetic of Reception* (Minneapolis: Univ. of Minnesota Press, 1982) to contextualize her argument.

19. Ammons, *Conflicting Stories,* 3–19; quoted, 9.

20. Lawrence Buell, *New England Literary Culture* (New York: Cambridge Univ. Press, 1986), 7. The Geertz quotation is from *The Interpretation of Cultures* (New York: Basic Books, 1973), 30.

21. Milette Shamir, "*The House of the Seven Gables*: Hawthorne's Romance and the Right to Privacy" (paper presented at Hawthorne Society Summer Conference, Concord, 17 June 1994). In her study of nineteenth-century legal judgments, Shamir found that legal decisions about the right to privacy moved beyond mind-space to property, thus suggesting that to cross the boundaries of the Pyncheon house is to invade the right to privacy.

22. Joel Pfister, "Hawthorne, O'Neill, Class and the Category of 'The Individual'" (paper presented at Hawthorne Society Summer Conference, 18 June 1994). Pfister uses his findings to understand Hawthorne's connection to the rise of popular psychology.

23. Freedman has worked with Olivia Frey and Frances Murphy Zauhar on several editorial projects involving autobiographical criticism, including *The Intimate Critique: Autobiographical Literary Criticism* (Durham, N.C.: Duke Univ. Press, 1992). Her own book using this method is *An Alchemy of Genres* (Charlottesville: Univ. Press of Virginia, 1992).

24. Joan Weimer, *Back Talk: Teaching Lost Selves to Speak* (New York: Random House, 1994). I am indebted to Weimer for sharing this book in galleys and for correspondence about Woolson and about her own goals for using the book to teach others to connect to those who might help them gain access to their inner selves.

25. Constance Fenimore Woolson, *Mentone, Cairo, and Corfu* (New York: Harper and Brothers, 1895).

1. A Woman in Search of a Home

1. Leon Edel, ed., *The Letters of Henry James* (Cambridge: Harvard Univ. Press, 1974–1980), vol. 3: 470. James's description of Woolson is from a letter to William James, dated 24 Mar. 1894.

2. Ibid. 3:461n. Letter from John Hay to Henry Adams.

3. Benedict 1:42, 94–101. Clara Benedict, Woolson's sister, said that Jarvis Woolson packed up his wife, who had almost lost her reason, though Woolson says they left Claremont because of the New England winters. According to Elinor Colby, the Woolson family physician suggested a trip away from Claremont. Jarvis and Hannah left the two oldest daughters in Claremont with Jarvis's sister and journeyed to Cleveland to visit old friends from Claremont. When they decided to remain there, Jarvis returned to sell his property, relocate his stove business, and fetch his two daughters (*The Woolsons of Claremont,* privately printed, 1983; available at the Fiske Free Library, Claremont, New Hampshire, and the Claremont New Hampshire Historical Society).

4. See Benedict 1:310–11 for a discussion of the Woolson family dogs.

5. The Fiske Free Library, Claremont, N.H., letter to O. F. R. Waite, Esq., dated 15 Aug. 1892.

6. Lydia Maria Child published *The Mother's Book* in 1831, which advocated freedom and outdoor recreation for children. The book was exceedingly popular, going through eight American and thirteen European editions (Carolyn L. Karcher, ed., *Hobomok and Other Writings on Indians by Lydia Maria Child* [New Brunswick, N.J.: Rutgers Univ. Press, 1986], xii). Horace Bushnell published *Work and Play* in 1864, a book that was inspired by watching his own children play and that advocated play and leisure for a fully developed life (Ann Douglas, *The Feminization of*

American Culture [New York: Knopf, 1977], 139). See Sharon O'Brien, "Tomboyism and Adolescent Conflict: Three Nineteenth Century Case Studies" in *Woman's Being, Woman's Place: Female Identity and Vocation in American History*, ed. Mary Kelley (Boston: G. K. Hall, 1979), 350–72 for a discussion of the problems adolescent girls had when they were forced to curb tomboyism and become ladylike. See Frances B. Cogan, *All-American Girl: The Ideal of Real Womanhood in Mid-Nineteenth-Century America* (Athens: Univ. of Georgia Press, 1989) for a reassessment of women's physical activity and health.

7. Moore, *Constance F. Woolson*, 23.

8. Edel, ed., *Letters of Henry James* 3:539. Letter dated 30 Aug. 1882.

9. WRHS. Hannah Woolson's letters dated 2 Jan. 1875 and 25 July 1878; Constance Woolson's letter is dated only 10 Jan. and would have been written between 1880 and 1882.

10. Torsney, *Constance Fenimore Woolson*, 161n.

11. Ibid., 17.

12. See Yannick Ripa, *Women and Madness: The Incarceration of Women in Nineteenth-Century France*, trans. Catherine DuPeloux Menage (Minneapolis: Univ. of Minnesota Press, 1991) for a discussion of the impact of alienism on women's incarceration in French asylums.

13. Benedict 2:393. Edel, ed., *Letters of Henry James* 3:536.

14. Edel, ed., *Letters of Henry James* 3:555. Letter dated 7 May 1883.

15. I am indebted to Joan Weimer for sharing this information with me. Permission to quote from the letter (Marie Holas to Sam Mather, 31 Jan. 1894) has been granted by its owner, who wishes to remain anonymous.

16. The source for Clara Hay's letter is the same as for Marie Holas's letter (chapter 1, note 15).

17. See Jean Strouse for a discussion of Alice James and suicide, *Alice James: A Biography* (Boston: Houghton Mifflin, 1980), 62, 186, 258–59, and Cheryl B. Torsney, "The Traditions of Gender: Constance Fenimore Woolson and Henry James," in *Patrons and Protégées: Gender, Friendship, and Writing in Nineteenth-Century America*, ed. Shirley Marchalonis (New Brunswick, N.J.: Rutgers Univ. Press, 1988), 166 (reprinted in Torsney, ed., *Critical Essays*, 152–71) for a discussion of Woolson's markings in *The Teachings of Epictetus.*

18. Constance Fenimore Woolson, "Dorothy," *Harper's New Monthly Magazine* 84 (Mar. 1892): 551–75, quoted, 553.

19. WRHS. Letter to Sam Mather, dated 20 Nov. 1893.

20. Benedict 2:411. Passage titled "Reflection."

2. Eden and the Anxiety of Influence

1. For example, whereas Cooper's *The Last of the Mohicans* sold 5,750 copies in 1826, Fanny Fern's *Fern Leaves from Fanny's Portfolio* sold 80,000 in 1853. See Douglas, *The Feminization of American Culture*, 80–117.

2. BHSM. Letter to Katharine Loring, dated 19 Sept. 1890. Woolson's child-hood coincided with the rapid rise of book publishing and selling made possible by new printing techniques and by the railroads, so she would have had access to large numbers of books.

3. WRHS. Letter from Hannah Woolson to Sam Mather, dated 22 Aug. 1878.

4. Constance Fenimore Woolson, "The Haunted Lake," *Harper's New Monthly Magazine* 44 (Dec. 1871): 20–30; reprinted in Benedict 1:49–57.

5. David S. Reynolds, *Beneath the American Renaissance: The Subversive Imagination in the Age of Emerson and Melville* (Cambridge: Harvard Univ. Press, 1989), 64–65. Other books Reynolds has located are George Bourne's *Lorette* (1833), Rebecca Reed's *Six Months in a Convent* (1835), and the anonymously published *Female Convents* (1834).

6. Moore, *Constance F. Woolson,* 148n.

7. I am indebted to Victoria Brehm for pointing me to the Ariadne connection.

3. Regionalism and the Bonds of Place

1. Dennis Berthold, "The Travel Sketches of Constance Fenimore Woolson" (paper presented at the American Literature Association Conference, San Diego, 29 May 1992).

2. I am indebted to Jim Moore of the United States Geological Survey, Menlo Park, California, and to my son Michael Dean, an intern for the USGS, for sharing this information with me. King's writings include *Report of the Geological Exploration of the Fortieth Parallel,* 7 vols. (1870–80) and *Mountaineering in the Sierra Nevada* (1872).

3. See Francis Paul Prucha, ed., *Documents of United States Indian Policy,* 2d ed. (Lincoln: Univ. of Nebraska Press, 1990) for a useful collection of primary documents on the development of United States Indian policies.

4. Elizabeth Ammons, ed., *How Celia Changed Her Mind & Selected Stories,* by Rose Terry Cooke (New Brunswick, N.J.: Rutgers Univ. Press, 1986), xv, xx–xxii.

5. See Cynthia Grant Tucker, *Prophetic Sisterhood: Liberal Women Ministers of the Frontier, 1880–1930* (Boston: Beacon Press, 1990) for a discussion of the rise and fall of female Unitarian and Universalist ministers.

6. Cited in Moore, *Constance F. Woolson,* 151n. and in Benedict 2:23. Letter is dated 25 Apr. 1875[?].

7. Henry James, *Partial Portraits* (1887; reprint, Ann Arbor: Univ. of Michigan Press, 1970), 177–92; quoted, 179–80.

8. Lori Askeland, "Remodeling the Model Home in *Uncle Tom's Cabin* and *Beloved,*" *American Literature* 64 (Dec. 1992): 785–805. Stowe and Beecher's *American Woman's Home* (1869) is available in a 1979 reprint, Watkins Glen, New York: Library of Victorian Culture.

9. Moore, *Constance F. Woolson,* 154n., rpt. in *Critical Essays,* ed. Torsney, 26–27.

10. Torsney, *Constance Fenimore Woolson,* 42–43. Pratt's discussion occurs in *Archetypal Patterns in Women's Fiction* (Bloomington: Indiana Univ. Press, 1981).

11. Phil Porter and Victor R. Nelhiebel, *The Wonder of Mackinac* (Mackinac Island State Park Commission, 1984) provides a pictorial overview of Mackinac Island.

4. Regional Bias and Ethnic Diversity

1. See Lucy Maddox, *Indian Removals: Nineteenth-Century American Literature and the Politics of Indian Affairs* (New York: Oxford Univ. Press, 1991), 15–49 for a discussion of how the policies of Indian removal were based on beliefs that offered the choice for American Indians to become civilized, that is, white, or to become extinct. See Richard Drinnon, *The Metaphysics of Indian-Hunting and Empire Building* (Minneapolis: Univ. of Minnesota Press, 1980), 508 for a discussion of the connection between Social Darwinism and white supremacy.

2. See a discussion of the Wakefield case in June Namias, *White Captives: Gender and Ethnicity on the American Frontier* (Chapel Hill: Univ. of North Carolina Press, 1993), 204–61.

3. Sidney Kaplan, "The Miscegenation Issue in the Election of 1864," in *American Studies in Black and White, Selected Essays of Sidney Kaplan, 1949–1989,* ed. Allan D. Austin (Amherst: Univ. of Massachusetts Press, 1991), 47–100. First published in *Journal of Negro History* 34 (July 1949): 273–343.

4. Ian Marshall, "Little Tree and Long Lance: The Indian Autobiography of Forrest Carter and Sylvester Long" (paper presented at the Northeast Modern Language Association Conference, Philadelphia, Mar. 1993).

5. The British did not surrender Fort Mackinac after the Revolution until 1796, then they recaptured it during the War of 1812. For the military history of the Fort, see Keith R. Widder, *Reveille Till Taps: Soldier Life at Fort Mackinac, 1780–1895* (Mackinac Island State Park Commission, 1972).

6. Beth L. Lueck, "Gender, Class, and Race in Early 19th-Century American Travel Writing" (paper presented at the American Literature Association Conference, San Diego, 29 May 1992).

7. See discussion of the controversies over Darwinism and religion in Tucker, *Prophetic Sisterhood,* 20.

8. Benedict 1:323–24. The letter became part of an article for the *Daily Cleveland Herald.*

9. Strouse, *Alice James,* 228. Letter to Frances Rollins Morse, dated Sunday 1884.

10. Peter Caccavari, "Literary Carpetbaggers: Region, Realism, and Race in the Fiction of Albion Tourgee and Constance Fenimore Woolson" (paper presented the Northeast Modern Language Association Conference, Philadelphia, Mar. 1993).

11. See discussions in *The Heath Anthology of American Literature,* 2d ed., ed. Paul Lauter, et al. (Lexington, Mass.: Heath, 1994), vol. 1: 1238–42, and James Mellon, ed., *Bullwhip Days: The Slaves Remember* (New York: Weidenfeld, 1989).

12. Hubbell 715–35; quoted 718, 726–27. Letters dated May Day 1875 and All Saints' Day, 1876.

13. See Deborah Gray White, *"Ar'n't I a Woman"* (New York: Norton, 1987) for a discussion of the life of female slaves.

14. See Reynolds, *Beneath the American Renaissance,* 351–57 for a discussion of fictional portraits of working-class women.

15. Quoted in Madelon Bedell, *The Alcotts* (New York: Clarkson N. Potter, 1980), 143. Bedell's reference to the Alcotts' servants names only one as Adeline.

16. Alice James, *The Diary of Alice James,* ed. Leon Edel (New York: Dodd, Mead, 1964), 169–70. Passage reprinted in Strouse, *Alice James,* 280.

17. Lizzie Boott was a model for Pansy Osmond in James's *The Portrait of a Lady.* For a discussion of the Boott family, see especially Edel, *The Life of Henry James* 3:194–98.

18. See chapter 1, note 15 for source of Holas's letter.

5. Woolson's Ambivalent Love Affair with Europe

1. Woolson's letters to members of the Mather family are still unpublished. They are housed at the Western Reserve Historical Society in Cleveland, Ohio. Four unpublished letters to Katharine Loring are housed at the Beverly Historical Society and Museum in Massachusetts. Letters to Edmund Clarence Stedman are at the Butler Library, Columbia University. Letters to Paul Hamilton Hayne, housed at Duke University, have been collected and edited by Jay B. Hubbell, "Some New Letters of Constance Fenimore Woolson." Letters to John and Clara Hay are at Brown University and have been collected and edited by Alice Hall Petry, "'Always, Your Attached Friend': The Unpublished Letters of Constance Fenimore Woolson to John and Clara Hay" (*Books at Brown* 29–30 [1982–83], 11–107); Petry's edition is indispensable for its identification of people Woolson names as friends and acquaintances. Benedict also quotes from many of Woolson's letters, but most of them are undated. A complete collection of Woolson letters would be most useful in furthering scholarship on her.

2. Torsney, "Traditions of Gender" and *Constance Fenimore Woolson,* 5–21. See also Joan Myers Weimer, "The 'Admiring Aunt' and the 'Proud Salmon of the Pond': Constance Fenimore Woolson's Struggle with Henry James," in *Critical Essays,* ed. Torsney, 203–16.

3. Edel, *Life of Henry James* 2:407.

4. Edel, ed., *Letters of Henry James* 3:xiv, 144; Edel, *Life of Henry James* 3:318–19.

5. WRHS. Clara's letter to her niece Kate Mather comments on her use of the desk James wrote on when he shared the Villa Brichieri with Woolson. Letter dated 27 Jan. 1889. Alice's letter is dated 3 Apr. 1887 and is collected in Ruth Bernard Yeazell, *The Death and Letters of Alice James* (Berkeley and Los Angeles: Univ. of California Press, 1981), 124.

6. Strouse, *Alice James,* 259. Letter to Aunt Kate dated 9 Dec. 1888; Letter to William dated 4 Nov. 1888.

7. Edel, ed., *Letters of Henry James* 3:28. Letter dated 21 Feb. 1884.

8. Ibid. 3:246–47. Letter dated 29 Oct. 1888.

9. Edel, *Life of Henry James* 3:318. Strouse quotes the letter, and though she says Alice's last message remains a mystery, in general she accepts Edel's version of Woolson, 312–13.

10. Strouse, *Alice James,* 307. Letter dated 5 Feb. 1892.

11. Edel, *Life of Henry James* 3:87–88.

12. Edel, ed., *Letters of Henry James* 3:528. Letter dated 12 Feb. 1882. Joan Weimer uses this reference for her title "The 'Admiring Aunt' and the 'Proud Salmon of the Pond,'" and reads it as evidence that Woolson adopted the role of aunt over her sexual or literary identity (*Critical Essays,* ed. Torsney, 204).

13. Edel, ed., *Letters of Henry James* 3:526. Letter dated 12 Feb. 1882.

14. Ibid. 3:557. Letter dated 7 May 1883.

15. Quoted in Moore, *Constance F. Woolson,* 126.

16. For an assessment of James's literary use of Woolson, see Sharon L. Dean, "Constance Fenimore Woolson and Henry James: The Literary Relationship," *Massachusetts Studies in English* 7, no.3 (1980): 1–9, and Rayburn S. Moore, "The Strange Irregular Rhythm of Life: James's Late Tales and Constance Woolson," *South Atlantic Bulletin* 41 (1976): 86–93.

17. Edel, ed., *Letters of Henry James* 3:559; Edel, *Life of Henry James* 3:89. Letter dated 24 May 1883.

18. Edel, ed., *Letters of Henry James* 3:551. Letter dated 7 May 1883.

19. Edel, *Life of Henry James* 3:384–87.

20. Strouse's biography of Alice James contains the fullest available discussion not only of Alice James but also of Katharine Loring.

21. R. W. B. Lewis, *The Jameses: A Family Narrative* (New York: Farrar, Straus and Giroux, 1991), 380–81.

22. Strouse, *Alice James,* 220. Letter to Catherine Walsh (Aunt Kate) dated 15 Nov. 1887[?].

23. See James, *Diary of Alice James,* for information on the fate of Alice's diary.

24. Edel, *Life of Henry James* 3:368.

25. Ibid. 4:142.

26. Moore, *Constance F. Woolson,* 148n. Letter dated 24 Feb. 1887.

27. See ibid., 77 for the dating of "A Transplanted Boy."

28. See Edel, *Life of Henry James* 2:407 for a discussion of James and Baldwin

and of his contact with Woolson in 1890. Woolson's sister Clara's journal also notes that "Connie always pronounced him (Dr. Baldwin) to be the cleverest doctor in existence for diagnosis" (Benedict 3:5).

29. Woolson may have intended a reference to another itinerant American, Margaret Fuller, in Roberta Spring. In Italy, Fuller knew a woman named Rebecca Spring. Spring later claimed to continue to dream of Fuller fifty years after her death. See Douglas, *Feminization of American Culture,* 287.

30. See especially a letter written on 3 Dec. 1893 by Woolson, just before her death, to Clare Benedict for her tone in speaking of Tello (Benedict 2:383–87). During Woolson's childhood, her family had conducted a funeral for a family dog and had invited all the neighborhood dogs to attend (Benedict 1:310–11).

6. The Marriage Question

1. James, *Partial Portraits,* 179, 182.

2. Victoria Woodhull, an Ohioan who had been involved with her mother in mesmeric exhibitions, was so outrageous by nineteenth-century standards that she ran for the presidency. She and her sister, Tennessee Claflin, published *Woodhull and Claflin's Weekly* between 1870 and 1876, a magazine that advocated suffrage, birth control, and free love.

3. For a discussion of divorce patterns, see Glenda Riley, *Divorce: An American Tradition* (New York: Oxford Univ. Press, 1991).

4. Alfred Habegger, *Henry James and the "Woman Business"* (New York: Cambridge Univ. Press, 1989), 27–62.

5. Joan Myers Weimer, "Women Artists as Exiles in the Fiction of Constance Fenimore Woolson," *Legacy* 3, no.2 (Fall 1986): 3–15, quoted 6.

6. Cited in Moore, *Constance F. Woolson,* 153–54. Letter dated 21 Jan. 1891.

7. Cited in *MG* xiii. Letter to Sam Mather dated 21 Jan. 1891.

8. Robert Gingras, "'Hepzibah's Story': An Unpublished Work by Constance Fenimore Woolson," *Resources for American Literary Study* 10 (1980): 33–46. Two other uncollected stories—"A Flower of the Snow" and "Black Point"—involve an incident in which a woman overhears the man she loves in a liaison with another woman, but in both stories, these are minor flirtations and the marriages take place. The pattern is frequent enough to invite speculation that Woolson overheard Zeph Spaulding in a liaison with another woman.

9. See Victoria Brehm, "Island Fortress: The Landscape of the Imagination," in *Critical Essays,* ed. Torsney, 172–86 for a discussion of western freedom represented in the female lighthouse keeper of Ballast Island.

10. Carolyn VanBergen, "Constance Fenimore Woolson and the Next Country," *Western Reserve Studies* 3 (1988): 86–92.

11. See Benedict 1:67 for a discussion of Emma's marriage.

12. For discussions of fictional presentations of women's domestic roles, see

especially Nina Baym, *Novels, Readers, and Reviewers: Responses to Fiction in Antebellum America* (Ithaca, N.Y.: Cornell Univ. Press, 1984); *Woman's Fiction: A Guide to Novels by and about Women in America, 1820–1870* (Ithaca, N.Y.: Cornell Univ. Press, 1978); and Mary Kelley, *Private Woman, Public Stage: Literary Domesticity in Nineteenth-Century America* (New York: Oxford Univ. Press, 1984).

13. *MG*.

14. WRHS. Letter to Sam Mather dated 24 Mar. 1887.

15. Leon Edel makes it seem as if Woolson is significantly older than James, but she is just three years older, hardly enough to be considered an older woman chasing a younger man. Edel, *Life of Henry James* 3:87.

16. John Dwight Kern, *Constance Fenimore Woolson: Literary Pioneer* (Philadelphia: Univ. of Pennsylvania Press, 1934), 42, identifies the model for Rast as John Biddle (1883–86), the son of Edward Biddle, who in 1819 married the stepdaughter of the French Joseph Bailey. Bailey's wife—the girl's mother—was an American Indian.

17. Torsney, *Constance Fenimore Woolson*, 44.

18. For a discussion of Catherine Walsh's marriage, see Strouse, *Alice James*, 33–35. For a discussion of the Beecher-Tilton scandal, which was exposed by Victoria Woodhull, see Douglas, *Feminization of American Culture*, 241–43.

19. Baym, *Novels, Readers, and Reviewers*, 184.

20. Margaret Fuller's sense of herself as a misfit led to enough unhappiness that her death on a burning ship may have been a choice to die rather than to be rescued and returned to the United States where she was so out of place. Her personality prompted her friend Rebecca Spring to continue to dream of her fifty years after her death. I have found no reference to Woolson meeting Rebecca Spring, but her choice of the name Roberta Spring for a woman who is a misfit in "A Transplanted Boy" is provocative. A letter from Woolson to Henry James dated 12 Feb. 1882 indicates that she had spoken to Richard Henry Dana about Fuller and Emerson (Edel, ed., *Letters of Henry James* 3:528). For a discussion of how much Margaret Fuller's life-style was at odds with the nineteenth century, see Douglas, *Feminization of American Culture*, 259–88. For a discussion of the Fuller-Emerson relationship, see Dorothy Berkson, "'Born and Bred in Different Nations': Margaret Fuller and Ralph Waldo Emerson," in *Patrons and Protégées*, ed. Marchalonis, 3–30.

21. Letter from John Hay to Henry Adams dated 22 Nov. 1882. Quoted in Fred Kaplan, *Henry James: The Imagination of Genius* (New York: William Morrow, 1992), 254.

22. Carolyn VanBergen, "Getting Your Money's Worth: The Social Marketplace in *Horace Chase*," in *Critical Essays*, ed. Torsney, 234–44.

23. Baym, *Novels, Readers, and Reviewers*, 181–90. Alfred Habegger (*Gender, Fantasy and Realism in American Literature* [New York: Columbia Univ.

Press, 1982], 15–20) thinks Baym overstates this prohibition against sexuality and reads the marriage proposal itself as a symbol of sexuality. Although his interpretation seems accurate, it does not negate the fact that any overt innuendo about sexuality remained taboo.

24. Woolson often spoke of herself as unattractive. Photographs of famous writers circulated widely in the nineteenth century, and those of Woolson indicate otherwise. The Granger Collection (381 Park Avenue South, New York, N.Y. 10016) possesses copies of some, including the ones reproduced in this text. All are in profile, apparently Woolson's way of responding to what Clare Benedict called her "curiously low opinion of her own personal appearance" (Benedict 2:xv).

25. The early model for Lanse (Lawrence) may be Lawrence Vickery in "Bro" (Rodman), a man who has European entanglements.

26. Petry, "'Always, Your Attached Friend,'" 88. The Howells' review appears in *Harper's*, Aug. 1886.

27. Moore, *Constance F. Woolson*, 97.

28. James, *Partial Portraits*, 190.

29. Weimer, "The 'Admiring Aunt,'" in *Critical Essays*, ed. Torsney, 203–16. Weimer reads *East Angels* in conjunction with James's *The Europeans*.

30. See Cathy N. Davidson, *Revolution and the Word: The Rise of the Novel in America* (New York: Oxford Univ. Press, 1986) for a discussion of wifely endurance of alcoholic husbands in Helena Well's *Constantia Neville; or the West Indian* (1800) and S. S. B. K. Wood's *Amelia; or the Influence of Virtue* (1802).

31. See Joanne Dobson, ed., *The Hidden Hand or, Capitola the Madcap,* by E. D. E. N. Southworth (New Brunswick, N.J.: Rutgers Univ. Press, 1988).

32. Information on the Walworth case is on exhibit at the Walworth Memorial Museum at Congress Park, Saratoga Springs, New York. See also Ruth Bordin, "'A Baptism of Power and Liberty': The Women's Crusade of 1873–1874," in *Woman's Being,* ed. Kelley, 283–95 for a discussion of Ohio's role in the temperance crusade of 1873–74.

33. Woolson believed in the hereditary nature of certain psychological traits and thought her own bouts of depression to be hereditary (Moore, *Constance F. Woolson,* 36). In a 16 Jan. 1876 letter to Paul Hamilton Hayne, she links "'Depression,' that evil spirit that haunts all creative minds" with the need for "the close appreciative warm belief & praise of . . . family" (Hubbell 728–29).

7. Parents, Children, and the Ties of Family

1. See O'Brien, "Tomboyism," 350–72.

2. Baym, *Woman's Fiction,* 17, 27.

3. Kelley, *Private Woman*. Since Kelley's study, Nina Baym has used the public career of Lydia Sigourney to challenge us to reconsider the as-

sumption that women avoided the public sphere. See "Reinventing Lydia Sigourney," *American Literature* 62 (Sept. 1990): 385–404.

4. Torsney, *Constance Fenimore Woolson,* 119–21; 143–45.

5. Sybil B. Weir, "Southern Womanhood in the Novels of Constance Fenimore Woolson," in *Critical Essays,* ed. Torsney (New York: G. K. Hall, Macmillan, 1992), 56; *MG* xi, xxix.

6. Benedict 2:19. The comment appears in an undated letter to Arabella Carter Washburn.

7. See Carroll Smith-Rosenberg, "The Hysterical Woman: Sex Roles and Role Conflict in 19th-Century America," *Social Research* 39 (1972): 652–78.

8. Torsney, *Constance Fenimore Woolson,* 62, 69.

9. Moore, *Constance F. Woolson,* 30. Weir, "Southern Womanhood," 145.

10. Benedict 3:12. Clare is about thirteen at this time. The letter is to a Mrs. Sherman and is undated.

11. Ann J. Lane, introduction to *The Charlotte Perkins Gilman Reader* (New York: Pantheon, 1980).

12. R. W. B. Lewis, *Edith Wharton: A Biography* (New York: Harper and Row, 1975; Fromm International Publishing, 1985).

8. The Social and Economic Position of Spinsters and Widows

1. See especially John Paul Harper, "Be Fruitful and Multiply: Origins of Legal Restrictions on Planned Parenthood in Nineteenth-Century America," in *Women of American History,* ed. Carol Ruth Berkin and Mary Beth Norton (Boston: Houghton Mifflin, 1979), 245–69.

2. See Davidson, *Revolution and the Word,* 110–50. According to Davidson, in 1800 the average number of live births per woman was 7.04; by 1850 the rate had declined 23 percent; and by 1900, 50 percent.

3. See Marylynn Salmon, "Equality or Submission? Feme Covert Status in Early Pennsylvania," in *Women of American History,* ed. Berkin and Norton, 93–95. See also Barbara Bardes and Suzanne Gossett, *Declarations of Independence: Women and Political Power in Nineteenth Century American Fiction* (New Brunswick, N.J.: Rutgers Univ. Press, 1990), 70–79.

4. See Bardes and Gossett, *Declarations of Independence,* for a full discussion of how the issue of property laws was reflected in nineteenth-century fiction.

5. Ibid., 130–37.

6. Linda L. Goldstein, "Women Enter Medicine in the Western Reserve: The Graduation of the First Six Women Doctors from Western Reserve College, 1852–56," *Western Reserve Studies* 3 (1988): 66–74. A good discussion of the conflict between male and female physicians and their attitudes toward gynecological care appears in Ann Douglas Wood, "'The Fashion-

able Diseases': Women's Complaints and Their Treatment in Nineteenth-Century America," *Journal of Interdisciplinary History* 4 (1973): 25–52.

7. Henry James Sr., "Woman and the 'Woman's Movement,'" *Putnam's Magazine*, 1 Mar. 1853, 279–88. Passage quoted in Strouse, *Alice James,* 45.

8. Habegger, *Henry James and the "Woman Business."*

9. Many good studies exist about women and education. See, for example, the following essays in Kelley, ed., *Woman's Being:* Joan G. Zimmerman, "Daughters of Main Street: Culture and the Female Community at Grinnell, 1884–1917," 154–70, and Lynn D. Gordon, "Co-education on Two Campuses: Berkeley and Chicago, 1890–1912," 171–93; and in Bernice A. Carroll, ed., *Liberating Women's History: Theoretical and Critical Essays* (Urbana: Univ. of Illinois Press, 1976): Adele Simmons, "Education and Ideology in Nineteenth-Century America: The Response of Educational Institutions to the Changing Role of Women," 115–26.

10. Kern, *Constance Fenimore Woolson,* 69–70; Moore, *Constance F. Woolson,* 58.

11. Not until the early 1950s did large numbers of married women become teachers, prompted especially by the need for teachers at the start of the baby boom.

12. Other uncollected teacher stories include "A Flower of the Snow," "The Waldenburg Road," "Mission Endeavor," "The Old Five," and "Barnaby Pass." The case of E. D. E. N. Southworth illustrates the hard life of a teacher. When her husband abandoned her, she tried to support herself and a sick child by teaching in the Washington public schools: she had eighty students in her class and was paid $250 per year. See Dobson, ed., *Hidden Hand,* xvii.

13. Adrienne Rich, "Taking Women Students Seriously" (delivered at New Jersey College and Univ. Coalition on Women's Education, 9 May 1978). Reprint in *On Lies, Secrets, and Silence: Selected Prose: 1966–1978* (New York: W. W. Norton, 1979).

14. See Jeannine Dobbs, "The Blue-Stocking: Getting It Together," *Frontiers* (Winter 1976): 81–93 for a discussion of the British Bluestockings.

15. Benedict 2:27. Undated letter to Miss Emily Vernon Clark.

16. Bardes and Gossett discuss the debate about women's public roles and their sexuality throughout *Declarations of Independence.* Of particular interest is their analysis of women as public speakers: in seeking a public voice, women were on the one hand seen as "desexed" and out of their sphere and, on the other, as having a "promiscuous relationship" with their audience (69). Public women also claimed themselves as subject rather than accept their positions as object.

17. W. A. Jones, "The Ladies' Library," *Graham's Magazine* 21 (1842):333. Quoted in Habegger, *Gender, Fantasy and Realism,* 116.

18. See Joyce W. Warren, ed., *Ruth Hall and Other Writings, by Fanny Fern*

(New Brunswick, N.J.: Rutgers Univ. Press, 1986) for a discussion of Fern's humor.

19. See Nancy A. Walker, *A Very Serious Thing: Women's Humor and American Culture* (Minneapolis: Univ. of Minnesota Press, 1988) for a discussion of women humorists.

20. In a letter to Sam Mather dated 25 Jan. 1880, Woolson complains that writing from 8:30 to 1:00 is not long enough, but that "Clara looks so tragic if I attempt anything more, that I don't dare to" (Benedict 2:161). She tends to shape her travels in Europe for her sister's needs just as she had shaped them in the United States for her mother's.

21. See Davidson, *Revolution and the Word;* Smith-Rosenberg, "Hysterical Woman"; and Wood, "Fashionable Diseases."

22. Diane Price Herndl, *Invalid Women: Figuring Feminine Illness in American Literature and Culture* (Chapel Hill: Univ. of North Carolina Press, 1993), 110–11. Abba Woolson's book was published by Roberts Brothers (Boston 1873). I am indebted to Joan Weimer for confirming Abba's possible relation to Woolson.

23. Edel, *Life of Henry James* 3:301.

9. The Challenge of Art

1. Moore, *Constance F. Woolson,* 157n. Letter dated 23 July 1877.

2. Edel, *Life of Henry James* 2:411, 414.

3. Torsney, *Constance Fenimore Woolson,* and Weimer, "Women Artists as Exiles," 3–15.

4. Torsney, *Constance Fenimore Woolson,* 108–26.

5. For a full discussion of the significance of the names in "The Street of the Hyacinth," see Torsney, *Constance Fenimore Woolson,* 108–26, and *MG* xxxvi.

6. See especially Kelley, *Private Woman.*

7. Edel, ed., *Letters of Henry James* 3:532; 535. Letter dated 12 Feb. 1882.

8. Torsney, *Constance Fenimore Woolson,* 70–73.

9. Susan Coultrap-McQuin, *Doing Literary Business: American Women Writers in the Nineteenth Century* (Chapel Hill: Univ. of North Carolina Press, 1990) quotes from a letter by Helen Hunt Jackson to the editors of the *Independent* (19 Jan. 1875): "I prefer, as you know, to confine myself to the three channels in which I have chiefly worked—the Ind[ependent], C[hristian] Union, & Scribners [*sic*]—I have a great dislike to [*sic*] the practice so many writers have, of having their names in *all* the papers and magazines—'infesting the magazines' as the cruel Nation said of Constance Woolson last month!" (154).

10. Edel discusses James's "Aspern Papers" in terms of his relationship to Woolson; however, James as easily could have been rewriting Woolson's vision of "Miss Grief" (*Life of Henry James* 2:416–17). Indeed, as Habegger

and others have shown, James was in the habit of using the plots of fiction by women for his own work. Habegger, *Gender, Fantasy and Realism*, 1–26, 230–38.

11. Torsney connects the physician image to the significance of "Miss Grief['s]" first name, Aaronna. The biblical Aaron had greater verbal powers than Moses and thus, for Torsney, Aaronna represents a new messiah, or physician, who could save the narrator and who is "a harbinger of an artistic era yet to come, when powerful women will direct their own creative destinies." Weimer provides a similar interpretation of the name Aaronna, saying that "Miss Grief" wears, metaphorically in her work, the priestly garb of Aaron but appears foolish to males. Torsney, *Constance Fenimore Woolson*, 77; *MG* xxxviii.

12. Edel, *Life of Henry James* 2:416–17.

13. Torsney, *Constance Fenimore Woolson*, 75.

14. Woolson wrote to Katharine Loring on 19 Sept. 1890 that she was reading *The World as Will and Idea* by Schopenhauer. BHSM. This letter was written three years after the publication of "At the Château of Corinne," so this reading of Schopenhauer's book is likely not Woolson's first encounter with him.

15. See Torsney for a discussion of the significance of Madame de Staël for women writers. Torsney sees "At the Château of Corinne" in terms of its intertextuality, with Woolson writing of Katharine Winthrop as Madame de Staël wrote of Corinne. She argues that the eighteenth century identified de Staël with Corinne and that Woolson used herself as a double for Katharine. *Constance Fenimore Woolson*, 87–107.

16. Torsney, *Constance Fenimore Woolson*, 106.

17. Constance Fenimore Woolson, "In Sloane Street," *Harper's Bazar* 25 (11 June 1892). It is interesting that this story of a male who makes a "female" choice is the only one of Woolson's stories to appear in what has been designated a "woman's magazine."

18. Benedict 2:27. Undated letter to Miss Emily Vernon Clark.

19. Woolson wrote a letter on 22 Jan. 1887 to Sam Mather, chastising Howells for "losing his mind about Tolstoi" and "apparently believ[ing] that Tolstoi really practices what he preaches!" She continues to say that she has it straight from Russia that Tolstoi never gave up any of his money for the masses and that as much as he dressed in peasant clothes it was all a facade. WRHS.

20. Gertrude's reference to *The Life of Louisa Alcott* must be to Ednah D. Cheney's *Louisa May Alcott: Her Life, Letters, and Journals* (Boston: Roberts Bros., 1889). If Woolson composed a draft of "In Sloane Street" earlier, she had to have revised it for the 1892 publication date.

21. Torsney, *Constance Fenimore Woolson*, 1–53.

22. Letter is to Ms. W. H. Riding, dated 12 July 1883. WRHS.

Bibliography

❧

Ammons, Elizabeth. *Conflicting Stories: American Women Writers at the Turn into the Twentieth Century*. New York: Oxford Univ. Press, 1991.

————. Introduction to *How Celia Changed Her Mind & Selected Stories*, by Rose Terry Cooke. New Brunswick, N.J.: Rutgers Univ. Press, 1986.

Askeland, Lori. "Remodeling the Model Home in *Uncle Tom's Cabin* and *Beloved*." *American Literature* 64 (Dec. 1992): 785–805.

Bardes, Barbara, and Suzanne Gossett. *Declarations of Independence: Women and Political Power in Nineteenth Century American Fiction*. New Brunswick, N.J.: Rutgers Univ. Press, 1990.

Barnett, Louise K. *The Ignoble Savage: American Literary Racism, 1790–1890*. Westport, Conn.: Greenwood Press, 1975.

Barrett, Eileen, and Mary Cullinan. *American Women Writers: Diverse Voices in Prose Since 1845*. New York: St. Martin's, 1992.

Baym, Nina. *Novels, Readers, and Reviews: Responses to Fiction in Antebellum America*. Ithaca, N.Y.: Cornell Univ. Press, 1984.

————. "Reinventing Lydia Sigourney." *American Literature* 62 (Sept. 1990): 385–404.

————. *Woman's Fiction: A Guide to Novels by and about Women in America, 1820–1870*. Ithaca, N.Y.: Cornell Univ. Press, 1978.

Bedell, Madelon. *The Alcotts*. New York: Clarkson N. Potter, 1980.

Benedict, Clare. *Appreciations*. Leatherhead, Surrey: F. B. Benger, 1941.

————. *Five Generations (1785–1923)*. 3 vols. London: Ellis, 1929–30, 1932. Vol. 1, *Voices Out of the Past*. Vol. 2, *Constance Fenimore Woolson*. Vol. 3, *The Benedicts Abroad*.

Berkin, Carol Ruth, and Mary Beth Norton, eds. *Women of American History*. Boston: Houghton Mifflin, 1979.

Berkson, Dorothy. "'Born and Bred in Different Nations': Margaret Fuller and

Ralph Waldo Emerson." *Patrons and Protégées: Gender, Friendship, and Writing in Nineteenth-Century America,* edited by Shirley Marchalonis, 3–30. New Brunswick, N.J.: Rutgers Univ. Press, 1988.

Blair, Walter, and Hamlin Hill. *America's Humor: From Poor Richard to Doonesbury.* New York: Oxford Univ. Press, 1978.

Bordin, Ruth. "'A Baptism of Power and Liberty': The Women's Crusade of 1873–1874." In *Woman's Being, Woman's Place,* ed. Kelley, 283–95.

Brehm, Victoria. "Island Fortress: The Landscape of the Imagination." In *Critical Essays,* ed. Torsney, 172–86. First published in *American Literary Realism* 22 (1990): 51–66.

Brown, Cheryl L., and Karen Olson. *Feminist Criticism: Essays on Theory, Poetry and Prose.* Metuchen, N.J.: Scarecrow Press, 1978.

Buell, Lawrence. *New England Literary Culture.* New York: Cambridge Univ. Press, 1986.

Carroll, Bernice A., ed. *Liberating Women's History: Theoretical and Critical Essays.* Urbana: Univ. of Illinois Press, 1976.

Chambers-Schiller, Lee. "The Single Woman: Family and Vocation Among Nineteenth-Century Reformers." In *Private Woman, Public Stage,* ed. Kelley, 334–50.

Chandler, Marilyn R. *Dwelling in the Text: Houses in American Fiction.* Berkeley and Los Angeles: Univ. of California Press, 1991.

Cheney, Ednah D. *Louisa May Alcott: Her Life, Letters, and Journals.* Boston: Roberts Bros., 1889.

Chodorow, Nancy. *The Reproduction of Mothering: Psychoanalysis and the Sociology of Gender.* Berkeley and Los Angeles: Univ. of California Press, 1978.

Cogan, Frances B. *All-American Girl: The Ideal of Womanhod in Mid-Nineteenth Century America.* Athens: Univ. of Georgia Press, 1989.

Colby, Elinor. *The Woolsons of Claremont.* Claremont: New Hampshire Historical Society, 1983.

Coultrap-McQuin, Susan. *Doing Literary Business: American Women Writers in the Nineteenth Century.* Chapel Hill: Univ. of North Carolina Press, 1990.

Crayon, Porte. "On Negro Schools." *Harper's New Monthly Magazine* 69 (Sept. 1874): 457–68.

Crèvecoeur, *Letters from an American Farmer: Letter III, "What Is an American?"* London: J. M. Dent, 1962.

Davidson, Cathy N. *Revolution and the Word: The Rise of the Novel in America.* New York: Oxford Univ. Press, 1986.

Dean, Sharon L. "Constance Fenimore Woolson and Henry James: The Literary Relationship." *Massachusetts Studies in English* 7, no. 3 (1980): 1–9.

———. "Constance Woolson's Southern Sketches." *Southern Studies* 25, no. 3 (1986): 274–83.

———. "Homeward Bound: The Novels of Constance Fenimore Woolson." *Legacy* 6, no. 2 (1989): 17–28.

———. "Women as Daughters; Women as Mothers in the Fiction of Constance Fenimore Woolson." In *Critical Essays,* ed. Torsney, 189–202.

Dobbs, Jeannine. "The Blue-stocking: Getting It Together." *Frontiers* (Winter 1976): 81–93.

Dobson, Joanne. Introduction to *The Hidden Hand or, Capitola the Madcap,* by E. D. E. N. Southworth. New Brunswick, N.J.: Rutgers Univ. Press, 1988.

Douglas, Ann. *The Feminization of American Culture.* New York: Knopf, 1977.

Drinnon, Richard. *The Metaphysics of Indian-Hunting and Empire Building.* Minneapolis: Univ. of Minnesota Press, 1980.

Dudden, Faye E. *Serving Women: Household Service in Nineteenth-Century America.* Hanover, N.H.: Wesleyan Univ. Press, Univ. Press of New England, 1983.

Edel, Leon. *The Life of Henry James.* 5 vols. Philadelphia: Lippincott, 1953–72.

Elliott, Emory, Linda Kerber, A. Walton Litz, and Terence Martin, eds. *The Prentice-Hall Anthology of American Literature.* 2 vols. Englewood Cliffs, N.J.: Prentice-Hall, 1992.

Epstein, Barbara Leslie. *The Politics of Domesticity: Women, Evangelism, and Temperance in Nineteenth Century America.* Middletown, Conn.: Wesleyan Univ. Press, 1981.

Erlich, Gloria C. *The Sexual Education of Edith Wharton.* Berkeley and Los Angeles: Univ. of California Press, 1992.

Fowler, Connie May. "No Snapshots in the Attic: A Granddaughter's Search for a Cherokee Past." *New York Times Book Review,* 22 May 1994, 49–50.

Fox-Genovese, Elizabeth. *Within the Plantation Household: Black and White Women of the Old South.* Chapel Hill: Univ. of North Carolina Press, 1988.

Freedman, Diane. *An Alchemy of Genres.* Charlottesville: Univ. Press of Virginia, 1992.

Freedman, Diane, Olivia Frey, and Frances Murphy Zauhar, eds. *The Intimate Critique: Autobiographical Literary Criticism.* Durham, N.C.: Duke Univ. Press, 1992.

Fryer, Judith. *Felicitous Space: The Imaginative Structures of Edith Wharton and Willa Cather.* Chapel Hill: Univ. of North Carolina Press, 1986.

Gates, Henry Louis. *The Signifying Monkey: A Theory of African-American Literary Criticism.* New York: Oxford Univ. Press, 1988.

Gebhard, Caroline. "Constance Fenimore Woolson Rewrites Bret Hart: The Sexual Politics of Intertextuality." In *Critical Essays,* ed. Torsney, 217–33.

Geertz, Clifford. *The Interpretation of Cultures.* New York: Basic Books, 1973.

Gilligan, Carol. *In a Different Voice: Psychological Theory and Women's Development.* Cambridge: Harvard Univ. Press, 1982.

Goldstein, Linda L. "Women Enter Medicine in the Western Reserve: The Graduation of the First Six Women Doctors from Western Reserve College, 1852–56." *Western Reserve Studies* 3 (1988): 66–74.

Gordon, Lynn D. "Co-education on Two Campuses: Berkeley and Chicago, 1890–1912." In *Woman's Being, Woman's Place,* ed. Kelley, 171–93.

Gwin, Minrose C. *Black and White Women of the Old South: The Peculiar Sisterhood in American Literature.* Knoxville: Univ. of Tennessee Press, 1985.

Habegger, Alfred. *Gender, Fantasy and Realism in American Literature.* New York: Columbia Univ. Press, 1982.

———. *Henry James and the "Woman Business."* New York: Cambridge Univ. Press, 1989.

Harper, John Paul. "Be Fruitful and Multiply: Origins of Legal Restrictions on Planned Parenthood in Nineteenth-Century America." In *Women of American History,* ed. Berkin and Norton, 245–69.

Harris, Susan K. "'But is it any *good?*: Evaluating Nineteenth-Century American Women's Fiction." *American Literature* 63, no. 1 (Mar. 1991): 43–61.

Harrison, Elizabeth Jane. *Female Pastoral: Women Writers Re-Visioning the American South.* Knoxville: Univ. of Tennessee Press, 1991.

Helmick, Evelyn Thomas. "Constance Fenimore Woolson: First Novelist of Florida." In *Feminist Criticism,* ed. Brown and Olson, 233–43. First published in *Carrell* 10 (1969): 8–18.

Hubbell, Jay B., ed. "Some New Letters of Constance Fenimore Woolson." *New England Quarterly* 14 (Dec. 1941): 715–35.

James, Alice. *The Diary of Alice James.* Edited by Leon Edel. New York: Dodd, Mead, 1964.

James, Henry. *The Letters of Henry James.* Edited by Leon Edel. 3 vols. Cambridge: Harvard Univ. Press, 1974–1980.

———. *Partial Portraits.* 1887. Reprint, Ann Arbor: Univ. of Michigan Press, 1970.

James, Henry Sr. "Woman and the 'Woman's Movement.'" *Putnam's Magazine,* 1 Mar. 1853, 279–88.

Jauss, Hans Robert. *Toward an Aesthetic of Reception.* Minneapolis: Univ. of Minnesota Press, 1982.

Jones, W. A. "The Ladies' Library." *Graham's Magazine* 21 (1842): 333.

Kaplan, Fred. *Henry James: The Imagination of Genius.* New York: William Morrow, 1992.

Kaplan, Sidney. "The Miscegenatin Issue in the Election of 1864." In *American*

Studies in Black and White, Selected Essays of Sidney Kaplan, edited by
Allan D. Austin, 47–100. Amherst: Univ. of Massachusetts Press, 1991. First
published in *Journal of Negro History* 34 (July 1949): 273–343.

Karcher, Carolyn L. Introduction to *Hobomok and Other Writings on Indians,*
by Lydia Maria Child. New Brunswick, N.J.: Rutgers Univ. Press, 1986.

Kelley, Mary, ed. *Private Woman, Public Stage: Literary Domesticity in Nineteenth-Century America.* New York: Oxford Univ. Press, 1984.

————. *Woman's Being, Woman's Place: Female Identity and Vocation in
American History.* Boston: G. K. Hall, 1979.

Kelton, D. H. *Annals of Fort Mackinac.* Chicago: Fergus Printing, 1882.

Kern, John Dwight. *Constance Fenimore Woolson: Literary Pioneer.* Philadelphia: Univ. of Pennsylvania Press, 1934.

Kolodny, Annette. *The Land Before Her: Fantasy and Experience of the American Frontiers, 1630–1860.* Chapel Hill: Univ. of North Carolina Press, 1984.

Lane, Ann J. Introduction to *The Charlotte Perkins Gilman Reader.* New York:
Pantheon, 1980.

Lauter, Paul et al., eds., *The Heath Anthology of American Literature,* 2d ed. vol.
1 Lexington, Mass.: Heath, 1990.

————. "Race and Gender in the Shaping of the American Literary Canon: A
Case Study for the Twenties." *Feminist Studies* 9 (Fall 1983): 435–64.

Le Guin, Ursula. "The Hand That Rocks the Cradle Writes the Book." *New York
Times Book Review,* 22 Jan. 1989, 1.

Lewis, R. W. B. *Edith Wharton: A Biography.* New York: Harper and Row, 1975;
Fromm International Publishing, 1985.

————. *The Jameses: A Family Narrative.* Farrar, Straus and Giroux, 1991.

Madden, David, and Peggy Bach, eds. *Classics of Civil War Fiction.* Jackson:
Univ. of Mississippi Press, 1991.

Maddox, Lucy. *Indian Removals: Nineteenth-Century American Literature and
the Politics of Indian Affairs.* New York: Oxford Univ. Press, 1991.

Marchalonis, Shirley, ed. *Patrons and Protégées: Gender, Friendship, and Writing in Nineteenth-Century America.* New Brunswick, N.J.: Rutgers Univ.
Press, 1988.

Mellon, James, ed. *Bullwhip Days: The Slaves Remember.* New York: Weidefeld,
1989.

Melville, Herman. "Hawthorne and His Mosses." In *Anthology of American Literature.* 5th ed. vol. 1, ed. George McMichael et al., 1467–71. New York:
Macmillan, 1993.

Mill, John Stuart. *The Subjection of Women.* London: Longmans, Green, Reader,
and Dyer, 1869.

Moers, Ellen. *Literary Women.* New York: Doubleday, 1976.

Moore, Rayburn S. *Constance F. Woolson*. New Haven, Conn.: Twayne, 1963.

————. "The Strange Irregular Rhythm of Life: James's Late Tales and Constance Woolson." *South Atlantic Bulletin* 41 (1976): 86–93.

Moore, Rayburn S., ed. *For the Major and Selected Short Stories*. New York: Harper and Brothers, 1883; New Haven, Conn.: College and Univ. Press, 1967.

Namias, June. *White Captives: Gender and Ethnicity on the American Frontier*. Chapel Hill: Univ. of North Carolina Press, 1993.

Nicholas, Edward. *The Chaplain's Lady: Life and Love at Fort Mackinac*. Mackinac Island State Park Commission, 1987.

O'Brien, Sharon. "Tomboyism and Adolescent Conflict: Three Nineteenth-Century Case Studies." In *Woman's Being, Woman's Place*, ed. Kelley, 350–72.

O'Grady, John P. *Pilgrims to the Wild: Everett Ruess, Henry David Thoreau, John Muir, Clarence King, Mary Austin*. Salt Lake City: Univ. of Utah Press, 1993.

Pattee, Fred Lewis. "Constance Fenimore Woolson and the South." *South Atlantic Quarterly* 38 (Apr. 1939): 130–41.

————. *The Development of the American Short Story: An Historical Survey*. New York: Harper, 1923.

Petry, Alice Hall. "'Always, Your Attached Friend': The Unpublished Letters of Constance Fenimore Woolson to John and Clara Hay." *Books at Brown* 29–30 (1982–83): 11–107.

Porter, Phil, and Victor R. Nelhiebel. *The Wonder of Mackinac*. Mackinac Island State Park Commission, 1984.

Pratt, Annis. *Archetypal Patterns in Women's Fiction*. Bloomington: Indiana Univ. Press, 1981.

Price Herndl, Diane. *Invalid Women: Figuring Feminine Illness in American Literature and Culture*. Chapel Hill: Univ. of North Carolina Press, 1993.

Prucha, Francis Paul, ed. *Documents of United States Indian Policy*. 2d ed. Lincoln: Univ. of Nebraska Press, 1990.

Quinn, Arthur Hobson. *American Fiction: An Historical Survey*. New York: D. Appleton-Century, 1936.

Reynolds, David S. *Beneath the American Renaissance: The Subversive Imagination in the Age of Emerson and Melville*. Cambridge: Harvard Univ. Press, 1989.

Rich, Adrienne. "Taking Women Students Seriously." In *On Lies, Secrets, and Silence: Selected Prose: 1966–1978*. New York: W. W. Norton, 1979. First presented at New Jersey College and University Coalition on Women's Education, 9 May 1978.

Richardson, Lyon N. "Constance Fenimore Woolson, 'Novelist Laureate' of
    America." *South Atlantic Quarterly* 39 (1940): 18–36.

Riley, Glenda. *Divorce: An American Tradition*. New York: Oxford Univ. Press,
    1991.

Ripa, Yannick. *Women and Madness: The Incarceration of Women in Nine-
    teenth-Century France*. Translated by Catherine Du Peloux Menage. Min-
    neapolis: Univ. of Minnesota Press, 1991.

Romines, Ann. *The Home Plot: Women, Writing, and Domestic Ritual*. Amherst:
    Univ. of Massachusetts Press, 1992.

Salmon, Marylynn. "Equality or Submersion? Feme Covert Status in Early Penn-
    sylvania." In *Women of American History*, ed. Berkin and Norton, 92–113.

Sayre, Robert F. *Thoreau and the American Indian*. Princeton, N.J.: Princeton
    Univ. Press, 1977.

Sherman, Sarah Way. *Sarah Orne Jewett: An American Persephone*. Hanover,
    N.H.: Univ. Press of New England, 1989.

Simmons, Adele. "Education and Ideology in Nineteenth-Century America: The
    Response of Educational Institutions to the Changing Role of Women." In
    Liberating Women's History, ed. Carroll, 115–26.

Slotkin, Richard. *Regeneration Through Violence: The Mythology of the Ameri-
    can Frontier, 1600–1860*. Middletown, Conn.: Wesleyan Univ. Press, 1973.

Smith-Rosenberg, Caroll. "The Hysterical Woman: Sex Roles and Role Conflict
    in 19th-Century America." *Social Research* 39 (1972): 652–78.

Strouse, Jean. *Alice James: A Biography*. Boston: Houghton Mifflin, 1980.

Sundquist, Eric I. *Home as Found: Authority and Geneology in Nineteenth-Cen-
    tury American Literature*. Baltimore: Johns Hopkins Univ. Press, 1979.

Tompkins, Jane. *Sensational Designs: The Cultural Work of American Fiction,
    1790–1860*. New York: Oxford Univ. Press, 1985.

Torsney, Cheryl B. *Constance Fenimore Woolson: The Grief of Artistry*. Athens:
    Univ. of Georgia Press, 1989.

———, ed. *Critical Essays on Constance Fenimore Woolson*. New York: G. K.
    Hall, Macmillan, 1992.

———. "In Anticipation of the Fiftieth Anniversary of Woolson House." *Legacy*
    2 (Fall 1985): 72–73.

———. "The Strange Case of the Disappearing Woolson Memorabilia." *Legacy*
    11, no. 2 (1994): 143–51.

———. "The Traditions of Gender: Constance Fenimore Woolson and Henry
    James." In *Critical Essays*, ed. Torsney, 152–71. First published in *Patrons
    and Protégées*, ed. Marchalonis, 161–83.

Tuchman, Gaye, with Nina F. Fortin. *Edging Women Out: Victorian Novelists,*

Publishers, and Social Change. New Haven, Conn.: Yale Univ. Press, 1989.

Tucker, Cynthia Grant. *Prophetic Sisterhood: Liberal Women Ministers of the Frontier, 1880–1930.* Boston: Beacon Press, 1990.

VanBergen, Carolyn. "Constance Fenimore Woolson and the Next Country." *Western Reserve Studies* 3 (1988): 86–92.

———. "Getting Your Money's Worth: The Social Marketplace in *Horace Chase.*" In *Critical Essays,* ed. Torsney, 234–44.

Vickers, Joanne F. "Woolson's Response to James: The Vindication of the American Heroine." *Women's Studies* 18 (1990): 287–94.

Vizenor, Gerald. *The People Named the Chippewa.* Minneapolis: Univ. of Minnesota Press, 1984.

Walker, Nancy A. *A Very Serious Thing: Women's Humor and American Culture.* Minneapolis: Univ. of Minnesota Press, 1988.

Warren, Joyce W., ed. Introduction to *Ruth Hall & Other Writings,* by Fanny Fern. New Brunswick, N.J.: Rutgers Univ. Press, 1986.

Weimer, Joan Myers. "The 'Admiring Aunt' and the 'Proud Salmon of the Pond': Constance Fenimore Woolson's Struggle with Henry James." In *Critical Essays,* ed. Torsncy, 203–16.

———. *Back Talk: Teaching Lost Selves to Speak.* New York: Random House, 1994.

———. "Women Artists as Exiles in the Fiction of Constance Fenimore Woolson." *Legacy* 3, no. 2 (Fall 1986): 3–15.

———, ed. *Women Artists, Women Exiles: "Miss Grief" and Other Stories,* by Constance Fenimore Woolson. New Brunswick, N.J.: Rutgers Univ. Press, 1988.

Weir, Sybil B. "Southern Womanhood in the Novels of Constance Fenimore Woolson." In *Critical Essays,* ed. Torsney, 140–47. First published in *Mississippi Quarterly* 29 (1976): 559–68.

White, Deborah Gray. *"Ar'n't I a Woman."* New York: Norton, 1987.

White, Robert L. "Cultural Ambivalence in Constance Fenimore Woolson's Italian Tales." In *Critical Essays,* ed. Torsney, 132–39. First published in *Tennessee Studies in Literature* 12 (1967): 121–29.

Widder, Keith R. *Reville Till Taps: Soldier Life at Fort Mackinac, 1780–1895.* Mackinac Island State Park Commission, 1972.

Wolff, Larry. *Postcards from the End of the World: Child Abuse in Freud's Vienna.* New York: Atheneum, 1988.

Wood, Ann Douglas. "'The Fashionable Diseases': Women's Complaints and Their Treatment in Nineteenth-Century America." *Journal of Interdisciplinary History* 4 (1973): 25–52.

Woolson, Constance Fenimore. *Anne.* New York: Harper and Brothers, 1882;
New York: Arno, 1977. First published in *Harper's New Monthly Magazine*
62–64 (Dec. 1880–May 1882).

———. "At the Château of Corrine." In *Women Artists, Women Exiles,* ed.
Weimer, 211–47. First published in *Harper's New Monthly Magazine* 75
(Oct. 1887): 778–96. Also in *Dorothy and Other Italian Stories,* by
Woolson; and *Five Generations,* by Benedict, vol. 2: 228–36.

———. "Ballast Island." *Appletons' Journal* 9 (28 June 1873): 833–39.

———. "Barnaby Pass." *Harper's New Monthly Magazine* 55 (July 1877): 261–71.

———. "Black Point." *Harper's New Monthly Magazine* 59 (June 1879): 84–97.

———. *Castle Nowhere: Lake Country Sketches.* Boston: J. R. Osgood, 1875.
(Published as *Solomon, and other "Lake country" sketches* [Odessa,
Ontario: J. Reish & Sons, 1897]). New York: Harper & Bros., 1899. New
York: Garrett Press, 1969.

———. "Cicely's Christmas." *Appletons' Journal* 6 (30 Dec. 1871): 753–58.

———. "Crowder's Cove." *Appletons' Journal* 15 (18 Mar. 1876): 357–62.

———. "A Day of Mystery." *Appletons' Journal* 6 (9 Sept. 1871): 290–93.

———. "Dorothy." *Harper's New Monthly Magazine* 84 (Mar. 1892): 551–75. Also
in *Dorothy and Other Italian Stories,* by Woolson.

———. *Dorothy and Other Italian Stories.* New York: Harper and Brothers,
1896, 1899.

———. "Duets." *Harper's New Monthly Magazine* 49 (Sept. 1874): 579–85.

———. *East Angels.* New York: Harper and Brothers, 1886. First published in
Harper's New Monthly Magazine 70–77 (Jan. 1885–May 1886).

———. "Fairy Island." *Putnam's Magazine,* n.s., 6 (July 1870): 62–69. Also in
Five Generations, by Benedict, vol. 2: 278–83.

———. "A Florentine Experiment." *Atlantic Monthly* 46 (Oct. 1880). Also in *Dorothy and Other Italian Stories,* by Woolson; and *Five Generations,* by
Benedict, vol. 2: 192–99.

———. "A Flower of the Snow." *Galaxy* 17 (Jan. 1874): 76–85.

———. *For the Major.* In *For the Major and Selected Short Stories,* ed. Moore,
259–367. First published in *Harper's New Monthly Magazine* 65–66 (Nov.
1882–Apr. 1883).

———. *The Front Yard and Other Italian Stories.* New York: Harper and Brothers, 1895; New York: Books for Libraries Press, 1969.

———. "The Happy Valley." *Harper's New Monthly Magazine* 41 (July 1870):
282–85. Also in *Five Generations,* by Benedict, vol. 1: 268–76.

———. "The Haunted Lake." *Harper's New Monthly Magazine* 44 (Dec. 1871):
20–30. Also in *Five Generations,* by Benedict, vol. 1: 49–57.

———. "'Hepzibah's Story': An Unpublished Work by Constance Fenimore

Woolson." Edited by Robert Gingras. *Resources for American Literary Study* 10 (1980): 33–45.

———. *Horace Chase*. New York: Harper and Brothers, 1894; Upper Saddle River, N.J.: Literature House, 1970. First published in *Harper's New Monthly Magazine* 86–87 (Jan. 1893–Aug. 1893).

———. "In Sloane Street." *Harper's Bazar* 25 (11 June 1892): 473–78.

———. *Jupiter Lights*. New York: Harper and Brothers, 1889; New York: AMS Press, 1971. First published in *Harper's New Monthly Magazine* 78–79 (Jan. 1889–Sept. 1889).

———. "Keller Hill." *Appletons' Journal*, n.s., 2 (May 1877): 414–21.

———. "King Log." *Appletons' Journal* 9 (18 Jan. 1873): 97–101.

———. "Lily and Diamond." *Appletons' Journal* 8 (2 Nov. 1872): 477–83.

———. "Margaret Morris." *Appletons' Journal* 7 (13 Apr. 1872): 394–99.

———. "Matches Morganatic." *Harper's New Monthly Magazine* 61 (Mar. 1878): 517–31.

———. *Mentone, Cairo, and Corfu*. New York: Harper and Brothers, 1895.

———. "A Merry Christmas." *Harper's New Monthly Magazine* 44 (Jan. 1872): 231–36.

———. "Miss Grief." In *Women Artists, Women Exiles*, ed. Weimer, 248–69. First published in *Lippincott's Magazine* 25 (May 1880): 574–85. Also in *For the Major*, ed. Moore, 123–43; and Cheryl B. Torsney, *Legacy* 4, no. 1 (Spring 1987): 11–25.

———. "Mission Endeavor." *Harper's New Monthly Magazine* 53 (Nov. 1876): 886–93.

———. "Miss Vedder." *Harper's New Monthly Magazine* 58 (Mar. 1879): 590–601.

———. "An October Idyll." *Harper's New Monthly Magazine* 41 (Nov. 1870): 907–12.

———. "The Old Five." *Appletons' Journal*, n.s., 1 (Nov. 1876): 438–46.

———. "The Old Palace Keeper." *Christian Union* 22 (10 Nov. 1880): 394–96. Also in *Five Generations*, by Benedict, vol. 2: 199–216.

——— [Anne March, pseud.]. *The Old Stone House*. Boston: D. Lothrop, 1873.

———. "One *Versus* Two." *Lippincott's Magazine* 10 (Aug. 1872): 213–21.

———. "On the Iron Mountain." *Appletons' Journal* 9 (15 Feb. 1873): 225–30.

———. "Raspberry Island." *Harper's New Monthly Magazine* 55 (Oct. 1877): 737–45.

———. "Reflection." In *Five Generations*, by Benedict, vol. 2: 411.

———. *Rodman the Keeper: Southern Sketches*. New York: D. Appleton, 1880; New York: Harper & Bros. 1886; New York: Garrett Press, 1969.

———. "The Story of Huron Grand Harbor." *Appletons' Journal* 11 (18 Apr. 1874): 484–90.

———. "A Transplanted Boy." In *For the Major,* ed. Moore, 217–58. First published in *Harper's New Monthly Magazine* 88 (Feb. 1894): 425–41. Also in *Dorothy and Other Italian Stories,* by Woolson; and *Five Generations,* by Benedict, vol. 2: 500–541.

———. "A Waitress." *Harper's New Monthly Magazine* 89 (June 1894): 88–102. Also in *Dorothy and Other Italian Stories,* by Woolson; and *Five Generations,* by Benedict, vol. 2: 301–2.

———. "The Waldenburg Road." *Appletons' Journal* 12 (4 July 1874): 5–11.

———. "Weighed in the Balance." *Appletons' Journal* 7 (1 June 1872): 589–94.

Yeazell, Ruth Bernard. *The Death and Letters of Alice James.* Berkeley and Los Angeles: Univ. of California Press, 1981.

Yellin, Jean Fagin. *Women and Sisters: The Anti-slavery Feminists in American Culture.* New Haven, Conn.: Yale Univ. Press, 1989.

Young, Mary E. "Women, Civilization, and the Indian Question." In *Clio Was a Woman: Studies in the History of American Women,* edited by Mabel E. Deutrich and Virginia C. Purdy, 98–110. Washington, D.C.: Howard Univ. Press, 1980.

Zimmerman, Joan G. "Daughters of Main Street: Culture and the Female Community at Grinnell, 1884–1917." In *Woman's Being, Woman's Place,* ed. Kelley, 154–70.

Index